ADMIRALTY
IN A NUTSHELL
Sixth Edition

By

FRANK L. MARAIST
Nolan J. Edwards Professor of Law
Holt B. Harrison Professor of Law
Louisiana State University Law Center

THOMAS C. GALLIGAN, JR.
President and Professor of Humanities
Colby–Sawyer College

CATHERINE M. MARAIST
Member of the Louisiana Bar

A Thomson Reuters business

Mat #40902013

Nutshell Series, In a Nutshell and the Nutshell Logo are trademarks registered in the U.S. Patent and Trademark Office.

COPYRIGHT © 1983, 1988, 1996 WEST PUBLISHING CO.
© West a Thomson business, 2001, 2005
© 2010 Thomson Reuters

> 610 Opperman Drive
> St. Paul, MN 55123
> 1–800–313–9378

Printed in the United States of America

ISBN: 978–0–314–92699–9

PREFACE TO
SIXTH EDITION

Most law school professors deal with discrete areas of the law such as contracts, torts, property, or commercial law. But one teaching admiralty has the opportunity to delve into many substantive, procedural and remedial aspects of the law and to analyze how those varied areas apply to one activity—maritime shipping and commerce. The admiralty professor must be concerned with such subjects as torts, contracts, worker compensation, insurance, commercial law, security devices, procedure, federal courts, constitutional law, international law and conflicts of law, as well as peculiar aspects of maritime law such as salvage, limitation of liability, and general average. Thus the maritime lawyer is truly a specialist in generality, a specialist in the law governing disputes that arise on or near, or affect commerce on water. It is easy to see how one falls in love with this wonderful area of the law.

Joining us in this Sixth Edition of the Admiralty Nutshell is Catherine Maraist, a co-author of our casebook in Maritime Law. We welcome her and her valuable contributions to this publication.

The authors are not sailors drawn to the subject by our love of the sea. We are lawyers who have occupied ourselves with maritime law because it is one of the most comprehensive and fascinating subjects imaginable. In this book, we have tried to bring our enthusiasm for the subject to those who may find this book useful. We have attempted to make our explanations clear and to avoid bogging down in needless detail. But we have also tried to identify and address significant maritime issues of current concern. In the spirit of the Nutshell Series, we have attempted to provide the newcomer to the material with a helpful introduction, but we also have attempted to provide all those who deal with maritime law with a helpful review and a useful presentation of cases decided since the fourth edition was published.

In this sixth edition we have strived to preserve the organization, clarity, tone, and style of the earlier editions. We have updated the citations where a more recent significant case has been decided or where Congress has acted. We also have made textual changes where the material demanded it. One of the significant demands is the renumbering of Title 46 of the U.S. Code; in this edition we provide the new citations and, where appropriate, reference to the prior citations. Generally, however, we have tried to preserve the inherent strengths of the previous editions (three of which Professor Maraist crafted until President Galligan joined him on the fourth edition).

President Galligan is grateful to his co-author, Professor Maraist, who not only has included him in this project and so many others over the years, but who convinced him about fifteen years ago that

PREFACE TO SIXTH EDITION

it would be wise for Galligan, as a Torts teacher, to
also teach a course in Admiralty. President Galligan
and Professor Maraist are also extremely excited
that Catherine Maraist is joining the authorial
team. Professor Maraist taught President Galligan
about Admiralty, Torts and teaching. And, President Galligan was lucky to have Catherine Maraist
as a student. Catherine Maraist also no doubt
learned much from her father, Frank Maraist, so
perhaps the educational loop comes full circle. The
authors owe unending thanks to Madeline Babin,
administrative assistant at LSU, without whose extraordinary effort this edition would not have been
completed in a timely fashion, and to Kevin Blanchard and Joshua Clayton, whose research assistance
on this sixth edition was invaluable.

V

OUTLINE

Page

TABLE OF CASES

References are to Pages

TABLE OF CASES

XX

TABLE OF CASES

TABLE OF CASES

ADMIRALTY
IN A NUTSHELL
Sixth Edition

CHAPTER I

INTRODUCTION

A. DEVELOPMENT OF THE GENERAL MARITIME LAW

In the broadest sense, admiralty is the great body of law—statutory and jurisprudential—which regulates the activity of carrying cargo and passengers over water. In a limited sense, admiralty or maritime law denotes those rules which govern contract, tort, and worker compensation claims arising out of travel on or over water.

Admiralty or maritime law is one of the world's oldest bodies of law. While its beginnings are obscure, most scholars agree that it began in countries bordering the Mediterranean Sea. Then, as now, the importance of transportation of goods over water was great. Additionally, the resolution of disputes over the transportation of goods among different countries presented jurisdictional and procedural problems not shared by controversies involving less transient parties. These factors apparently led to the establishment of special courts in coastal towns to resolve disputes among those engaged in the business of transporting goods over water, and, subsequently, to the codification of the substantive rules developed in those courts. Some of the codes were recognized as authoritative in other ports; among the remembered are The Tablets of Amalfi, near Naples, and the Rules of Oleron, an island off the French west coast. From these codes there eventually developed a body of general maritime law which was in many respects uniform among the seafaring nations.

This maritime law—with its special courts and its international rules—spread to the Atlantic and Baltic nations of Europe, including England. When the maritime courts in English ports were unable to make satisfactory disposition of piracy and spoil claims, they were replaced by courts under the jurisdiction of the Lord of the Admiralty. By way of this English experience, the Mediterranean concept of maritime law reached during the colonial period what was to become the United States.

The British crown established in its American colonies vice-admiralty courts to which it granted power over maritime disputes. After the Revolution, the Articles of Confederation gave the Congress the power to regulate prizes and piracies, and to establish an appeals court for dealing with prizes and captures. Original jurisdiction over these cases, however, was vested in the state courts. It was an unhappy experience. Some state courts employed procedures foreign to admiralty. Some states prohibited appeals and refused to comply with decrees of the federal appellate tribunal which reversed state court decisions. This history undoubtedly prompted the inclusion in the United States Constitution of federal power over admiralty and maritime matters, and the resulting establishment of special federal courts and substantive laws to resolve maritime disputes. It is these courts and substantive laws—American admiralty law—that are the focus of this work.

The reader should be aware at the outset that there is a body of general maritime law that for the most part has been accepted by all seafaring nations, including the United States. Although this treatise focuses upon American law, mention is made of the general maritime law, particularly when it differs from the American law. With this brief historical and functional perspective, we turn to the American admiralty experience.

B. DEVELOPMENT OF AMERICAN ADMIRALTY LAW

The framers of the United States Constitution included in Article III, the judiciary article, a clause extending the judicial power of the federal sovereign to "all Cases of admiralty and maritime Jurisdiction." Article III, § 2. The language of the clause and its placement within the Constitution suggest that it may have been intended only as a delegation to the federal sovereign of the power to prescribe the courts which could adjudicate cases involving maritime matters, and not a delegation to the federal courts of the power to develop substantive rules of decision in admiralty cases. Other grants of power contained in the same article and section, such as jurisdiction over cases between citizens of different states, have been construed as granting only the power to prescribe the courts in which those kinds of disputes will be heard. The argument that the grant of jurisdiction over maritime cases extended only to the power to prescribe judicial competence was reinforced by the language of the first Judiciary Act, in which Congress conferred upon federal courts the power to hear maritime causes,

> saving to suitors, in all cases, the right of a common law remedy, where the common law is competent to give it.... Sec. 9 of the Judiciary Act of 1789, 1 Stat. 76–77.

As late as the turn of the twentieth century, there was respectable authority for the proposition that if a maritime matter was brought in federal court, federal substantive law would govern, but if it was brought in state court, state substantive law would be dispositive.

The dispute was resolved by a pair of cases decided by the United States Supreme Court during World War I. In *Southern Pacific Co. v. Jensen*, 244 U.S. 205 (1917), and *Chelentis v. Luckenbach Steamship Co.*, 247 U.S. 372 (1918), the Court construed the "admiralty and maritime jurisdiction" clause of the Constitution as conferring upon the federal sovereign two separate powers—the power to determine what courts will hear maritime cases *and* the power to prescribe the substantive law governing the disposition of such cases.

The Court's interpretation of Article III, Section 2, as a grant of both substantive and procedural competence over maritime matters may have been influenced by both historical and practical considerations. As we have observed, from pre-Renaissance times, seafaring nations maintained special admiralty courts which disposed of maritime disputes by applying rules and principles common to all seafaring nations. More importantly, however, the Supreme Court may have been motivated by the desire to provide the federal sovereign with power over maritime shipping and commerce, a power not then generally available under the Constitution (the interstate commerce clause was not to receive its expansive interpretation until the middle of the twentieth century). The wisdom of providing the federal sovereign with such power is obvious. Without it, domestic and foreign participants in maritime shipping and commerce would be subject to varying state laws, and the differences resulting therefrom could have an adverse effect on the nation's maritime shipping and commerce. Regardless of the motivation, the question of the scope of the power delegated to the federal sovereign by Article III, Section 2, is well-settled. It was summarized by Justice Felix Frankfurter in *Romero v. International Terminal Operating Co.*, 358 U.S. 354 (1959):

Article III, § 2, cl. 1 (3d provision) of the Constitution and section 9 of the Act of September 24, 1789, have from the beginning been the sources of jurisdiction in litigation based upon federal maritime law. Article III impliedly contained three grants. (1) It empowered Congress to confer admiralty and maritime jurisdiction on the "Tribunals inferior to the Supreme Court" which were authorized by Art. 1, § 8, cl. 9. (2) It empowered the federal courts in their exercise of the admiralty and maritime jurisdiction which had been conferred on them, to draw on the substantive law "inherent in the admiralty and maritime jurisdiction," *Crowell v. Benson*, 285 U.S. 22 [1932], and to continue development of this law within constitutional limits. (3) It empowered Congress to revise and supplement the maritime law within the limits of the Constitution. *See Crowell v. Benson, supra.*

The careful reader will note that Justice Frankfurter's third point deals with legislative power. Thus the Court interpreted the admiralty jurisdiction clause in the judiciary article of the Constitution (Article III) as also providing a source of federal legislative power.

Although Congress has been sparing in the exercise of its power to prescribe substantive rules governing "cases within the admiralty and maritime jurisdiction," some areas of maritime law, such as the carriage of goods under bills of lading, maritime liens, ship mortgages, and worker's compensation for non-seaman maritime workers, have been the subject of comprehensive legislation. However, Congress has said little or nothing about what rules govern most admiralty tort or contract claims. Thus the federal judiciary, fashioning a "federal admiralty common law," has provided much of the substantive law of admiralty. Some of this judge-made law has been handed down by the Supreme Court, but for the most part the prevailing law is a consensus of decisions by the lower federal courts. These decisions usually reflect a synthesis of the general maritime law of nations, analogies from Congressional pronouncements, and the courts' own views of what is reasonably needed to promote American shipping and maritime commerce.

The jurisdiction of admiralty in England traditionally was limited to seagoing vessels and to events occurring on the high seas. In the United States, however, it has been extended to all "navigable waters," including many inland rivers and lakes. The potential conflict with state law has presented the judiciary with the difficult task of accommodating the sometimes competing policies of state and federal sovereigns. Thus "comity" is an important factor in the determination of the reach of the federal admiralty power and in the development of maritime common law. Where Congress has adopted legislation, or where the federal interest in promoting maritime shipping and commerce requires a uniform national rule, state interests must bow. However, where the matter is "maritime" but there is neither a federal statute nor a perceived need for uniformity, a court applying maritime law may adopt the state law as the appropriate rule of decision. Justice John M. Harlan described this non-preemption (often called "maritime but local") approach as one of "accommodation . . . somewhat analogous to the normal conflict of laws situation where two sovereignties assert divergent interests in a transaction as to which both have some concern." *Kossick v. United Fruit Co.*, 365 U.S. 731 (1961).

The non-preemption or "maritime but local" doctrine has endured. *See, e.g., Askew v. American Waterways Operators, Inc.*, 411 U.S. 325 (1973); *American Dredging Co. v. Miller*, 510 U.S. 443 (1994). *See, also, Yamaha Motor Corp. v. Calhoun*, 516 U.S. 199 (1996) (federal maritime law does not preempt a state remedy in certain wrongful death actions). It has been applied to both state statutes and state common law. In *Sprietsma v. Mercury Marine*, 537 U.S. 51 (2002), the U.S. Supreme Court ruled that a state tort claim based on a boat manufacturer's failure to install propeller guards on outboard motors is neither expressly nor impliedly preempted by the Federal Boat Safety Act, 46 U.S.C. Sec. 4306 In *Palestina v. Fernandez*, 701 F.2d 438 (5th Cir. 1983), the court was faced with the question of whether the owner of a commercial fishing boat who left a key in the ignition was liable to a third party for harm resulting from the subsequent unauthorized use of the boat. Although the collision between the fishing boat and the vessel in which the victim was riding was within admiralty jurisdiction (*see* Chapter III), the court elected to apply the rule developed by Louisiana jurisprudence, observing

> This case is within our admiralty jurisdiction because the collision occurred on … a navigable Louisiana waterway…. In all other respects, however, it is a garden variety state tort claim, and in such instances, where there is no uniform

federal rule, "even though admiralty suits are governed by federal substantive and procedural law, courts applying maritime law may adopt state law by express or implied reference or by virtue of the interstitial nature of federal law."
... We conclude that this case is an appropriate one for applying the law of Louisiana.

Palestina (citations omitted). *See, also, Zbylut v. Harvey's Iowa Management Co., Inc.*, 361 F.3d 1094 (8th Cir. 2004) (admiralty law does not preempt a state wrongful discharge claim); *Favorito v. Pannell*, 27 F.3d 716 (1st Cir. 1994) (state law applies to a claim against a vessel owner for negligent retention of an engineer who invited passengers to the yacht without the owner's permission and who injured passengers in a collision between his inflatable tender and another vessel while he was returning passengers to shore); *Green v. Industrial Helicopters, Inc.*, 593 So.2d 634 (La. 1992) (applying state tort law to a claim against the owner of a helicopter which crashed approximately 150 miles offshore). *Compare Churchill v. F/V Fjord*, 857 F.2d 571 (9th Cir. 1988) (admiralty law "completely" preempts a state statute providing that the owner of a vessel is not liable unless the craft was used with his consent, and creating presumptions of such consent). *See, also, Calhoun v. Yamaha Motor Corp., U.S.A.*, 216 F.3d 338 (3d Cir. 2000), holding that federal maritime law applies in determining the standard for tort liability, but state law applies on the issue of damages in a claim for the death of a nonseafarer in state territorial waters.

Many of the considerations that apply in determining whether a matter is "maritime but local" also are relevant to the search for the maritime "flavor" or "nexus" which brings some matters into the federal admiralty power. (*See, e.g.,* Chapter II, *infra*). The relationship between the two is frequently overlooked and not clearly articulated. One may view this as a "reverse" *Erie* doctrine. The case is in state court but maritime law applies, except where the controversy or issue falls under the "maritime but local" doctrine, but even there state law is being applied "in admiralty."

Congress' allocation of judicial competence over maritime matters has remained essentially unchanged since the first Judiciary Act in 1789; it presently is contained in 28 U.S.C.A. § 1333, which provides in part

[T]he district courts shall have original jurisdiction, exclusive of the courts of the States, of:

(1) Any civil case of admiralty or maritime jurisdiction, saving to suitors in all cases all other remedies to which they are otherwise entitled.

The first clause gives federal courts the power to hear any matter which is "in admiralty," without regard to the existence of a federal statute creating the maritime right or to diverse citizenship or any minimum amount in controversy. This jurisdictional grant originally had the effect of continuing the colonial admiralty court as one "side" of the new federal circuit or district court. (*See* Chapter XIX, *infra*). One characteristic feature of that admiralty "side" of federal court was special admiralty procedures. Another difference between the law and admiralty "sides" of federal court was that a litigant was not entitled to trial by jury on the admiralty "side," while the Seventh Amendment guarantees jury trial in most matters brought on the law "side." In 1966, by amendment to the Federal Rules of Civil Procedure, the separate "sides" were merged. Despite the merger, however, several important procedural features (including the non-availability of jury trial) remain applicable when the jurisdiction of the federal court is premised solely upon the admiralty power and 28 U.S.C.A. § 1333. Thus when a matter is brought as an admiralty claim (i.e., the federal court is exercising jurisdiction only by virtue of the admiralty power), it is not entirely inaccurate to speak, as some still do, of the case as being on the admiralty "side" of the court.

The second clause of section 1333—"saving to suitors ... all other remedies to which they are otherwise entitled" (the language was changed in 1948 from "such remedy as the common law is competent to give")—has the effect of granting state courts subject matter jurisdiction, concurrent with federal courts, over most maritime matters. The contention that this clause also grants states the right to apply their own substantive law to maritime matters pending in their courts probably has been laid to rest; it now appears settled that what has been "saved" is judicial competence only.

Thus a matter which falls within the federal admiralty power may be brought on the admiralty "side" of federal court, in state court and, if there is an independent basis of jurisdiction (diversity of citizenship or federal question), as a law claim in federal court. Regardless of the court in which the matter is brought, if the rule of decision is not prescribed by federal statute, the court must determine the applicable admiralty substantive rule. It does this by a selective process similar to that by which the common law developed. Since the source of this power to create a body of admiralty "common law" is Article III, Section 2, one could assume that all cases arising under the admiralty "common law" fall within the federal question jurisdiction of federal courts, 28 U.S.C.A. § 1331. However, that argument by the Supreme Court was rejected in *Romero v. International Terminal Operating Co.,* page 5, *supra.*

In summary, a determination that a matter is "in admiralty," i.e., that it comes within the admiralty and maritime jurisdiction granted to the federal sovereign under Article III, Section 2, produces these results:

1. Congress has the power to provide the substantive law governing the resolution of the dispute. If Congress has not done so, the courts must fashion a dispositive "federal admiralty common law." In fashioning this law, the courts will accord deference to, but are not bound by, the general maritime law of nations. If there is no federal statute and no need for a uniform national law, the courts may

apply the law of the state with the most significant relationship to the controversy, under the "maritime but local" (non-preemption) doctrine.

2.   The case may be heard in federal court without regard to diversity of citizenship or the amount in controversy, but the litigants ordinarily will not be entitled to trial by jury unless there is some basis of federal jurisdiction other than section 1333. Most admiralty cases also may be brought in state court under the "saving to suitors" clause, with trial by jury if the litigants are otherwise entitled to jury trial under state law. If an admiralty claim arises under a federal statute, or if it arises under the maritime common law but the requirements of diversity jurisdiction are satisfied, the claim may be heard in federal court as a law claim, with the right to trial by jury. Regardless of the court in which an admiralty matter is brought, the substantive law which governs is federal admiralty law, unless the non-preemption or "maritime but local" doctrine applies.

Chapter III examines how one determines when a matter is "in admiralty," and the chapters which follow discuss the substantive and procedural laws which govern the disposition of a matter which is "in admiralty." Defining the bounds of admiralty jurisdiction, i.e., determining whether a matter is "in admiralty," involves the application of both geographical and conceptual factors. The geographical factors—"navigable waters" and "vessels"—continue to play important major roles in the inclusion or exclusion of some matters from the maritime jurisdiction. The conceptual factor is a determination of whether the matter has potential impact upon maritime shipping and commerce sufficient to invoke the attention of, and the expenditure of resources by, the federal sovereign. This factor, sometimes referred to in a shorthand way as "maritime nexus" or "flavor," is of ascending importance. In the past, the geographical factors have produced some certainty in determining the bounds of admiralty jurisdiction, frequently at the cost of absurd results. While the conceptual approach produces more logical results, it injects uncertainty into the determination of whether a particular matter is "in admiralty." Throughout this treatise, the reader will be concerned with whether a structure is a vessel, whether waters are navigable, and whether the matter has "maritime flavor." In Chapter II we discuss briefly the features of these indicia of maritime jurisdiction.

CHAPTER II

INDICIA OF JURISDICTION

A. VESSELS

In many cases, whether a matter is "in admiralty" depends upon whether it has a sufficient relationship to a "vessel." Maritime liens and preferred ship mortgages attach only to "vessels," and limitation of liability (which may drastically reduce a person's liability for maritime claims; *see* Chapter XVIII) is available only to the owner or demise charterer of a "vessel." An injured employee may qualify as a seaman, thereby gaining the benefits of maintenance and cure, the Jones Act, and the warranty of seaworthiness (*see* Chapter XIII), only if his employment has the requisite connection with a "vessel."

Congress has defined "vessel" as including "every description of watercraft or other artificial contrivance used, or capable of being used, as a means of transportation on water." 1 U.S.C.A. § 3. The Supreme Court initially defined vessels as "all navigable structures intended for transportation." *Cope v. Vallette Dry–Dock Co.*, 119 U.S. 625 (1887). Judge Brown in *Burks v. American River Transp. Co.,* 679 F.2d 69 (5th Cir. 1982) stated that the definition was broad enough to encompass the tub carrying the three men in the nursery rhyme. Additionally, more than a century later, the Court applied the definition of a vessel in 1 U.S.C. Sec. 3 in a manner consistent with Judge Brown's prediction, and concluded that a dredge, with extremely limited ability to move itself but which was normally towed from place to place, is a vessel for the purposes of an action under the Jones Act and the Longshore and Harbor Workers' Compensation Act, 33 U.S.C.A. § 905(b). The Court observed that the requirement of 1 U.S.C. Sec. 3 that a vessel must be "used, or capable of being used, as a means of transportation on water" does not mean that the vessel must be used primarily for that purpose, or that it must be in motion at the time of the event. "The question remains in all cases whether the watercraft's use 'as a means of transportation on water' is a practical possibility or merely a theoretical one." *Stewart v. Dutra Constr. Co.*, 543 U.S. 481 (2005).

Stewart apparently will apply to all "what is a vessel" issues in maritime law. Prior to *Stewart* the lack of a generally recognized definition was inconsequential in those cases—by far the greater number—in which the structure in question was actually engaged in the transportation of goods or passengers over water. The issue of whether a structure is a "vessel" often arises in cases involving ships under construction, ships which have been withdrawn from navigation, and certain special function structures used for harbor work, the production of minerals from the seabed and subsoil of navigable waters, and harbor recreation (such as houseboats and gambling casino boats). Prior to *Stewart*, the United States Fifth Circuit Court of Appeals, which gets most of the offshore mineral production cases, apparently settled upon a test which looked to "the purpose for which the craft is constructed and the business in which it is engaged." *Blanchard v. Engine & Gas Compressor Servs., Inc.*, 575 F.2d 1140 (5th Cir. 1978). The Fifth Circuit emphasized such circumstances as the manner in which the structure was attached to the shore or the ocean bottom, whether it was registered and equipped for navigation, and the extent to which it was moved. *See, e.g., Ducrepont v. Baton Rouge Marine Enters., Inc.*, 877 F.2d 393 (5th Cir. 1989). Other courts suggested additional functional inquiries, such as whether the structure was subject to the "perils of the sea," and whether it performed a function that might be performed equally well by a land-based structure. Now, these tests, while potentially relevant to certain aspects of the inquiry, will be subsumed under the more functional *Stewart* inquiry: is the vehicle at issue capable of serving as a means of maritime transportation?

Indeed, the Fifth Circuit itself, in *Holmes v. Atlantic Sounding Co., Inc.*, 437 F.3d 441 (5th Cir. 2006), stated that *Stewart* forced it to broaden its vessel status test in cases involving unconventional vehicles on water and held that a quarterbarge with no means of self-propulsion was a vessel. Alternatively, in *Cain v. Transocean Offshore USA, Inc.*, 518 F.3d 295 (5th Cir. 2008), the court held that

Stewart did not change Fifth Circuit jurisprudence holding that a structure under construction remains a non-vessel until it is complete and ready for duty upon the sea. There, a drilling rig that had been towed from the Far East to the United States was held not to be a vessel.

As noted, a "vessel" may be without motive power of its own (*see Holmes, supra*) and the goods which it transports may be aboard temporarily or may be permanently attached to it. Traditionally non-maritime equipment, such as an oil drilling rig or a piledriver, may be classed as a vessel when mounted on a barge or other structure that floats. Thus drilling barges and jack-up rigs, which may be moved, are vessels; oil drilling platforms, which are not as mobile, are not vessels. A floating dry dock generally is not considered a vessel because it ordinarily is not capable of transporting vessels or other property over water. Other structures which have been classified as vessels include derrick boats, canning barges, houseboats, floating bathhouses, dredges, scows, rafts, and a car shuttle ferry permanently anchored on both sides of the river. A pontoon bridge operated as part of a state highway system is not a vessel. Although aircraft frequently serve the same function as vessels—transportation of goods and passengers over water—the courts generally do not treat them as "vessels." One exception is that a seaplane may be a "vessel" when actually on the water. Small recreational vessels, such as jet skis, generally are treated as vessels. *Complaint of Messina,* 574 F.3d 119 (2nd Cir. 2009). All of the pre-

Stewart jurisprudence may be reassessed in light of the Court's pronouncement in *Stewart, supra.*

In the wake of the rebirth of legalized riverboat gambling and other gambling on water, an important modern issue has been whether floating gambling structures can be classified as vessels for maritime purposes. The matter is of great significance to workers aboard those vessels (a croupier could then be a seaman, *see* Chapter XIII) and to land-based merchants dealing with the structures (*see* Chapter V). Some structures are basically floating docks and may not meet the test, either before or after *Stewart. See, e.g., Pavone v. Mississippi Riverboat Amusement Corp.*, 52 F.3d 560 (5th Cir. 1995); *Howard v. Southern Illinois Riverboat Casino Cruises, Inc.*, 364 F.3d 854 (7th Cir. 2004). Others that are required to or do in fact navigate while hosting gambling activities should satisfy the vessel test, either before or after *Stewart*; *Weaver v. Hollywood Casino–Aurora, Inc.*, 255 F.3d 379 (7th Cir. 2001). Under the *Stewart* test, if the vehicle is practicably capable of navigation it should be a vessel, unless withdrawn from navigation. *See also, Board of Com'rs of Orleans Levee Dist. v. M/V BELLE OF ORLEANS*, 535 F.3d 1299 (11th Cir. 2008).

A contract to sell a vessel is not maritime. *Natasha, Inc. v. Evita Marine Charters, Inc.*, 763 F.2d 468 (1st Cir. 1985). A vessel may not engage in certain activities, such as foreign trade, coastwide trade, or fishing, unless it is registered (documented) under federal law. A vessel is eligible to be documented if it has a size of at least five net tons, is not registered under the laws of a foreign country or titled in a state, and is owned by the federal or a state government, an American citizen, a corporation established in the United States and controlled by American citizens, or a partnership controlled by American citizens. 46 U.S.C.A. § 12102. The owner selects the port of documentation of his vessel from among those designated by the head of the department in which the Coast Guard is operating; that port becomes the vessel's "home port." An undocumented vessel equipped with propulsion machinery of any kind must be "numbered" by the state in which it principally is operated. 46 U.S.C.A. § 12301.

Because a contract to build a vessel is not a maritime contract (*See* Chapter III), one question which frequently arises is whether a structure under construction is sufficiently advanced to be treated as a vessel by admiralty law. While the matter is not free from doubt, the weight of authority classifies a structure as a vessel when it is sufficiently advanced to perform the functions for which it is designed, although, as noted above, the Fifth Circuit has held that until a vessel has completed sea trials and while it is still under construction, it is not yet a vessel for purposes of maritime law. *Cain v. Transocean Offshore USA, Inc.*, 518 F.3d 295 (5th Cir. 2008).

A vessel which is permanently withdrawn from navigation is a "dead ship" and is not a vessel for maritime purposes. Some examples of "dead ships" are those in "mothballs," those connected to shore-side utilities or transportation facilities, those in use as floating wharves, and some casino boats. *Stewart* expressly recognizes that a ship that is permanently withdrawn from navigation is no longer a vessel.

A vessel which is undergoing major repairs may be sufficiently withdrawn from navigation to lose temporarily its status as a "vessel" for maritime matters. The issue essentially is one of fact, and the factors which bear upon the decision include the nature and cost of the repairs, whether the owner remains in control of the vessel, and whether the repairs require an invasion of the "watertight integrity" of the vessel.

B. NAVIGABLE WATERS

Unique historical developments limited admiralty jurisdiction in England to matters occurring on navigable waters. The English admiralty courts were drawn into the conflict between the law and equity courts. During that struggle, writs of prohibition issued by the common law courts blocked or hindered admiralty courts from exercising jurisdiction over acts or transactions that did not take place on navigable waters. Out of this struggle grew the limitation of the jurisdiction of British admiralty courts to matters occurring on navigable waters. While the colonial admiralty courts were not always subjected to the same restrictions as their English counterparts, the concept of "navigable waters" as a limitation upon some aspects of admiralty jurisdiction carried over into American maritime law.

In England, most inland streams were susceptible to significant commercial use only within the ebb and flow of the tide; as a result, navigable waters in English admiralty law generally were defined as those waters subject to the ebb and flow of the tide. This limitation was acceptable for an American nation composed of states along the Atlantic coast, where inland streams generally were not used for commerce beyond the reach of tidal fluctuations. However, the expansion of the American nation resulted in the use for water-borne commerce of a number of important streams—most notably the Mississippi River—to carry goods and people far beyond the effect of tidal waters. Thus, while "navigable waters" in American maritime law still includes those areas seaward of the mean high water mark of tidal waters (*see, e.g.*, *Hassinger v. Tideland Elec. Membership Corp.*, 781 F.2d 1022 (4th Cir. 1986) and cases cited therein), the concept of "navigable waters" has been broadened greatly. In *The Daniel Ball*, 77 U.S. 557 (1870), the Court provided what has become the accepted definition of navigable waters for the purpose of determining admiralty jurisdiction. The Court wrote that:

Those rivers must be regarded as public navigable rivers in law which are navigable in fact. And they are navigable in fact when they are used, or are susceptible of being used, in their ordinary condition, as highways for commerce, over which trade and travel are or may be conducted in the customary modes of trade and travel on water. And they constitute navigable waters of the

United States within the meaning of the acts of Congress, in contradistinction from the navigable waters of the States, when they form in their ordinary condition by themselves, or by uniting with other waters, a continued highway over which commerce is or may be carried on with other States or foreign countries in the customary modes in which such commerce is conducted by water.

This definition is applied in determining whether waters which are not within the ebb and flow of the tide are "navigable" for the purposes of admiralty and maritime jurisdiction. It also is used to ascertain whether waters are "navigable" for other purposes, such as determining ownership of the beds of streams or the exercise of the servitude of navigation by which the federal government regulates the construction of dams, locks, slips and other structures affecting the flow of water. A case classifying a stream as "navigable" for one of these purposes should not be applied automatically to classify the stream as "navigable" for another purpose, inasmuch as the underlying policy considerations may differ. However, a ruling on navigability for one purpose may be "significant" in determining navigability for another purpose. *Sanders v. Placid Oil Co.*, 861 F.2d 1374 (5th Cir. 1988).

The core of *The Daniel Ball* definition is "use" as a "highway of commerce." Each of these elements has generated its share of jurisprudence. Some courts have held that areas of wetlands are navigable waters for purposes of admiralty jurisdiction. *In re Everglades Island Boat Tours, LLC*, 484 F.Supp.2d 1259 (M.D.Fla. 2007).

1. Use

Waters actually in use, or susceptible of use, for maritime shipping and commerce clearly fall within the definition of "navigable waters." If a stream or body of water formerly was used or susceptible of use, but is no longer so, some courts have held that it remains navigable. This concept of "indelible navigability" has not prevailed; later decisions require the stream to be presently in use or capable of use for maritime commerce in order to qualify as "navigable waters."

Under the concept of "future navigability," a stream which is not now navigable in fact and has not been so in the past nevertheless is navigable if it may be made navigable in fact by the expenditure of resources which would be reasonable in relation to the benefits anticipated. This concept has been applied in classifying water as "navigable" for some purposes, such as federal regulation of the construction of dams, bridges and other structures, but it should not be applied in determining the bounds of American admiralty jurisdiction.

A stream may be navigable in fact for only part of its length; such a stream is classified as "navigable waters" only to the extent of its navigability in fact, and not beyond.

A waterway which was once navigable may cease to be so. A stream which is navigable throughout most of the year is not non-navigable solely because it loses its navigability in fact during certain low water periods. Navigability generally extends to the ordinary high water mark, and is not expanded by the fact that flooding sometimes makes adjacent land navigable in fact.

A vessel or other structure afloat on navigable waters is treated as a part of "navigable waters" for the purposes of admiralty jurisdiction. However, piers, jetties, bridges, ramps, railways running into the sea, and other structures firmly attached to land are "extensions of land" and are not "navigable waters" for the purpose of admiralty jurisdiction, unless they are used primarily in aid of navigation. This "extension of the land" doctrine also applies to fixed structures that are used in the production of minerals and are completely surrounded by water, but which are firmly attached to the sea bed or other water bottom. The exclusion of these fixed structures from the definition of navigable waters produces the anomaly that drilling platforms constructed on the sea bed or subsoil of navigable waters constitute land for the purposes of admiralty jurisdiction, although some are located many miles from the nearest shore, while movable drilling structures, temporarily attached to the seabed or subsoil and performing the same function as the platforms, are treated as vessels and fall within admiralty jurisdiction. Of course, if attached for an extended period the structure may cease to be a vessel. Additionally, after the decision in *Demette v. Falcon Drilling Co., Inc.*, 280 F.3d 492 (5th

Cir. 2002), it may be that a jack-up rig ceases to be a vessel when jacked up on the Outer Continental Shelf. Alternatively, one might read *Demette* for the proposition that a jack-up rig, while jacked up on the Outer Continental Shelf can be a vessel for some purposes (i.e., seaman status) but a non-vessel for others such as the Outer Continental Shelf Lands Act and the LHWCA.

2. Highways

The stream or body of water, either alone or by uniting with other streams or bodies of water, must be capable of serving as a "highway" between two or more states, or between a state and a foreign country. This excludes "landlocked" lakes located wholly within one state, but includes bodies of water that are located wholly in one state but empty into one of the oceans, the Great Lakes, or the Gulf of Mexico.

3. Maritime Commerce

There is a dearth of jurisprudence defining "commerce." Some early cases indicate that the floating of logs is sufficient, but later cases require that the waters be capable of use for the transportation of goods or passengers or some significant commercial activity. A footnote in one Supreme Court case suggests that mere pleasure fishing and pleasure boating may not be sufficient, however. *Foremost Insurance Co. v. Richardson*, 457 U.S. 668 (1982). The declining use of "navigable waters" as the sole criterion for determining maritime jurisdiction has lessened the importance of this issue.

C. MARITIME FLAVOR

The boundaries of American admiralty jurisdiction sometimes are fixed solely by the relationship of an event or occurrence to a vessel, navigable waters, or to the high seas. In most cases, however, the existence of admiralty jurisdiction rests in whole or in part upon a finding that the event or occurrence has "maritime flavor," sometimes referred to as maritime "nexus." In maritime contract jurisdiction, the key inquiry is whether the subject of the contract is maritime. Although this determination technically involves maritime flavor, for most maritime contract cases, special rules have developed that place the contract either inside or outside admiralty jurisdiction, and thus there is no need for a general inquiry into maritime flavor. However, in most maritime tort cases, the court must determine if the tort has a sufficient maritime flavor to justify the exercise of admiralty jurisdiction. Technically, the question in tort cases is whether the activity involved bears a substantial relationship to a traditional maritime activity, but that definition does little more than restate the question. The quest is to identify those events and occurrences which have an effect or potential effect upon maritime shipping and commerce substantial enough to justify the exercise of the federal power, despite the resulting drain on federal judicial resources and strain upon federal-state relations.

While "maritime flavor" is incapable of precise definition, certain observations may be helpful. Generally, courts find "maritime flavor" in those events and transactions which are major concerns of the shipping industry. This is tempered by the realization that exercise of federal control will not necessarily promote maritime shipping with the same vigor as control by a coastal or predominantly maritime state. Since federal law will not necessarily be more favorable, courts may find "maritime flavor" only when there is a perceived need for a uniform national rule, which, of course, can only be provided by the federal sovereign. Even if there is maritime flavor and maritime jurisdiction, a court may nevertheless apply state law in particular cases (*See* Chapter I, *supra*). In such cases, the conclusion that an incident or relationship has sufficient maritime flavor to justify admiralty jurisdiction but does not present a need for a uniform maritime rule may prove frustrating. Notably, the mere fact that a court determines there is maritime jurisdiction does not mean that maritime law necessarily applies. If there is not a need for uniformity, state law may be applied. *Wilburn Boat Co. v. Fireman's Fund Ins. Co.*, 348 U.S. 310 (1955).

Having examined the three criteria—"vessels," "navigable waters," and "maritime flavor"—by which the boundaries of admiralty jurisdiction are ascertained, we next look to the manner in which those criteria are applied to determine whether contracts, torts, and other legal relationships fall within the federal maritime power.

CHAPTER III

SCOPE OF THE MARITIME JURISDICTION

A. JURISDICTION OVER MARITIME CONTRACTS

Significant consequences flow from classifying a contract as "maritime" or "in admiralty." A maritime contract may be enforced in federal court without any other basis of subject matter jurisdiction, *Farwest Steel Corp. v. Barge Sea Span 241*, 769 F.2d 620 (9th Cir. 1985), and it usually is secured by a maritime lien, which may be enforced only in an *in rem* action in federal court. *See* Ch. XIX. A maritime contract is not subject to some land-based formal "contract" requirements such as the "statute of frauds," and its validity and interpretation are governed by federal maritime law, unless the "maritime but local" or "non-preemption" doctrine applies. *See Kossick v. United Fruit Co.*, 365 U.S. 731 (1961).

When is a contract "maritime"? The early English rule—an aftermath of the defeat of the admiralty courts in a seventeenth-century struggle with courts of law and equity—was that a contract was not maritime unless it was made on and was to be performed on navigable waters. The English rule was not generally applied in the colonies, and modern American jurisprudence rejects this stringent geographical test in favor of a conceptual approach. In American admiralty law, the nature and subject matter of the contract, not the place of making or performance, govern. If the contract is maritime, it is subject to maritime jurisdiction. Unfortunately, neither Congress, the judiciary nor academia have provided adequate guidelines for determining when the nature and subject matter of a contract are maritime. There are many less than helpful definitions, such as "an agreement which concerns transportation by sea, relates to navigation or maritime employment, or involves navigation and commerce on navigable waters," *General Engine & Machine Works, Inc. v. Slay*, 222 F.Supp. 745 (S.D.Ala.1963) (citing 2 C.J.S. Admiralty § 24 n.23), and "a contract [which] is ... directly or substantially related to navigation." *Id*. In applying these general tests, the courts usually draw the line between contracts for goods and services furnished directly to the vessel and pertaining to the actual navigation and management of the vessel, and those which indirectly affect a vessel or its voyage. Thus, contracts to furnish repairs or stevedoring services for a vessel are maritime, but contracts to procure such services are not. A marine insurance contract is in admiralty, but a contract to obtain marine insurance is not. Frequently, a vessel employs an agent to procure goods and services for the vessel for one of its voyages. Traditionally, these contracts between vessel and agent were not treated as maritime, because the agent did not directly furnish the goods and services. However, there now is no "per se" rule excluding these agency contracts from maritime jurisdiction; instead, "courts should look to the subject matter of the agency contract and determine whether the services performed under the contract are maritime in nature." *Exxon Corp. v. Central Gulf Lines*, 500 U.S. 603 (1991).

One helpful guide in determining whether a contract is maritime is precedent, which abounds. A contract to insure, supply, load or unload, tow, pilot or dock a vessel is in admiralty. A seaman's contract of employment is maritime. Contracts to build or to sell vessels are not in admiralty, but contracts to lease vessels (charter parties) are. *See Cooper v. Meridian Yachts*, 575 F.3d 1151 (11th Cir. 2009); *Clem Perrin Marine Towing, Inc. v. Panama Canal Co.*, 730 F.2d 186 (5th Cir. 1984). Additionally, courts have ruled that the following are maritime contracts: (1) a contract to lease containers to a vessel, *Foss Launch & Tug Co. v. Char Ching Shipping U.S.A.*, 808 F.2d 697 (9th Cir. 1987); (2) a contract to provide catering services to a movable drilling rig, *Stoot v. Fluor Drilling Servs., Inc.*, 851 F.2d 1514 (5th Cir. 1988), (3) a vessel operator's contractual obligations to make contributions to a seaman's union trust funds, *Nehring v. Steamship M/V Point Vail*, 901 F.2d 1044 (11th Cir. 1990), and (4) an indemnity contract between consignee and carrier, *Great Eastern Shipping Co. v. Binani Cement, Ltd.*, 655 F.Supp.2d 395 (S.D.N.Y. 2009). In addition, a declaratory judgment suit under a comprehensive general liability (CGL) insurance policy is within admiralty jurisdiction since the assured's business was primarily maritime and the claim by the assured under the policy was for the defense of the assured in a maritime personal injury suit. *Folksamerica Reinsurance Co. v. Clean Water of New York, Inc.*, 413 F.3d 307 (2d Cir. 2005).

The rule that an agreement to build a ship is not a maritime contract is an historical anomaly which has produced much apology, but appears firmly entrenched. The original rationale behind the rule was that the product contemplated by the contract did not become a vessel until it was launched, and thus was not a concern of admiralty before that time. Even though the historical reasoning supporting the rule is questionable, the rule survives to this day. The present rationale supporting the rule likely has less to do with its history but rather the lack of a need for any maritime federal law governing the validity or interpretation of a contract to build a ship, since such a contract usually is specially negotiated between parties with equal expertise and bargaining power. The prevailing rule is that a ship under construction becomes a vessel, and thus may be the object of a maritime contract, when it is sufficiently advanced in construction to be capable of performing its intended use. *The Francis McDonald*, 254 U.S. 242 (1920). The minority view is that the construction becomes a vessel when it is launched.

Contracts with both maritime and non-maritime elements, sometimes called "mixed contracts," have caused much difficulty. The general rule is that a "mixed" contract is not within admiralty jurisdiction unless it is "wholly maritime." *See, e.g., Marine Logistics, Inc. v. England*, 265 F.3d 1322 (Fed. Cir. 2001). Generally, the courts have determined the "primary" or "principal" purpose of the contract; if that is maritime, the contract is treated as "wholly maritime," despite its non-maritime elements. Even if the "primary" or "principal" purpose is non-maritime, the court may exercise maritime jurisdiction over the contract if the maritime and non-maritime portions are "separable" ("severable") from each other. *See, e.g., Lucky–Goldstar, International, Inc. v. Phibro Energy International, Ltd.*, 958 F.2d 58 (5th Cir. 1992); *Thypin Steel Co. v. Asoma Corp.*, 215 F.3d 273 (2d Cir. 2000); *Folksamerica, supra*. One frequently occurring "mixed" contract is a lease-purchase agreement on a vessel. Since the contract to lease (charter party) is in admiralty and the contract to sell is not, courts have experienced difficulty in the enforcement of these agreements.

In *Norfolk Southern Railway Co. v. Kirby*, 543 U.S. 14 (2004), the Court dealt with one frequent "mixed contract," the transportation of goods over land and water through a single contract. There, the Court first observed that when a contract is a maritime one, and the dispute is not inherently local, federal law governs. Even if there is a strong local interest, federal substantive law governs where the state interest cannot be accommodated without defeating the federal interest. Finding that the "primary objective" of a particular contract was maritime—transportation of goods by sea from Australia to the United States—the Court applied maritime law to a damage claim arising during the land transportation "leg" of the contract. The case undoubtedly will impact upon the lower courts' "mixed contract" doctrine. It should govern where the maritime elements of the contract cannot be adequately promoted by applying state law to some aspects. However, where the state interest is strong and application of state law to some of the elements would not defeat the federal interest, an adequate solution may be to use supplemental jurisdiction and apply state law to some of the non-maritime aspects as "maritime but local."

Much of the jurisprudence on "mixed" contracts has arisen out of offshore mineral exploration, where a single contract may combine the maritime element of transportation by water and the non-maritime element of mineral production from a fixed platform. Many of these contracts contain clauses indemnifying against the indemnitee's negligence. These clauses are valid under maritime law but sometimes are invalid under the otherwise applicable state law. The jurisprudence on the subject has not crystallized into any helpful rule. *See, e.g.*, *Davis & Sons, Inc. v. Gulf Oil Corporation*, 919 F.2d 313 (5th Cir. 1990). *See also*, *Alleman v. Omni Energy Services Corp.*, 570 F.3d 680 (5th Cir. 2009) (holding that a contract to ferry workers to an offshore oil platform by air is not a maritime contract and any indemnity provision therefrom may be invalid under state statute).

Because of abundant particularized precedent, the lack of an adequate overarching formula for determining when a contract is "maritime" has not been of great significance. In the absence of governing precedent, there are some inquiries which may aid a court in its determination. Where the contract is one which is highly likely to be negotiated in detail between parties of equal bargaining power (such as a shipbuilding contract), the parties usually will provide through contract language the substantive law they deem important. In such cases, it is doubtful that maritime shipping and commerce will be promoted significantly by calling the contract maritime, unless there is a perceived need for enforcement in, or interpretation by, a federal court, or for the security of a maritime lien. Where the contract is not one which is likely to be specially negotiated between parties of equal bargaining power (such as a contract for supplies to a vessel, or a seaman's contract of employment), the inquiry then should focus upon whether the parties to the agreement would reasonably anticipate that their rights and liabilities will be governed by a general or uniform maritime law with which they are likely to be somewhat familiar.

B. JURISDICTION OVER MARITIME TORTS

Since 1972, the United States Supreme Court has grappled with the problem of providing a workable test for the presence of maritime tort jurisdiction. After nearly thirty years and four judicial decisions, the Court apparently settled upon a general test that requires (1) that the tort occurred on navigable waters, i.e., on a maritime locality, and (2) that the relevant activity had a maritime connection or flavor. This latter inquiry, maritime "flavor," is further bifurcated into two subparts: (a) does the type of incident involved have the potential to disrupt maritime commerce, and (b) does the general activity involved bear a relationship to a traditional maritime activity? A full understanding of the current test requires some historical explanation.

Perhaps the most quoted language in American maritime law was Justice Samuel Nelson's pronouncement in *The Plymouth*, 70 U.S. 20 (1865), that "[e]very species of tort, however occurring, and whether on board a vessel or not, if upon the high seas or navigable waters, is of admiralty cognizance." From this language and the reaffirmation of it by the Supreme Court, American scholars and judges assumed for more than a century that, in the absence of a congressional statute, the place where the tort occurred was conclusive as to whether it was "in admiralty." If the tort occurred on navigable waters, it was maritime; otherwise, it was not.

Congress seldom has spoken on the issue of maritime tort jurisdiction. In 1920, it enacted the Death on the High Seas Act ("DOHSA"), now 46 U.S.C.A. §§ 30302 et seq., extending the federal admiralty power to torts occurring on the high seas and causing death. Except for those cases coming under

DOHSA, maritime tort jurisdiction was measured by the maritime common law "locality alone" test until the middle of the twentieth century.

Acceptance of the "locality alone" rule was not unanimous. Erastus C. Benedict, one of America's earliest admiralty scholars, expressed doubt with this language:

> Cases of torts on the high seas ... have always been held, even in England, to be within the jurisdiction of the Admiralty. And the jurisdiction in such cases has usually been held to depend upon locality, embracing only civil torts and injuries done on sea, or on waters of the sea, where the tide ebbs and flows. It depends upon the place where the cause of action arises, and that place must be the sea or tide waters. In this country, under the influence of English authority, the same language has been held. It may, however, be doubted whether the civil jurisdiction, in cases of torts, does not depend upon the relation of the parties to a ship or vessel, embracing only those tortious violation (sic) of maritime right and duty which occur in vessels to which the Admiralty jurisdiction, in cases of contracts, applies. If one of several landsmen bathing in the sea, should assault, or imprison, or rob another, it has not been held here that the Admiralty would have jurisdiction of the action for the tort.

(Erastus C. Benedict, The American Admiralty 173 (1850).)

Support for Benedict's "celebrated doubt" (the origin of this phrase was Charles M. Hough, *Admiralty Jurisdiction Of Late Years*, 37 Harv. L. Rev. 529, 531 (1924)) came from the Supreme Court in 1914, when, in *Atlantic Transport Co. v. Imbrovek*, 234 U.S. 52 (1914), it wrote, in dicta:

> But the petitioners urge that the general statements which we have cited, with respect to the exclusiveness of the test of locality in cases of tort, are not controlling; and that in every adjudicated case in this country in which the jurisdiction of admiralty with respect to torts has been sustained, the tort apart from the mere place of its occurrence has been of a maritime character. . . .

> We do not find it necessary to enter upon this broad inquiry.

Despite these warnings, the "locality alone" rule appeared firmly entrenched as the test for determining maritime jurisdiction over torts. Its application often produced anomalous and sometimes absurd results. One of the intolerable results of the "locality alone" rule arose when a vessel struck a pier. If a victim standing on a pier was struck by a ship's sling and knocked into the water, there was no admiralty jurisdiction because the tort "occurred" on "land," i.e., when the sling struck the victim on the pier. *T. Smith & Son v. Taylor*, 276 U.S. 179 (1928). However, if a victim on a vessel was struck by a hoist and knocked onto a pier, the matter was within admiralty jurisdiction, since the tort "occurred" on navigable waters, i.e., the vessel. *Minnie v. Port Huron Terminal Co.*, 295 U.S. 647 (1935). Similarly, the claim for damage to the vessel in a vessel-pier collision was in admiralty but the claim for damage to the pier was not. This often gave rise to an inequitable result since, at that time, most state law barred any recovery by a plaintiff who was at fault to any degree, but maritime law merely reduced the faulty plaintiff's recovery by 50% under the rule of divided damages. (*See* Chapter XII, *infra*). Thus if a vessel struck a bridge and both the vessel and the bridge owner were at fault, the bridge owner would recover nothing, while the vessel could recover one half of its damages.

Congress spoke to this problem in 1948 in the Admiralty Extension Act, now 46 U.S.C.A. § 30101, extending maritime jurisdiction to "all cases of damage or injury caused by a vessel on navigable water, notwithstanding that such damage or injury be done or consummated on land." Even after the adoption of the Admiralty Extension Act, considerable protest against the "locality alone" test developed in the lower courts. Some courts held that a tort was not "in admiralty" unless it had both "locality" and a maritime "flavor" or "nexus." The leading case was *Chapman v. City of Grosse Pointe Farms*, 385 F.2d 962 (6th Cir. 1967).

The Supreme Court scuttled the "locality alone" test for domestic air crash cases in 1972. In *Executive Jet Aviation, Inc. v. Cleveland*, 409 U.S. 249 (1972), a land-based plane, commencing the first leg of a journey from Ohio to Maine to New York, stalled on take-off, struck land, and came to rest in Lake Erie, a short distance from the airport. An action to recover damages for the alleged negligence of the air controller was brought in federal court, with jurisdiction premised solely upon admiralty. The district court dismissed the case, finding neither "locality" nor the maritime "nexus" required by *Chapman v. City of Grosse Pointe Farms, supra.* The Sixth Circuit, affirming, found an absence of "locality" and did not reach the "nexus" question. The Supreme Court granted writs and affirmed, but used its opinion to promulgate a "locality plus nexus" test for determining jurisdiction over maritime torts. In a strict sense, *Executive Jet* merely adopted the "locality plus" rule for domestic airplane accidents. However, the Court expressed such a strong distaste for the "locality alone" rule that the lower courts thereafter unanimously concluded that *Executive Jet* abolished it.

The Supreme Court confirmed the lower courts' conclusions in *Foremost Insurance Co. v. Richardson*, 457 U.S. 668 (1982). There, the Court expressed what it had implied in *Executive Jet*; in the absence of a federal statute, a tort is not "in admiralty" unless it has "maritime flavor." Critically, the case involved a collision between two pleasure boats on navigable water; the Court found the requisite maritime flavor although neither vessel was engaged in maritime commerce at the time of the collision.

After *Executive Jet*, the United States Fifth Circuit developed a test that frequently was followed by other appellate courts. In *Kelly v. Smith*, 485 F.2d 520 (5th Cir.1973), the court identified the following factors that should be considered in determining maritime flavor: (1) the functions and roles of the parties; (2) the types of vehicles and instrumentalities involved; (3) the causation and the type of injury and (4) the traditional concepts of the role of admiralty. In *Sisson v. Ruby*, 497 U.S. 358 (1990) and *Jerome B. Grubart, Inc. v. Great Lakes Dredge & Dock Company*, 513 U.S. 527 (1995), the Supreme Court rejected this test by formulating its own two-part test for determining maritime tort jurisdiction.

In *Sisson*, the Court ruled that admiralty jurisdiction extended to claims arising out of a fire on a pleasure yacht that damaged both the marina at which the yacht was docked and several neighboring vessels. In *Grubart,* a case arising under the Admiralty Extension Act, the Court concluded that admiralty jurisdiction applied to claims for building damage in downtown Chicago resulting from a tunnel flood caused by a vessel's activity in driving piles from a barge into a river bed and by the city's improper maintenance of the tunnel. In finding admiralty jurisdiction in both instances, the Court developed in *Sisson* and refined in *Grubart* the following test for the maritime "connection" (flavor) necessary for admiralty jurisdiction over tort claims: (1) a court first must "assess the general features of the type of incident involved" to determine whether the incident has "a potentially disruptive impact on maritime commerce," and, if so,

(2) the court must determine whether "the general character" of the "activity giving rise to the incident" shows a "substantial relationship to traditional maritime activity."

Following these Supreme Court decisions, the boundaries of admiralty tort jurisdiction may be summarized in this manner:

1. Under the Admiralty Extension Act (AEA), maritime tort jurisdiction extends to all damages "caused by a vessel on navigable water, notwithstanding that such damage ... be done ... on land." Two important questions in applying the statute are (a) does the AEA require "maritime flavor," and (b) how far inland does the AEA extend admiralty jurisdiction?

The answer to the first question probably is that maritime flavor is required, whether the damage caused by the vessel occurs on navigable water or on land. *See, e.g., Grubart, supra; Sohyde Drilling & Marine Co. v. Coastal States Gas Producing Co.*, 644 F.2d 1132 (5th Cir. 1981).

The answer to the second question was addressed in *Grubart*. In that case, the Supreme Court held that the traditional "proximate cause" concept should be applied to determine whether the damage was "caused by a vessel" within the meaning of the AEA, rather than any temporal or spatial limitation on the jurisdictional limit. One obvious concern in using "proximate cause" as a test for subject matter jurisdiction is that a court would have to decide the causation question, usually reserved for the trier of fact, in determining the threshold question of jurisdiction. Recognizing this potential problem, the *Grubart* Court instructed that the jurisdiction issue should be resolved "by means of a nonfrivolous assertion of jurisdictional elements" and a "comparatively summary procedure before a judge alone."

Application of maritime jurisdiction to torts consummated on land increases the possibility that the fault of the vessel will be joined with that of a land-based tortfeasor to cause harm. In *Grubart*, the defendants argued that the presence of a non-maritime tortfeasor weakened the "maritime flavor" of the tort caused by the vessel on navigable waters. In rejecting this argument, the Court concluded that "as long as one of the putative tortfeasors was engaged in traditional maritime activity the allegedly wrongful activity will 'involve' such traditional maritime activity" and will satisfy the "substantial relationship to traditional maritime activity" required for maritime tort jurisdiction.

However, finding maritime jurisdiction over a land-based tortfeasor does not mean that maritime law will apply to all aspects of the case involving that tortfeasor. Difficult issues are certain to arise in cases in which the applicable state law differs from maritime law, such as on the important issue of joint and several liability, since maritime law retains full joint and several liability (*see* Chapter XVII, *infra*), while many states now limit a tortfeasor's liability to that tortfeasor's percentage of the fault. In other words, what law should govern where one tortfeasor is maritime and the other is land based?

Often the application of the AEA produces as much jurisdictional uncertainty as that which prompted the passage of the Act. *Compare Anderson v. United States*, 317 F.3d 1235 (11th Cir.2003) (AEA applies to claim of plaintiff injured on land by bomb fired by an aircraft which was launched from an aircraft carrier; aircraft was an appurtenance of carrier so that plaintiff's injuries were caused by vessel on navigable waters), with *Scott v. Trump Ind., Inc.*, 337 F.3d 939 (7th Cir. 2003) (plaintiff injured when struck by life raft being lifted onto pier by pier-based crane during life raft drill on vessel; neither crane nor raft was appurtenance of vessel). *See also Dahlen v. Gulf Crews, Inc.*, 281 F.3d 487 (5th Cir. 2002) (AEA deemed not applicable to claim for injury sustained while unloading improperly packed groceries from a box on a platform after it was unloaded from supply boat; the AEA does not apply if the defect is not in an appurtenance but is due to personnel performing services for the vessel); *Tagliere v. Harrah's Illinois Corp.*, 445 F.3d 1012 (7th Cir. 2006) (the AEA will apply to a tort action brought against riverboat casino operator by riverboat casino patron who was injured when the stool the patron was leaning against collapsed, causing her to fall, if the riverboat was indefinitely, and not permanently, moored to a pier on a navigable river when the fall occurred). Courts also differ on whether the AEA applies to circumvent a state "dram shop" statute in cases in which casino patrons are injured or caused injury on land as a result of their intoxication aboard the casino vessel.

2. Through the Death on the High Seas Act, maritime tort jurisdiction arguably extends to any tort occurring on the high seas and causing death, even though it does not have "maritime flavor." This conclusion is supported by the language of the Supreme Court in *Executive Jet* and in *Offshore Logistics, Inc. v. Tallentire*, 477 U.S. 207 (1986). *See also, Zicherman v. Korean Air Lines Co.*, 516 U.S. 217 (1996); *Motts v. M/V Green Wave*, 210 F.3d 565 (5th Cir. 2000).

3. In the absence of a statute, maritime tort jurisdiction arguably exists if there is a sufficient maritime "nexus" or "flavor," even though the tort occurs on land. This approach is supported by lower court cases sustaining admiralty jurisdiction over torts consisting of "boycotts" by insurers of seamen who failed to reach satisfactory settlements of their compensation claims, *Carroll v. Protection Maritime Ins. Co., Ltd.*, 512 F.2d 4 (1st Cir. 1975), "retaliatory discharges" by employers of seamen who prosecute their maritime remedies, *Smith v. Atlas Off–Shore Boat Service, Inc.*, 653 F.2d 1057 (5th Cir. 1981), and medical advice given on land to seamen, *Parker v. Gulf City Fisheries*, 803 F.2d 828 (5th Cir. 1986). However, the better view of the Court's opinion in *Foremost Insurance Co. v. Richardson*, page 40, *supra,* is that both "locality" and "flavor" are required. *See also, Broughton v. Florida Int'l. Underwriters, Inc.*, 139 F.3d 861 (11th Cir. 1998);

Smith v. Pan Air Corp., 684 F.2d 1102 (5th Cir. 1982).

4.   In the absence of a statute, maritime tort jurisdiction extends to all torts that (a) occur on navigable waters and (b) have a sufficient maritime "flavor" or "nexus," as refined by the two-part test set forth in *Sisson* and *Grubart*. The standard approach is that a tort occurs when the last act necessary to give rise to a cause of action takes place. Under this approach, an intentional tort is complete when the act is done, and negligence "occurs" when damage has been sustained, i.e., when the instrumentality negligently set into motion by the defendant has an effect upon the person or property of the victim. In a maritime setting involving vessels, piers, and docks, it may be difficult to determine whether that effect takes place on land or on navigable waters. In the overwhelming number of cases, however, there is no difficulty in determining whether there is "locality," and thus the question is whether there is a sufficient "nexus" or "flavor" to support a finding of admiralty jurisdiction.

The lesson of *Sisson* and *Grubart* is that there is a sufficient "nexus" or "flavor" if (1) the general feature or character of the type of incident involved is such that it is likely to disrupt commercial activity, and, if so, (2) there is a substantial relationship between the general activity giving rise to the incident and traditional maritime activity. The incidents involved in *Sisson* and *Grubart* were damages to or by vessels on navigable waters, and the activities which were found to relate to traditional maritime activity were storage and maintenance of a vessel and work performed from a vessel. One may only speculate whether sufficient "flavor" will be found if vessel operation or maintenance is not involved.

In *Executive Jet* the Court emphasized that it was not excluding all accidents involving airplanes and hinted strongly that jurisdiction in admiralty might lie where an aircraft is engaged in a function traditionally performed by waterborne vessels and the tort occurs over navigable waters. The lower courts have followed the Court's lead and will evaluate jurisdiction in such cases based on the purpose of the aircraft's flight. *See, e.g., United States Aviation Underwriters, Inc. v. Pilatus Business Aircraft, Ltd.,* 582 F.3d 1131 (10th Cir. 2009) (holding that admiralty jurisdiction did not extend to a product liability claim arising from an airplane crash in international waters where the crash occurred during a promotional excursion by airplane enthusiasts for the express purpose of aircraft evaluation and demonstration).

A product incorporated into a ship, or the ship itself, may fail at sea and cause damage. If the injured party seeks to recover in tort from the shipbuilder or the supplier of a component part, application of the "locality plus flavor" test may bring the claim within admiralty tort jurisdiction. However, if the injured party seeks to recover against the shipbuilder in contract, state law may govern, because a contract to build a ship is not maritime. The damages sought may be critical to the determination of jurisdiction. The Supreme Court has ruled that when a defective product purchased in a commercial transaction malfunctions, injuring only the product itself and causing purely economic loss (cost of repairs and lost income while the ship is out of service), admiralty tort law does not apply, and the purchaser's remedy is in contract. *East River Steamship Corp. v. Transamerica Delaval, Inc.*, 476 U.S. 858 (1986). If the product is a vessel sold pursuant to a shipbuilding contract, the non-maritime nature of the contract, coupled with the *East River* rule, means there would be no maritime tort jurisdiction over the claim. If the claim is for injury to the person or to other property, then there is a maritime tort claim and possibly maritime tort jurisdiction, depending upon the "locality/flavor" test. (*See* Chapter XI, *infra*).

5.   Maritime law permits certain persons to limit their liability to the value of the vessel involved in the case. 46 U.S.C. § 30505 et seq. (*See* Chapter XVIII, *infra*). In *Sisson* and *Grubart*, the Supreme Court reserved decision on whether the Limitation Act provides an independent basis of federal jurisdiction, or whether there must be maritime jurisdiction over the event which provokes the limitation. In *Richardson v. Harmon*, 222 U.S. 96 (1911), the Court indicated that the Limitation Act conferred an independent basis of federal jurisdiction. The lower courts generally hold that the Act does not confer independent federal jurisdiction. *See, e.g.*,

Three Buoys Houseboat Vacations U.S.A. Ltd. v. Morts, 921 F.2d 775 (8th Cir. 1990).

C. JURISDICTION OVER WORKER INJURY CLAIMS

The third area in which the federal admiralty power has had a great impact upon private American law is in worker injury claims, i.e., claims by employees against their employers or the vessels on which they are employed, or both, for injuries arising out of the employment relationship. Such claims are "in admiralty" and thus governed by maritime law if the employee is either a "seaman" or a "maritime worker." Otherwise, the claims ordinarily are governed by state law.

Since state and maritime law treat worker injury claims differently, definition of the terms "seaman" and "maritime worker" has spawned a staggering volume of litigation. A worker qualifies as a seaman if he or she has a sufficient "employment-related" connection with a vessel in navigation. A seaman may seek traditional tort damages against his negligent employer (through the Jones Act) and from the operator of the vessel as to which he or she is a seaman (through the maritime common law doctrine of unseaworthiness). The seaman's other remedy (primarily against his employer) is maintenance and cure, which provides medical treatment, together with living expenses while undergoing such treatment. Generally, the seaman also may pursue tort actions (under maritime tort law, if applicable) against third party tortfeasors. For a more detailed discussion of who is a "seaman," and the remedies available to seamen, *see* Chapter XIII.

Employees who are engaged in maritime-related activities but who do not qualify as "seamen" may be "maritime workers" entitled to the benefits provided by the Longshore and Harbor Workers' Compensation Act, 33 U.S.C.A. §§ 901–950. Persons covered by the act, which has the attributes of the usual worker's compensation law, include (1) employees injured on the Outer Continental Shelf in the course of mineral exploration and production activities, and (2) employees who fall within the Congressional definition of a "maritime worker," and who are injured on "navigable waters" or designated adjacent property. For a more detailed discussion of which workers qualify for coverage under the Longshore and Harbor Workers' Compensation Act, and the benefits available to them, *see* Chapter XIII.

Employees who do not qualify as seamen and who are not within the coverage of the Longshore and Harbor Workers' Compensation Act ordinarily will recover from their employers through state worker's compensation. For a discussion of the interaction of state worker's compensation and the maritime compensation remedies, *see* Chapters XIII and XV.

CHAPTER IV

SUBSTANTIVE MARITIME LAW: CONTRACTS FOR CARRIAGE OF GOODS

A. GENERALLY

Contracts involving the operation and management of merchant vessels and the carriage of goods and passengers by water are maritime contracts. Consequently, they are within admiralty jurisdiction, and are governed by a comprehensive body of maritime law, both statutory and jurisprudential. These contracts include the lease of a vessel (charter party), the carriage of goods under a bill of lading (regulated by the Harter Act and the Carriage of Goods by Sea Act), and the furnishing of repairs, supplies and other services to vessels. The general principles of these areas of maritime law are discussed in this chapter and in Chapter V.

B. CHARTER PARTIES

A charter is an agreement under which a shipowner places a ship at the disposal of another; it is an agreement to let another use a ship. The instrument by which a vessel is leased is a charter party. The term is derived from *charta partita*, i.e., a deed of writing divided. In earlier times the *charta partita*, like the indenture agreement, was prepared in two parts, with the ship owner retaining one part and the charterer the other.

The three kinds of charter parties which have developed are the demise charter, the time charter, and the voyage charter. The demise charter differs from the latter two in that it is a lease of a vessel which makes the lessee (charterer) the operator of the vessel. In the other two kinds of charters, the owner or lessor remains the operator of the vessel, but the charterer acquires the services of all or part of the vessel for a fixed period of time or for a specified voyage. While a charter party need not be in writing, most charters today are detailed written documents drawn to accommodate the particular needs of shipper and carrier in a certain type of trade or commerce. A charter comes into existence like any other contract—when the parties reach an objective meeting of the minds about the essential terms of the agreement.

1. Demise Charter

The essence of the demise charter is that the owner surrenders possession and control of the vessel to the charterer, who then succeeds to many of the rights and obligations of the owner. Thus the demise charterer is sometimes called the owner *pro hac vice. See, e.g., Matute v. Lloyd Bermuda Lines, Ltd.*, 931 F.2d 231 (3d Cir. 1991). In many demise charters, the charterer also obtains the services of the owner's master and crew, who become employees of the charterer during the term of the charter. In other cases, the owner furnishes a vessel without master or crew; this type of demise is called a bareboat charter. The difference is semantic, since the rights and obligations of the parties to a bareboat charter do not differ from those arising out of other demise charters.

To create a demise charter, the owner of the vessel must "completely and exclusively relinquish possession, command and navigation [of the vessel]. It is therefore tantamount to, though just short of, an outright transfer of ownership. However, anything short of such a complete transfer is a time or voyage charter party or not a charter party at all." *Guzman v. Pichirilo*, 369 U.S. 698 (1962).

Since the owner and charterer are deemed to possess equal bargaining power, an agreement allocating risks between them ordinarily is enforced. In the absence of agreement, admiralty law provides that the owner impliedly warrants that the vessel is seaworthy, i.e., reasonably fit for its intended use, at the commencement of the charter. This warranty may be negated by plain, clear terms in the charter party. In addition, the owner may not be responsible for a defect in the vessel which exists when the vessel is delivered to the charterer, if the charterer inspects the vessel and either discovers or should discover the defect. Descriptions of the vessel in the charter party may constitute warranties if they tend to induce the charterer to enter into the agreement.

In the absence of agreement to the contrary, the obligations of the charterer are to pay the rent and to return the vessel in the same condition as the charterer received it, ordinary wear and tear excepted. The demise charter is a kind of bailment; thus if the owner proves that the vessel was delivered to the charterer in good condition and returned in a damaged condition, the charterer bears the burden of producing evidence that the damage was caused by something other than his negligence. *See, e.g., Commercial Molasses Corp. v. NY Tank Barge Corp.*, 314 U.S. 104 (1941). In the absence of a stipulation in the charter to the contrary, the rent is not reduced when the vessel is taken out of service for repairs during the term of the charter.

A demise charterer may sublease, unless the charter party provides otherwise. Any sublease, of course, must be on terms not inconsistent with those of the initial charter, which sometimes is referred to as the "head" charter.

If a demise charter has been perfected, the owner is relieved of his obligations as owner and operator of the vessel for the term of the charter; liability for the contracts and torts of the master, crew, and vessel falls upon the charterer and upon the vessel *in rem. See, e.g., Agrico Chem. Co. v. M/V Ben W. Martin*, 664 F.2d 85 (5th Cir. 1981). The owner, however, may be liable to third persons for unseaworthiness or negligence predating the commencement of the charter, and one prestigious admiralty court has ruled that the owner is liable to a seaman for damages caused by an unseaworthy condition arising after the commencement of the demise charter. *See Baker v. Raymond Int'l, Inc.*, 656 F.2d 173 (5th Cir. 1981). However, this probably is the minority view. *See, e.g., Backhus v. Transit Cas. Co.*, 549 So.2d 283 (La. 1989) ("the *Baker* rationale is contrary to the [majority] of federal case law.").

2. Time Charter

Under a time charter the owner retains the management and control of the vessel, but the charterer designates the ports of call and the cargo carried. *See, e.g., Moore v. Phillips Petroleum Co.*, 912 F.2d 789 (5th Cir. 1990). The vessel owner provides the crew, equips and maintains the vessel, makes repairs, and pays for normal operating expenses. Each party bears the expenses related to, and the damages generated by, his functions.

The parties may agree that the length of the time charter will be measured by the duration of one or more voyages. In such a case, the amount of charter hire will vary with the amount of time encompassed by the voyage, but the charter remains a time charter with respect to the rights and obligations of the parties. Ordinarily, however, the parties will enter into a time charter for a stated period of time, preceded by the word "about"; the use of that word indicates an intention to provide the charterer with reasonable leeway as to the date of surrender of the vessel at the conclusion of the charter. If a voyage terminates at the port of redelivery near the end of the fixed period, the charterer may elect to surrender the vessel before the expiration of the full term, thus creating an "underlap." Conversely, the charterer may require the vessel to embark upon another "reasonable" voyage near the end of the fixed term, even though the voyage is certain to "overlap" beyond the term. *See, e.g., Wong Wing Fai Co., S.A. v. United States*, 840 F.2d 1462 (9th Cir. 1988). Where there is an "overlap" or "underlap," charter hire is adjusted.

In the absence of contractual agreement, the owner warrants that he will furnish a seaworthy vessel at the commencement of each voyage and that the vessel is reasonably fit to load, carry, and unload the contemplated cargo. Under the particular circumstances, declarations as to the ship's capacity, nationality, class, speed, and fuel consumption may constitute warranties by the owner. The obligation of the charterer is to pay the rent, which usually is based upon the vessel's "deadweight" capacity, i.e., the total weight of cargo, fuel, supplies and ballast that the vessel may carry without being overloaded. Under a time charter (and in some voyage charters) the charterer has the right to designate the port at which the vessel will call. The charter may provide a "safe berth" clause, which imposes upon the charterer the duty to use due diligence in selecting a port and a berth at that port.

Most time charters are confected through the use of standard forms, and any subsequent disputes are resolved through arbitration. Common to these charters, however, is one central theme: since the charterer is leasing the vessel for a fixed period of time at a fixed fee, and must offset his expenses with the value of, or revenue from, freight, he usually is concerned with the efficient operation of the vessel. Thus the charterer ordinarily will insist upon clauses requiring that the vessel proceed with reasonable dispatch during the voyage and that it load and unload "night and day." The charter also may provide for a suspension of rent—sometimes called "off hire"—when the vessel is out of service for repairs. If the time required for repairs is extensive, or other conditions arise that make accomplishment of the commercial object of the charter impossible, the charter is said to be "frustrated," and the agreement may be canceled. Where a vessel under time charter is damaged by the negligence of a third person, the owner may recover any damages sustained through loss of charter hire. The charterer ordinarily may not recover for loss of use or profits caused by damage to the vessel. *Robins Dry Dock & Repair Co. v. Flint*, 275 U.S. 303 (1927). However, the charterer may be able to recover against the tortfeasor where there is no suspension of charter hire during the period in which the vessel is out of service. *Venore Transp. Co. v. M/V Struma*, 583 F.2d 708 (4th Cir. 1978).

The master of a vessel under time charter is the agent of both the shipowner and the charterer. He is the shipowner's agent for the navigation of the vessel, but he acts as agent of the charterer in the handling of the cargo and the selection of loading and discharging ports and berths. Conflict may arise between the interest of the owner in the safety of the vessel and the interest of the charterer in obtaining maximum use of the vessel during the term of the charter. Such a conflict may place the master in the unenviable position of either following the charterer's orders and subjecting the vessel to unreasonable risks, or refusing such orders and providing the charterer with grounds for cancellation of the charter. Some of the difficulty may be alleviated by insertion of a "protest clause" providing that where the charterer orders actions which the master believes will unreasonably endanger the vessel, the master may register a protest with the charterer or the charterer's representative, and if the charterer nevertheless orders the master to proceed, the risk of loss or damage resulting therefrom falls upon the charterer. *See, e.g., Landry v. Oceanic Contractors, Inc.*, 731 F.2d 299 (5th Cir. 1984).

A time charterer or a voyage charterer may be liable to third persons for its negligence in the exercise of its right to control the vessel or the vessel's movement during the term of the charter. *See, e.g., Hodgen v. Forest Oil Corp.*, 87 F.3d 1512 (5th Cir. 1996).

3. Voyage Charter

Under the voyage charter the owner provides a ship, master and crew, and places them at the disposal of the charterer for the carriage of cargo to a designated port. The voyage charterer may lease all of the vessel for a voyage or series of voyages, or he may (by "space charter" or "slot charter") lease only a part of the vessel.

The voyage charter usually is reduced to a detailed written agreement which regulates the rights and liabilities of the parties. The use of brokers to arrange charters between owners and shippers, and the frequency with which some kinds of voyage charters are utilized, has led to some standardization of provisions in voyage charters. These standard forms usually are referred to by code name or short title; thus parties may agree through a broker to charter a vessel under the "Uniform General Charter As Revised 1922," with its code name of "Gencom," or the "Chamber of Shipping Australian Grain Charter 1928," with its code name of "Austral." In the absence of a provision in the charter party to the contrary, the owner who executes a voyage charter warrants that he will furnish a seaworthy vessel at the commencement of the charter and will pay all operating expenses. The obligation to furnish a seaworthy vessel is absolute, but the parties frequently will stipulate that the charter shall be subject to the provisions of the Carriage of Goods by Sea Act, page 51, *infra*, which has the effect of lessening the owner's obligation to that of using due diligence to furnish a seaworthy vessel. A provision subjecting a charter to the Carriage of Goods by Sea Act is called a "clause paramount."

The charterer is obligated to pay the freight, i.e., the rental charges for the voyage. Freight usually is payable only on the cargo actually carried. However, the charter may obligate the charterer to furnish a "full and complete" cargo; if the charterer fails to do so, he will be obligated to pay "dead freight," the freight that would have been due if the cargo had been carried, minus the cost of carrying it.

Frequently the charter will contain a "cesser clause," under which the charterer pays part of the freight in advance and is relieved of any further liability to the vessel owner for the remainder of the freight. In such circumstances, the owner will look to the consignee of the cargo (who is jointly and severally liable with the shipper for the freight) and to the vessel's lien on the cargo (*see* Chapter V) for payment of the remainder of the freight.

Because the owner receives a fixed fee for the voyage, he ordinarily will attempt to complete the voyage as quickly as possible. Thus the owner's primary concern in a voyage charter is that there is no significant delay in commencement of the voyage. The charter normally will specify the expected date upon which the ship will arrive at the loading port. Even though the vessel arrives late, the charterer must load, unless the arrival is so late as to frustrate the charter. However, the charter may provide that if the vessel does not arrive on the specified date, the charterer may cancel. Since a charterer with that option could wait until a tardy vessel arrives before electing to cancel (thus causing the vessel to make an unnecessary stop at the port where the charter was to have commenced) another clause of the charter may require that if it becomes apparent that the vessel will not arrive on the specified date, the charterer must exercise his option to cancel at some fixed time prior to the vessel's arrival.

After the vessel arrives, the shipowner usually has the greater concern about any delay in the commencement of the voyage. The charter will provide that loading will be accomplished within a specific period, called "lay days" or "lay times." When ready to load or discharge, the master or agent of the shipowner will give the charterer a "notice of readiness," which commences the running of "lay days." The charter may require loading or unloading within a certain number of "running" (calendar) days, "workdays," or "weather working days." The contract also may provide that if loading is achieved in a shorter period than that fixed by the charter, the shipowner will pay the charterer a bonus called "dispatch," or if the loading time exceeds that fixed by the charter, the charterer will pay a liquidated compensation termed "contract demurrage." The shipowner's right to recover demurrage may require that he show actual damage from the delay.

Most charters provide for arbitration of the disputes between the owner and the charterer. If the arbitration clause is in writing, it may be enforced in federal court. 9 U.S.C.A. § 1 et seq. A special statute, 9 U.S.C.A. Sec. 8, permits a claimant with a maritime lien to provoke seizure of the vessel or other property in admiralty court, and then compel arbitration, with the admiralty court retaining jurisdiction over the seized property for subsequent enforcement of the arbitration award.

C. BILLS OF LADING

1. The Allocation of Risks Between Shipper and Carrier

A merchant who ships a large volume of goods over water can charter a vessel for the carriage of his goods, and since they ordinarily enjoy equal bargaining power, maritime law permits the shipper and carrier to allocate between themselves the risks of the voyage. Their contract, the charter party, governs, and maritime law is primarily concerned with interpreting and enforcing the contract and with allocating the risks about which the contract is silent.

The smaller shipper, however, may be at some bargaining disadvantage. Since the volume of goods that he ships may not justify chartering a vessel or a part of it, he cannot induce a carrier to make a specific voyage. He must rely upon those vessels which make more or less regular voyages to designated ports on fixed schedules, and which offer themselves as willing to carry the goods of any shipper to any one of the ports of call. These vessels are called common carriers, or liners, as distinguished from private carriers, which haul cargo only for certain designated shippers, and tramp steamers, which carry goods between ports anywhere in the world on voyage or time charters.

When a common carrier receives goods for shipment, it usually issues a bill of lading to the shipper. This bill of lading can serve several functions. First, the bill of lading is the shipper's receipt from the carrier for the goods delivered for shipment. Second, the bill of lading may be negotiable. In a legal sense, this essentially means that the document represents the goods themselves. A federal statute, 49 U.S.C.A. Sec. 80101, et seq., formerly the Pomerone Act, 49 U.S.C.A. § 81, et seq., provides that a bill of lading for transportation of goods between the United States and a foreign country is negotiable unless the parties specifically agree otherwise. If the bill is issued in a foreign country for shipment of goods into the United States, negotiability depends upon the law of that country; however, ocean bills of lading usually are treated as negotiable by the maritime law of seafaring nations. Since the bill of lading usually is negotiable, the shipper may use it to borrow money on the goods while they are in transit, pledging the bill to the lender. The shipper also may use the bill to obtain payment for his goods from the consignee in a distant port by forwarding and tendering the bill, with draft attached, to the consignee's bank at the port of destination.

The final critical function of the bill, and the one with which we are here concerned, is that it serves as the contract allocating the risks of the voyage between the shipper and carrier. However, it is a contract extensively regulated by legislation. A little history will explain how American and international law developed this regulation. Early maritime common law imposed upon the carrier all of the risks of the loss of the goods during the voyage except damages caused by Acts of God or by the fault of the shipper. Predictably, common carriers began limiting that broad liability by inserting clauses in bills of lading relieving them from some of the risks of the voyage. Because of their superior bargaining power, the carriers, through such clauses, eventually were able to exculpate themselves from all liability to the shipper or his consignee, even those damages caused by the negligence of the master and crew during the voyage. American courts refused to honor these exculpatory clauses, holding them invalid because of the inequality of bargaining power between shippers and common carriers. However, courts of other maritime nations upheld such clauses, thus giving foreign carriers an economic advantage over American carriers. To lessen the advantage, Congress adopted the Harter Act, 46 U.S.C.A. § 190 et seq. (now 46 U.S.C.A. § 30701, et seq.), making a statutory allocation of the risks between shipper and carrier.

In its basic allocation of risks, the Harter Act requires the carrier to use due diligence in sending out a seaworthy vessel at the commencement of the voyage and holds the carrier responsible for its negligence in the handling of the cargo during the voyage. If the carrier uses due diligence to send out a seaworthy vessel, it is not responsible for damage caused by other designated risks, such as errors in navigation or management of the vessel and insufficiency of packaging, and it may by contract (clauses in the bill of lading) exculpate itself from risks other than negligence in handling the cargo. Under Harter, the exercise of due diligence to send out a seaworthy vessel is a prerequisite to the carrier's freedom from responsibility for the other statutorily identified risks (*e.g.,* error in navigation), even if there is no causal relationship between the unseaworthiness and the loss.

The compromise struck by Congress in the Harter Act impressed other nations, and served as the blueprint for proposed legislation regulating shipments between foreign ports. This proposal was adopted at an international diplomatic conference in 1924 under the name of the Brussels Convention for the Unification of Certain Rules of Law Relating to Bills of Lading. The United States and most of the other maritime nations subsequently adopted the suggested legislation, the American version being the Carriage of Goods By Sea Act (COGSA), 46 U.S.C.A. § 1300 et seq. Subsequent proposals for modification of the Brussels Convention, such as the 1976 Visby Amendments and the 1978 Hamburg Rules and the Hague–Visby Amendment, met with modest success. A later version of the rights and obligations of parties involved in maritime shipping, called the Rotterdam Rules, has been signed by a number of nations, including the United States, and will become international law upon ratification by 20 nations. The United States Senate has not yet ratified the Rotterdam Rules, which make substantial changes in the law, including increasing the limitation amount of carriers, defining "packages" for purposes of the limitation of the carrier's liability, and providing greater details for the liability for losses, claims procedures and the obligations of the various parties involved in maritime shipping. This work does not provide details of the Rotterdam Rules but continues the discussion of the governing American law, the Harter Act and the Carriage of Goods By Sea Act. Even such discussion, however, has been complicated. In 2006, the substantive provisions of the codified American admiralty law were reenacted from the appendix of Title 46 of the U.S. Code to the main portion of Title 46. The Harter Act was generally recodified as 46 U.S. Code Sec. 30710, et seq. The Carriage of Goods By Sea Act, formerly located in 46 U.S. Code Secs. 1300–1315, was not codified with new section numbers, but a historical note to Section 30701 sets forth the original provisions of the Carriage of Goods By the Sea Act, listing them by section numbers (1 through 16 of the original act) and an appended comment states that although the Harter Act was recodified, Secs. 1300 to 1315 were not recodified but "were not repealed, omitted or restated by" the codifying act. An argument can be made that COGSA is no longer in effect, but lower courts have reached the conclusion that COGSA was not repealed by Public Law 109–304 but continues as viable. *See, e.g.*, *CNA Ins. Co. v. Hyundai Merch. Marine Co.*, 2009 WL 700206, 2009 A.M.C. 738 (W.D.Ky. 2009). These issues demand legislative or authoritative judicial clarification. In this work, we continue discussion of the Harter Act and COGSA, citing the new codification numbers for the Harter Act and the initial codification numbers of the COGSA (since those numbers appear in all of the prior jurisprudence and in some of the subsequent jurisprudence).

In adopting COGSA, Congress provided that the Harter Act would remain applicable to situations not within the reach of the new legislation. Thus the student of maritime law must understand both Harter and COGSA. COGSA applies to "[e]very bill of lading ... which is evidence of a contract for the carriage of goods by sea to or from ports of the United States." 46 U.S.C.A. § 1300. The Harter Act applies to all voyages, including those between American ports and between American and foreign ports. COGSA applies only to the risks of the voyage between loading at the port of departure and unloading at the port of destination, while the Harter Act allocates the risks from delivery to the carrier until redelivery to the consignee at a fit and customary wharf. Consequently, the acts apply in the following manner. On a voyage between an American port and a foreign port, the Harter Act applies from delivery to the shipper until loading, and from unloading at the port of destination until delivery to the consignee; COGSA applies between loading and unloading. On a voyage between American ports, absent permissible agreement discussed below, the Harter Act applies at all times between delivery and redelivery. The parties may not by their contract lessen the duties imposed upon the carrier by COGSA or Harter. However, when Harter applies, the parties may stipulate that their rights will be governed by COGSA, either (1) from delivery to loading and from unloading to redelivery, in voyages between American and foreign ports; or (2) for the entire voyage, in shipments between American ports. (When the latter stipulation is made, the parties are said to have exercised a "coastwise option.") Parties may not avoid COGSA and Harter by stipulating to foreign law which imposes less responsibility upon the carrier or by adopting a "forum selection" clause which would have the same effect. However, a clause calling for foreign arbitration is *not* in and of itself unenforceable. The party seeking to avoid enforcement of the forum selection clause must establish that litigation in the agreed upon forum would lessen the carrier's responsibility below that which is provided for in COGSA.

The co-existence of the Harter Act and COGSA has not produced much difficulty, partly because the parties frequently stipulate that COGSA applies and partly because the acts generally make the same allocation of risks. As noted above, there are some major differences, however. The Harter Act provides that

If the owner of [a] vessel ... shall exercise due diligence to make the ... vessel in all respects seaworthy ... the vessel ... shall ... [not] be held responsible for damage[s] ... resulting from faults or errors in navigation or in the management of said vessel nor ... for losses arising from dangers of the sea or ... acts of God....

46 U.S.C.A. § 192 (new 46 U.S.C. § 30706). Seizing upon this language, the courts have held that if the vessel owner defaults in its duty to use due diligence to send out a seaworthy vessel, it may not claim the benefit of the exculpatory language in Harter or in the bill of lading, even though the unseaworthiness did not play any part in the loss or damage to the cargo. Alternatively, under COGSA, the carrier's failure to use due diligence to send out a seaworthy vessel imposes liability upon the carrier only if the unseaworthiness was a cause of the damage to the goods. 46 U.S.C.A. § 1304(1) (Sec. 3, COGSA).

Secondly, under the Harter Act, a carrier may limit its liability for damage to any amount, but COGSA prohibits a carrier from limiting its liability to less than "$500 per package, or customary freight unit." (Judicial interpretation of the terms "package" and "customary freight unit" are discussed elsewhere in this chapter.) Under either Harter or COGSA, any limitation of the carrier's liability to an amount less than the actual loss sustained is valid only if the carrier gives the shipper "a fair opportunity to choose between higher or lower liability by paying a correspondingly greater or lesser charge." *New York, New Haven & Hartford R.R. Co. v. Nothnagle*, 346 U.S. 128 (1953); *Tessler Bros. (B.C.) Ltd. v. Italpacific Line*, 494 F.2d 438 (9th Cir. 1974).

COGSA contains a one-year statute of limitations on claims by shippers for loss or damage to cargo. 46 U.S.C.A. § 1303(6) (Sec. 3(6), COGSA). The one-year period begins to run at delivery of the goods. Delivery may occur when the goods are delivered to the person entitled to receive the goods from the carrier, even though that person is not the consignee. *See Servicios–Expoarma v. Industrial Maritime Carriers, Inc.*, 135 F.3d 984 (5th Cir. 1998) (delivery to authorized customs warehouse triggered the one year limitations period). The Harter Act does not contain a statute of limitations; hence the general maritime rule of laches—unreasonable delay and prejudice to the defendant—applies.

In general, allocation of risks under the Harter Act and COGSA is that the carrier must use due diligence to send out a seaworthy vessel and must "properly and carefully load, handle, stow, carry, keep, care for, and discharge the goods carried." 46 U.S.C.A. § 1303(2), Sec. 3, COGSA. The remaining risks of the voyage—including damage caused by negligence in the operation or management of the vessel—fall upon the shipper, either through the statutory allocation of risks in COGSA, or, where Harter applies, through statutory or contractual allocation of risks (under Harter these risks fall on the shipper only if the carrier has exercised due diligence to send out a seaworthy vessel).

Seaworthiness connotes that the vessel is reasonably fit for its intended use; in carriage contracts, this means the vessel is "reasonably fit to carry the cargo which she has undertaken to transport." *The*

Silvia, 171 U.S. 462 (1898). Seaworthiness extends to the construction of the vessel and to its equipment, master, and crew. A vessel also may be unseaworthy because of the manner in which it is loaded. The vessel must be able to withstand the expected weather conditions of the voyage; if cargo is lost or damaged because of weather conditions, and the weather which was encountered was not unusual, it is presumed that the vessel was unseaworthy.

There is no absolute duty to send out a seaworthy vessel; the carrier's duty is only to use due diligence to do so. However, the duty which is imposed may be non-delegable. If so, a shipowner who engages a competent shipyard to inspect and repair its vessel prior to sailing is not relieved of liability for the negligence of the shipyard in failing to discover or to repair properly a condition that was discoverable in the exercise of due diligence and that makes the vessel unseaworthy.

Under American maritime law, the duty to use due diligence to send out a seaworthy vessel ends with the commencement of the voyage. Determining when a voyage begins has been made difficult by new methods of shipping, such as the utilization of barges loaded on a "mother ship" for the ocean voyage but detached and navigated separately in inland waters for loading and delivery of goods at dockside. Even after the voyage has begun, the duty to exercise due diligence to send out a seaworthy vessel may re-arise if the owner regains control after the voyage has begun. *May v. Hamburg–Amer-*

ikanische Packetfahrt Aktiengesellschaft, 290 U.S. 333 (1933).

The carrier's duty to use due diligence may arise as to each shipper at the port at which his or her cargo is loaded. The operator of a vessel on a voyage from Houston to New York via New Orleans will owe the duty to cargo loaded at Houston until the vessel breaks port there, but will owe the duty to cargo loaded in New Orleans until departure at that port. Thus, if the discoverable unseaworthy condition arises during the Houston to New Orleans "leg" of the journey, but is not discovered before the ship breaks ground at New Orleans, the carrier may have breached his duty to cargo loaded at New Orleans, but not to cargo loaded at Houston.

A carrier is not liable to the shipper or consignee for damages to the goods caused by negligence in the operation and management of the vessel. Since the concept of "seaworthiness" extends to the soundness of procedures utilized in the operation and management of the vessel, nice disputes arise as to whether an improper procedure constitutes mere negligence in operation and management, or makes the vessel unseaworthy. *See, e.g., Usinas Siderugicas de Minas Geras, S.A.–Usiminas v. Scindia Steam Nav. Co., Ltd.*, 118 F.3d 328 (5th Cir. 1997).

The second risk falling upon the carrier is that it is liable for negligence in failing to "properly and carefully load, handle, stow, carry, keep, care for, and discharge the goods carried." 46 U.S.C.A.

§ 1303(2), Sec. 3, COGSA. The carrier must know the characteristics of the cargo which it agrees to carry and must afford the cargo the type of stowage which those characteristics require. Issuance of a bill of lading which does not provide for storage on deck—a "clean" bill of lading—requires storage below decks, except in some limited cases in which custom dictates otherwise. The duty to "properly . . . discharge the goods" imposed by COGSA, 46 U.S.C.A. § 1303(2), Sec. 3, COGSA, and to make "proper delivery" required by the Harter Act, 46 U.S.C.A. § 30704 (formerly Secs. 190–91), is fulfilled when the carrier unloads the cargo onto a dock, segregates it, and makes it accessible to the consignee.

The carrier is not responsible for loss arising from "act, neglect, or default of the master, mariner, pilot, or the servants of the carrier in the navigation or in the management of the ship." 46 U.S.C.A. § 1304(2)(a). The distinction between negligence in the stowage and handling of cargo, for which the carrier is responsible, and error in the operation and management of the vessel, for which it is not, is sometimes elusive. Gilmore & Black suggest that the distinction should turn upon whether the negligent act imperils only cargo, or whether it places both cargo and vessel in danger. Gilmore & Black, *supra,* p. 159. Benedict on Admiralty suggests that the issue may hinge upon whether the negligent act also would be an ordinary incident of storage on land; if not, then the negligence properly should be classified as that in management of the vessel. Michael F. Sturley, 2A Benedict on Admiralty § 136 at 13–20.

The shipper bears the risk of "insufficiency of packing." 46 U.S.C.A. § 1304(2)(n); Sec. 4, COGSA. The goods must be packed in such a manner that they are fit to endure the ordinary hazards of the voyage. Customs in the industry, as well as federal and industry regulations, are relevant but not controlling on the issue of whether the packing is sufficient. Since almost all goods can be packed, or can be stowed and handled, in such a manner as to avoid damage through ocean carriage, the overlap of these two risks obviously requires drawing a line at some reasonable place.

Other specific provisions in COGSA relieve the carrier from liability for a number of other losses, including acts of war and public enemies, "restraint of princes," strikes or lockouts, and riots.

Three types of risks allocated to the shipper raise issues somewhat different from the other risks allocated to the shipper. By statute under COGSA, 46 U.S.C.A. § 1304(2)(c) and (d), Sec. 4, COGSA, and through the common law or a customary provision in the bill of lading where the Harter Act applies, the shipper bears the risk of loss caused by an "Act of God" or a "peril of the sea." A peril of the sea has been defined as a fortuitous action of the elements at sea of such force as to overcome the strength of a well-founded ship or the usual precautions of good seamanship. *Chiswick Products, Ltd. v. S.S. Stolt Avance*, 257 F.Supp. 91 (S.D.Tex.

1966). An Act of God has been defined as an accident "due to natural causes directly and exclusively, without human intervention, ... [which] ... could not have been prevented by any amount of foresight and ... care reasonably to be expected from [the carrier]." *Mamiye Bros. v. Barber Steamship Lines, Inc.*, 241 F.Supp. 99 (S.D.N.Y. 1965). Thus a carrier attempting to avoid liability through these exceptions essentially must prove that it was not negligent.

Congress initially allocated the risk of loss by fire in the "Fire Statute," adopted in 1851. That statute, formerly 46 U.S.C.A. § 182 (now 46 U.S.C. Sec. 30564), exempts the carrier (either shipowner or demise charterer) from liability to the shipper for loss caused by fire on board the vessel unless the fire was caused by the "design or neglect" of the owner. COGSA, while expressly saving the Fire Statute from repeal, exempts the carrier (the shipowner or any charterer, including a time or voyage charterer) from liability for damage caused by fire, unless caused by "the actual fault or privity" of the carrier. 46 U.S.C.A. § 1304(2)(b), Sec. 4(2)(a), COGSA. The courts have concluded that "design or neglect" and "actual fault or privity" have the same meaning, i.e., personal negligence of the owner (or, in the case of a corporate owner, negligence of its managing officers and agents), as distinguished from the negligence of the master and crew. *See, e.g., Nissan Fire & Marine Ins. Co., Ltd. v. M/V Hyundai*, 93 F.3d 641 (9th Cir. 1996). Since heat without fire also may damage cargo, the courts usually require that the damage be accompanied by some visible flame before the "fire" provision applies. A carrier seeking exoneration under the "fire" provisions first must prove that the damage was caused by fire. If it meets this burden, the weight of authority is that the shipper then must prove that the fire was caused by the "design or neglect" of the shipowner. *See, e.g., Westinghouse Electric Corp. v. M/V Leslie Lykes*, 734 F.2d 199 (5th Cir. 1984). A minority view is that the carrier also must prove that it exercised due diligence to send out a seaworthy vessel—akin to the general Harter scheme.

COGSA also contains a "catch all" exception which relieves the carrier from liability for "[a]ny other cause arising without the actual fault and privity of the carrier . . . [or his agents] . . . but the burden of proof shall be on the person claiming the benefit of this exception" to show that carrier fault did not contribute to the loss or damage. 46 U.S.C.A. § 1304(2)(q), Sec. 4(2)(q), COGSA.

2. Proof of Claims; The Burden of Proof

As with many other areas of law, the manner in which the burden of proof is allocated in cargo damage claims plays a major role in determining who bears the loss. The initial burden is with the plaintiff (shipper or consignee, hereinafter called the shipper), who must establish a *prima facie* case that the goods were damaged or lost while in the possession of the carrier. The shipper can meet the burden by showing that the goods were delivered to the carrier in an undamaged condition and were not redelivered, or were redelivered in a damaged condition. When the carrier issues the bill of lading, it must show "[t]he apparent order and condition of the goods." 46 U.S.C.A. § 1303(3)(c), Sec. 3(3), COGSA. If the defective or damaged condition could have been observed by the carrier at the time the goods were shipped, the shipper may meet his or her burden of establishing that the goods were received by the carrier in good condition by introducing the bill of lading reflecting receipt "in apparent good condition." The shipper also must prove the failure of the carrier to redeliver the goods, or their receipt in a damaged condition. On this issue, however, COGSA may provide the carrier, and not the shipper, with a favorable presumption. If the shipper fails to give notice of

loss or damage and the general nature of such loss or damage ... in writing to the carrier ... at the port of discharge before or at the time of the removal of the goods into the custody of the person entitled to delivery thereof ... such removal shall be prima facie evidence of the delivery by the carrier of the goods as described in the bill of lading.

46 U.S.C.A. § 1303(6), Sec. 3(6), COGSA. If the loss or damage is not apparent, the presumption applies if notice is not given within three days of delivery.

When the shipper has made a *prima facie* showing that the goods were damaged or lost in transit, the burden shifts to the carrier to prove that the loss or damage resulted from a cause for which it is not responsible. Its first option is to prove that the loss or damage was caused by vessel negligence for which it is not responsible (neglect in navigation or management of the ship). 46 U.S.C.A. § 1304(2)(a), Sec. 4(2)(a), COGSA. Its second option is to show that the loss or damage resulted from other causes for which it is not chargeable under COGSA, such as unseaworthiness which developed after the voyage began, pre-voyage unseaworthiness which could not have been discovered in the exercise of due diligence, fire, a peril of the sea, an Act of God, or some other risk imposed upon the shipper by the provisions of 46 U.S.C.A. § 1304(2)(b)–(p), Sec. 4(2), COGSA. If the carrier chooses this second option, it probably need not also negate its own negligence, although in some cases, proof of an exculpatory cause necessarily will negate vessel negligence, such as where the carrier establishes that the loss was caused by a "peril of the sea." 46 U.S.C.A. § 1304(2)(c), Sec. 4(2)(c), COGSA. *See, e.g., Taisho Marine & Fire Ins. Co. v. M/V Sea–Land Endurance*, 815 F.2d 1270 (9th Cir. 1987). The carrier's third option is to prove that the loss or damage was the result of some other cause under the "q" clause, but in that case it bears the burden of proving that "neither the actual fault or privity of the carrier nor the fault or neglect of the agents or servants of the carrier contributed to the loss or damage." 46 U.S.C.A. § 1304(2)(q), Sec. 4(2)(q), COGSA. If the carrier's proof of an exculpatory cause does not negate vessel negligence for which it remains responsible under the act, the shipper, at least theoretically, then has the opportunity to establish such negligence and the fact that negligence also was a cause of the damage to the goods.

The evidence may establish that the goods were damaged by risks chargeable to both carrier and shipper. In such a case, if the damages are divisible—a rare occasion—liability should be imposed upon each for that damage caused by the risk chargeable to him. But if, as in nearly all cases, the damages are indivisible, maritime law imposes upon the carrier liability for the full amount of the damages. *See, e.g., Sun Company Inc. v. S.S. Overseas Arctic*, 27 F.3d 1104 (5th Cir. 1994). The suggestion that this rule should be modified, because of the "pure" comparative negligence which now pervades maritime law, apparently has gone unheeded.

3. Damages

At common law the carrier is liable for the market value of the lost cargo at destination or, if the cargo is damaged, for the difference between market value and value, damaged, at destination. Before and after the Harter Act, carriers inserted provisions in bills of lading limiting their liability to the value of the goods as declared in the bill or to a stated sum "per package." These restrictions probably are valid under Harter, if the shipper is afforded the opportunity to pay a higher freight rate and obtain the liability of the carrier for a greater amount. A limitation of liability may be so low as to violate public policy, however.

COGSA, 46 U.S.C.A. § 1304(5), Sec. 4(5), COGSA provides:

> Neither the carrier nor the ship shall in any event become liable for any loss or damage ... in an amount exceeding $500 per package ... or in case of goods not shipped in packages, per customary freight unit ... unless the nature and value of such goods have been declared by the shipper before shipment and inserted in the bill of lading.... By agreement between the carrier ... and the shipper another maximum amount ... may be fixed: Provided, That such maximum shall not be less than the figure above named. In no event shall the carrier be liable for more than the amount of damage actually sustained.

Section 1303(8), Sec. 3(8), COGSA provides that any clause which lessens the liability of the carrier of the ship "otherwise than as provided in this chapter" shall be null and void.

Under these provisions the carrier must give the shipper an opportunity to declare the value of the goods. The carrier bears the initial burden of proving that the shipper was given a "fair opportunity" to declare the value. Some courts hold that the carrier makes out a *prima facie* case of "fair opportunity" if he shows that the shipper had "constructive notice," i.e., if the bill of lading refers to COGSA, or to a long form bill of lading or a tariff which advises him of the opportunity. Other courts reject the "constructive notice" approach and hold that the bill is *prima facie* evidence of fair opportunity only if the language appears on the face of the bill of lading issued to the shipper. For a discussion of the cases, *see Henley Drilling Co. v. McGee*, 36 F.3d 143 (1st Cir. 1994); *Ferrostaal, Inc. v. M/V Sea Phoenix*, 447 F.3d 212 (3d Cir. 2006). Where the shipper declares a value higher than $500 per package, he may recover the amount of his loss or the value he has declared, whichever is less. However, under COGSA (see discussion of Harter, *infra*) any declaration of value which is less than $500 per package is void, and the shipper may recover the full amount of his loss. If the shipper does not declare the value of the goods, the carrier is liable for the amount of the shipper's loss or $500 per package, whichever is less.

If the goods are encased—or perhaps partially encased—they will be treated as a single "package" for the purposes of these provisions limiting liability; otherwise, the "customary freight unit" provision is applicable. For example, if freight is computed at a lump sum for carriage of a railroad locomotive, and the locomotive is not shipped in a "package," the lump sum on which the freight is computed will be the "customary freight unit" for the purpose of determining the carrier's liability. Freight on bulk cargo usually is computed on a tonnage basis, and the limitation of $500 per ton applies. If the freight charge is a lump sum, the entire shipment may be treated as the customary freight unit.

Much litigation has arisen over the terms "package" and "customary freight unit"; as Gilmore &

Black observe, "[t]hese words have created a wilderness of problems." Gilmore & Black, p. 187. The underlying premise is that at or prior to shipment, both shipper and carrier should be able to determine the effect of the $500 limitation, and then may respond, either by an adjustment of the carrier's liability and freight charges, or by the shipper's purchase of additional insurance. "Package" and "customary freight unit," terms of art, do not always provide the carrier or shipper with the foresight with which to respond.

One nice problem: when the carrier repacks the goods, is the "package" that in which the shipper delivered the goods, or that in which they are repacked by the carrier? The jurisprudence has not produced a satisfactory answer. The proper focus should be the reasonable expectations of the shipper at the time the goods leave his hands, since he presumably will obtain insurance that reflects those expectations. The shipper's reasonable expectations turn upon such factors as the manner in which the goods are described in the bill of lading and whether the goods were packed by the shipper in such a manner as to withstand the foreseeable perils of the contemplated voyage. If the bill describes the goods as consisting of a certain number of packages, and the shipper delivers that number of cargoworthy packages, subsequent action by the carrier should not operate to reduce the shipper's protection. Even where the goods require repacking for shipment, the shipper's description of the number of packages in the bill of lading probably should prevail, since the carrier ordinarily has the last opportunity to obtain a clarification and thus avoid the controversy which may arise if the goods are lost or damaged after repackaging. Any ambiguity in the bill of lading regarding the number of COGSA packages probably will be resolved in favor of the shipper. *See, e.g., Sony Magnetic Products Inc. of America v. Merivienti O/Y*, 863 F.2d 1537 (11th Cir. 1989).

The advent of containerized maritime shipping has injected additional uncertainty into the "package" problem. The courts hold that the entire container may be the relevant "package" for the purposes of section 1305 of COGSA. *See, e.g., Fishman & Tobin, Inc. v. Tropical Shipping & Construction Co., Ltd.*, 240 F.3d 956 (11th Cir. 2001). *Compare Monica Textile Corp. v. S.S. Tana*, 952 F.2d 636 (2d Cir. 1991). If the shipper delivers to the carrier a certain number of packages suitable for shipment without repacking, and describes that number of packages in the bill of lading, the carrier should not be able to lessen its liability by placing the packages in a container. Arguably, where the shipper delivers a sealed container and does not reveal the contents, the carrier should be entitled to treat the container as a single package. Between those "poles" are situations which may best be decided on a case by case basis, with the important inquiry being the reasonable expectations of the parties.

A provision in a bill of lading limiting the carrier's liability to less than $500 per package or customary freight unit may be valid under the Harter Act but invalid under COGSA. What if damage occurs after unloading but before delivery to the consignee and the parties have not stipulated to coverage by COGSA during that period? Some courts have held that the Harter Act "springs back" and the limitation clause applies, but others have concluded that the limitation clause, invalid under COGSA while the goods were aboard the vessel, cannot be revived by subsequent reapplication of the Harter Act.

Carriers frequently will attempt to extend the defenses and protections of COGSA to their agents and contractors. Bill of lading clauses extending such protection, known as Himalaya clauses, are valid. In *Robert C. Herd & Co. v. Krawill Machinery Corp.*, 359 U.S. 297 (1959), the Supreme Court said that such a clause would be "strictly construed and limited to intended beneficiaries." That case involved an attempt to extend a Himalaya clause to stevedores. More recently, in *Norfolk Southern Railway Company v. Kirby*, 543 U.S. 14 (2004), the Court gave a Himalaya clause a more expansive and literal meaning, applying it to "downstream carriers." *Kirby* did not resolve all of the issues arising out of intermodal shipping. Courts are divided on whether maritime law applies to the land portion if a separate bill of lading is issued for that portion, and whether the Carmack Amendment, a federal statute governing liability of land carriers, applies to the carrier's liability for damage to the goods during the land based portion of the trip. *Compare Sompo Japan Ins. Co. of America v. Union Pacific R. Co.*, 456 F.3d 54 (2d Cir. 2006), and *Altadis USA*

Inc. v. Sea Star Line LLC, 458 F.3d 1288 (11th Cir. 2006).

4. Deviation

The bill of lading specifies the voyage upon which the goods will be carried and frequently designates the method of stowage during the voyage. At common law, any deviation by the carrier from the specified voyage, or from the designated method of stowage, made the carrier liable for damage to the cargo, regardless of whether the deviation was related causally to the damage. The reason for the rule was that the insurance coverage then available to cargo provided that any deviation voided the policy. Deviation no longer voids the shipper's policy; the "held covered" clause in the policy provides for coverage notwithstanding the deviation, with a subsequent rate adjustment to reflect increased risks caused by the deviation. COGSA is silent on the issue of whether impermissible deviation makes the carrier liable for damages to the cargo when there is no causal connection between the deviation and the damage. The jurisprudence has not provided a clear answer. Some cases hold that deviation will "oust the contract" and impose liability upon the carrier only if the deviation was the cause of the damage to the goods. The weight of authority is that an unreasonable deviation will deprive the carrier of the $500 per package limitation provided by § 1304(5) of COGSA (*see* page 69, *supra*). *See also, Minerais U.S. Inc. v. M/V Moslavina*, 46 F.3d 501 (5th Cir. 1995). Intentional unexcused destruction of the cargo constitutes deviation. *Vision Air Flight Service, Inc. v. M/V Nat'l. Pride*, 155 F.3d 1165 (9th Cir. 1998).

COGSA provides by implication that only an unreasonable deviation is a breach of the contract of carriage. It also makes certain deviations—those for the purpose of attempting to save life or property at sea—*per se* reasonable, and makes others—those for the purpose of loading and unloading cargo and passengers—*prima facie* unreasonable. 46 U.S.C.A. § 1304(4) (Sec. 4(4), COGSA).

An unreasonable delay in the commencement or prosecution of the voyage constitutes deviation. The bill of lading will specify the ports of call on the voyage and the carrier is expected to proceed to those ports along the customary shipping routes. A bill of lading may contain a clause which sanctions every conceivable kind of deviation by the vessel from the customary routes and ports of call. This "liberty clause" has been construed by the courts to authorize only reasonable departures from the normal route. *See, e.g., Rainbow Nav., Inc. v. United States*, 937 F.2d 105 (3d Cir. 1991). Courts have been hesitant to recognize other non-geographic but fundamental breaches of the contract of carriage as deviations.

The bill of lading may specify stowage below deck or some other special method of stowage. A departure from the method specified will constitute a deviation. If the bill of lading specifies stowage above deck, COGSA does not apply. The maritime common law prior to COGSA was that if the bill specified stowage above deck, the carrier was liable only for negligence causing damage to the goods. Apparently both shipper and carrier were satisfied with that allocation of risk, and it was continued by excluding such stowage from coverage under COGSA. 46 U.S.C.A. § 1301(C).

Frequently, goods will be shipped under a "clean" bill of lading, i.e., a bill which (1) does not indicate that the goods or their container were in any manner defective when received by the carrier, and (2) does not prescribe the place or manner of stowage of the goods. A "clean" bill of lading imports that the goods will be stowed below deck. Where goods shipped under a "clean" bill of lading are not stowed below deck and are damaged, the courts must determine whether the stowage constituted deviation. The search generally is for the intent of the parties as to the manner in which the goods would be carried. Some courts determine intent from the customary method of carrying such goods, while others hold that a method of stowage constitutes an "unreasonable deviation" only when such stowage is in an area of the vessel which is not intended for stowage, and which exposes the cargo to a greater risk.

5.   Bills of Lading in Charter Parties

The question of whether COGSA regulates the rights of the shipper and carrier when a bill of lading is issued in conjunction with a charter party apparently is unresolved. The parties to the charter may stipulate for the application of COGSA through a "clause paramount." If there is no such stipulation, COGSA provides some hazy guidelines. Section 1300 (Sec. 1, COGSA) limits the effect of COGSA to a bill of lading "which is evidence of a contract for the carriage of goods by sea," and Section 1301(b) (Sec. 1(B), COGSA) provides that a "contract of carriage" includes "any bill of lading ... issued ... pursuant to a charter party from the moment at which such bill of lading ... regulates the relations between a carrier and the holder of the same." Section 1305 of COGSA (Sec. 1(B), COGSA), provides that "if bills of lading are issued in the case of a ship under a charter party, they shall comply with the terms of this chapter." The prevailing view probably is that if the bill remains in the hands of the shipper, the charter, and not the bill of lading, is the "contract of carriage" between the parties, but if the bill is negotiated to a third person, it becomes the "contract of carriage," and any provisions of the charter in conflict with COGSA are unenforceable. What if there are provisions in the charter party which are not in conflict with COGSA? The better view appears to be that such provisions can be given effect against the third-party holder of the bill only if he knew or should have known of the existence of the charter.

6. Freight

Absent a contractual provision to the contrary, freight is not earned until the cargo is delivered at the port of destination. Anyone who contracts to pay for ocean freight can be held liable in accordance with ordinary contract law as applied in maritime matters. *EIMSKIP v. Atlantic Fish Market, Inc.*, 417 F.3d 72 (1st Cir. 2005). Most bills of lading contain "guaranteed freight provisions," which specify that the freight is earned even though not delivered, unless the failure to deliver results from a cause for which the carrier is liable. Abandonment of a voyage is a cause for which the carrier is liable unless the decision to abandon was based upon the exercise of "reasoned judgment" under the circumstances existing and reasonably foreseeable at the time the decision was made.

CHAPTER V

LIENS ON MARITIME PROPERTY

The diverse nationalities and geographical locations of shipowners, their customers, and their suppliers increase the importance of the ability of each to assert a lien upon the property of the other wherever such property is found. Thus it is not surprising that substantive maritime law is devoted to determining when a lien may be asserted against vessels and cargo. Interestingly, much of the development of the law relating to maritime liens arose long before the advent of modern American law relating to security devices in personal property—Article 9 of the Uniform Commercial Code.

A. LIENS ON CARGO

A vessel and its operator have a lien upon the charterer's or shipper's cargo for the freight due for carriage of the cargo. The lien often is described as "possessory," i.e., existing only while the goods are aboard the vessel. Courts, however, have held that the lien arises before the goods are loaded and while the goods are still on the dock, if they have been delivered into the control of the master of the vessel. Frequently, the nature of the goods or of the shipping contract is such that the consignee must inspect the goods before deciding to accept them from the shipper or from the carrier. In such cases, the bill of lading may provide that the carrier's lien will not be lost by delivery to a warehouse adjacent to the dock or delivery to the consignee, and such a stipulation will be upheld. Even in the absence of an express stipulation, the vessel's lien on cargo is not lost by the cargo's removal from the vessel if the court is satisfied that the parties intended that the lien continue after unloading. The Supreme Court long ago stated that in determining whether a lien on cargo is lost by unloading, courts

> must look to the substance and good sense of the transaction; to the contract, as understood and intended by the parties, and as explained by its terms, and the attending circumstances out of which it arose. . . .

Bulkley v. The Naumkeag Steam Cotton Co., 65 U.S. 386 (1860).

A maritime lien does not arise out of the breach of an "executory" maritime contract. Thus, the failure of the shipper to deliver cargo gives rise to a maritime contract claim, but that claim is not secured by a maritime lien on the cargo contemplated by the carriage contract. A nice question is presented when some of the cargo contemplated by a contract of carriage is delivered and loaded, but the carrier refuses to accept, or the shipper fails to deliver, the remainder of the contemplated cargo. The prevailing view is that no lien arises to secure the payment of damages for nonperformance of the unexecuted portion of the contract. *Osaka Shosen Kaisha v. Pacific Export Lumber Co.*, 260 U.S. 490 (1923). This doctrine has been applied to deny lien claims of passengers who have paid in advance for passage on a voyage that subsequently is cancelled. *Effjohn International Cruise Holdings, Inc. v. A & L Sales*, 346 F.3d 552 (5th Cir. 2003).

When the charterer arranges for the vessel to carry the cargo of a third person and collects the freights, the vessel does not have a lien on the cargo of the third person carried pursuant to the charter. However, the charter may provide that in the event of nonpayment of the charter hire, the vessel owner will be subrogated to the charterer's lien on the cargo for payment of the freight or sub-freight. If the shipper or consignee receives notice that the subrogation has taken place, payment of freight thereafter to the charterer will not discharge the obligation. *Lykes Lines Ltd. v. M/V BBC SEALAND*, 398 F.3d 319 (5th Cir. 2005). After receiving such a notice, the shipper or consignee may obtain possession of the cargo by placing the amount of the freight in escrow.

When the carrier executes a charter or issues a bill of lading containing a "cesser clause" (*see* Chapter IV), he usually will require prepayment by the shipper of some of the freight, and, pursuant to the clause, will look to the consignee or to his lien on the cargo for payment of the remainder of the freight.

B. LIENS ON VESSELS

Maritime liens on vessels may be either express (by mortgage) or implied by the occurrence of a maritime tort or the performance of a maritime service. State law also may create maritime liens on vessels in limited instances.

1. Express Liens—The Ship Mortgage Act

In the mid-nineteenth century the Supreme Court, in *Bogart v. The John Jay*, 58 U.S. 399 (1854), ruled that a ship mortgage was not a maritime contract. The result was that ship mortgages could not be enforced *in personam* or *in rem* in admiralty court. Maritime common law did provide a lien to secure a bottomry bond (a loan on the security of the vessel) and a respondentia bond (a loan on the security of the cargo). However, because those loans were discharged if the vessel did not successfully complete the voyage, the bottomry and respondentia bonds were of limited utility and faded from use; Gilmore & Black observed in 1974 that "most probably no living admiralty lawyer has ever seen an example of either." Gilmore & Black, *supra*, page 632.

The lack of an adequate device by which a shipowner could borrow on the credit of the vessel undoubtedly discouraged private financing of vessels. In 1920, Congress, in an effort to develop a stronger American merchant marine and, perhaps, to facilitate disposal of the merchant vessels which the federal government had acquired during World

War I, passed the Ship Mortgage Act, now 46 U.S.C.A. §§ 31301, et seq., providing for a "preferred mortgage," now 46 U.S.C.A. § 31301(6), on a vessel and for its enforcement in an *in rem* proceeding in admiralty. The Act was met with the objection that it was unconstitutional because a ship mortgage was not a maritime contract, and thus Congress could not provide for such a contract under its admiralty power. Rejecting this contention, the Supreme Court, in *Detroit Trust Co. v. The Thomas Barlum*, 293 U.S. 21 (1934), ruled that ship mortgages are within the federal admiralty power and that earlier decisions, such as *Bogart,* meant only that the maritime common law did not permit enforcement *in rem* of a ship's mortgage. The Ship Mortgage Act has become a vital part of the financing of American maritime shipping; predictably, it was amended after World War II to facilitate its greater use, and subsequently was amended in the recodification of Title 46. In 1988, the Act was modified and recodified as the Commercial Instruments and Maritime Liens Act, 46 U.S.C. Sec. 31301, et seq.

As the Act derogates from the maritime common law, strict compliance with its provisions may be essential to the validity of a maritime preferred mortgage. Among the more important requirements and provisions of the Act are:

(a) A maritime preferred mortgage can be granted only on a "documented vessel" as defined in 46 U.S.C.A. §§ 12101–12122. Since vessels under five tons cannot be documented, that constitutes the minimum weight limit for a maritime preferred mortgage on a "documented vessel." However, a mortgage granting a security interest perfected under state law on a vessel titled in the state may be deemed a preferred mortgage under certain circumstances. 46 U.S.C.A. § 31322(d). In addition, mortgages on certain foreign vessels may be enforced in American admiralty courts. 46 U.S.C.A. §§ 31325–26.

(b) The mortgage must be given on the "whole of the vessel," including appurtenances. However, the owner of an undivided interest in a vessel may mortgage his interest. The interest of the mortgagor in the vessel must be stated in the mortgage. 46 U.S.C.A. § 31321(b).

(c) The mortgagee must be a citizen of the United States or some other designated entity, including "a person approved by the Secretary of Transportation." 46 U.S.C.A. § 31322(a)(1)(D).

(d) The mortgage may include more than one vessel or may include non-maritime property. The mortgage may provide for separate discharge of each vessel or for discharge of mortgaged non-maritime property by the payment of a part of the mortgage indebtedness. If it does not, the mortgage will constitute a lien on a vessel covered by the mortgage in the full amount of the outstanding mortgage indebtedness. 46 U.S.C.A. § 31322(c).

(e) There is no limitation upon the interest rate which may be charged. 46 U.S.C.A. § 31322(b).

Congress eliminated the former prohibition against waiver of the preferred status. 46 U.S.C.A. § 31305.

"Substantial compliance" (*See* 46 U.S.C.A. §§ 31321–22) with the following steps is necessary for perfection of a preferred mortgage:

(a) Execution of a mortgage, with an acknowledgment. 46 U.S.C.A. § 31321(b)(6).

(b) The mortgagor's affidavit of "good faith" is no longer required. However, the mortgagor may be required to disclose the existence of obligations on the mortgaged vessel, and may not incur certain liens on the vessel until the mortgagee has had a reasonable time to record his preferred mortgage. Criminal penalties are imposed for violation of these duties. 46 U.S.C.A. §§ 31323, 31330.

(c) Recordation of the mortgage and affidavit with the Secretary of Transportation. 46 U.S.C.A. § 31321(a)(1).

(d) The requirement of indorsement of a memorandum of the mortgage on the ship's documents apparently has been eliminated. However, the Secretary of Transportation must maintain an appropriate index of mortgages "for use by the public." 46 U.S.C.A. § 31321(e).

(e) If the mortgaged vessel is self-propelled, the mortgagor shall use "diligence in keeping a certified copy of the mortgage on the vessel." 46 U.S.C.A. § 31324(b). The owner or master of the vessel shall permit a person to examine the mortgage if the person has business with the vessel that may give rise to a maritime lien on or other encumbrance of the vessel. 46 U.S.C.A. § 31324(a).

The Act does not require that the construction of the vessel be completed before the mortgage attaches. *United States v. TRIDENT CRUSADER*, 366 F.3d 391 (5th Cir. 2004).

In *Mullane v. Chambers*, 333 F.3d 322 (1st Cir. 2003), the court held that section 31321 rendered an unrecorded bill of sale or conveyance invalid as against a seller's judgment creditors who, without notice, levied upon the vessel. The court did state that if the creditors had actual notice of the transfer, state fraudulent conveyance law might be applied.

Despite its title as "preferred," the maritime ship mortgage is primed by all maritime liens arising prior to the recordation of the mortgage, and by all subsequently arising maritime liens except those securing maritime contracts. 46 U.S.C.A. §§ 31301(5), 31326(b)(1). Because of this, the mortgagee may require that all pre-existing liens be paid before funds are advanced under the mortgage and that no other contract liens be placed on the vessel before the mortgage is recorded.

A mortgage may be enforced *in rem* or *in personam*. 46 U.S.C.A. § 31325(b)(2). Foreclosure *in rem* must be brought in federal court, 46 U.S.C.A. § 31325(c), and is achieved in the same manner as foreclosure of an implied maritime lien, except that actual notice of the commencement of the foreclosure on the mortgage must be given, in such manner as the court directs, to the master or individual in charge of the vessel, to any lienholder who has recorded his lien, 46 U.S.C.A. § 31343, and to the mortgagee on any mortgage recorded with the Secretary of Transportation. 46 U.S.C.A. § 31325(d). A self-help repossession and resale remedy provided by state law also may be available. 46 U.S.C.A. § 31325(b)(3); *Dietrich v. Key Bank, N.A.*, 72 F.3d 1509 (11th Cir. 1996).

If the sale of the vessel in an *in rem* proceeding does not generate funds sufficient to satisfy the mortgage, the mortgagee may seek a deficiency judgment in an *in personam* action against the mortgagor. 46 U.S.C.A. § 31325. State statutes prohibiting a deficiency judgment if the property is sold without appraisal apparently will not apply to maritime mortgages. Maritime law, however, permits the court to reduce the mortgagor's liability for a deficiency by the sale price, or, if there is a significant disparity between the sale price and the fair value of the property, by the latter amount. *Bollinger & Boyd Barge Service, Inc. v. M/V Captain Claude Bass*, 576 F.2d 595 (5th Cir.1978); *Walter E. Heller & Co. v. O/S Sonny V.*, 595 F.2d 968 (5th Cir. 1979). *See also*, 46 U.S.C.A. § 31325(b)(2).

Upon discharge of the indebtedness, the mortgagor must on demand provide a certificate of discharge. 46 U.S.C.A. § 31321(f), (h).

A foreign ship mortgage executed and registered in accordance with the laws of the country in which the vessel is documented may be recognized and enforced as a "preferred mortgage" under American law. 46 U.S.C.A. § 31301(6)(A). However, it will be subordinate to those liens which prime the American preferred mortgage and to any maritime liens for necessaries supplied in the United States. 46 U.S.C.A. § 31325–26.

2. Implied Liens

a. *Nature of the Implied Maritime Lien*

The implied maritime lien that arises from breach of some maritime contracts or the commission of some maritime torts is one of the law's most unusual security devices. The lien arises at the moment of the occurrence of the debt or damages which it secures, exists without recordation, does not require possession of the vessel, and can be judicially discharged only by an *in rem* proceeding in admiralty court. The often expressed rationale is that the purpose of the lien is "to enable a vessel to obtain supplies or repairs necessary to her continued operation by giving a temporary underlying pledge of the vessel which will hold until payment can be made or more formal security given." *Lake Charles Stevedores v. Professor Vladimir Popov MV*, 199 F.3d 220 (5th Cir. 1999).

Another unique characteristic of the lien is that it may arise even though the owner of the vessel is not personally liable for the debt or damage. Thus a vessel in the control of a demise charterer may be liable *in rem* for the debts of the voyage, although the owner of the vessel is not personally liable. Similarly, the vessel may be liable for the torts of a compulsory pilot, although its owner or operator is not. This characteristic, and the rule that an action can be brought against the vessel *in rem* without the necessity of joining the owner or some other person as a defendant, has given rise to the theory of "personification of the *res.*" This theory, that maritime law elevates the vessel to the status of a juridical person, is neither helpful nor accurate. In every case in which a vessel is liable *in rem,* some person—the owner, charterer, or compulsory pilot— also is liable *in personam.* Carried to its logical conclusion, the "personification of the *res*" theory would permit a litigant who has lost his *in personam* claim against the operator of the vessel to relitigate the same issues in an action *in rem* against the vessel; however, the courts generally do not permit that result.

The implied maritime lien is considered an extraordinary remedy and is *stricti juris*, i.e., a lien claim will not be extended by construction or analogy. Thus attorney's fees or other penalties otherwise due on a claim may not be secured by the lien. *Gulf Marine & Industrial Supplies, Inc. v. GOLDEN PRINCE M/V*, 230 F.3d 178 (5th Cir. 2000).

b.   *Transactions or Occurrences Giving Rise to the Implied Maritime Lien*

A seaman has a lien on the vessel for his wages. 46 U.S.C.A. § 31301(5)(d). The maritime common law did not give the master a lien on the vessel for his wages, because during voyages the master usually possessed funds belonging to the operator of the vessel which he could use to pay his wages. Now, by statute the master of a documented vessel has the same lien, and lien priority, for his wages as any other seaman serving aboard the vessel. 46 U.S.C.A. § 11112.

A maritime tort committed in the operation of a vessel gives rise to a lien upon the offending vessel. 46 U.S.C.A. § 31301(5)(B). However, the seaman's negligence action against his employer (a statutory claim arising under the Jones Act) does not provide a lien on the vessel. Likewise, a maritime worker does not have a lien on a vessel as security for his compensation benefits. 33 U.S.C.A. § 905(a).

There is no lien for the breach of an executory contract. Thus negligent failure to perform a contract of affreightment does not create a lien on the offending vessel. A salvage claim is secured by a lien on the vessel, as are sums due under general average. 46 U.S.C.A. §§ 31301(5)(E), (F). Other contracts are secured by liens on vessels if they come within the maritime lien for "necessaries." 46 U.S.C.A. § 31301(4). This lien, developed at common law and adjusted by Congress through the adoption of the Maritime Lien Act, now 46 U.S.C.A. §§ 31341–43, is of great importance to maritime shipping and commerce and has spawned a large body of jurisprudence. A breach of a time charter gives rise to a maritime lien which may attach at the moment the owner places the vessel at the charterer's disposal, and not at the later time at which the charter party is breached. *Bank One, Louisiana N.A. v. MR. DEAN M/V*, 293 F.3d 830 (5th Cir.2002).

Under 46 U.S.C.A. § 31342(a)(1), "a person providing necessaries to a vessel on the order of the owner or a person authorized by the owner—(1) has a maritime lien on the vessel...." 46 U.S.C.A. § 31301(4) defines "necessaries" as including "repairs, supplies, towage, and the use of a dry dock or marine railway." The key word is "necessaries," and the other items listed in the statute are illustrative. Repairs, towage, and use of dry dock facilities are treated as "necessaries" without further inquiry, but courts scrutinize lien claims asserted by furnishers of supplies to determine whether they are "necessary." The courts usually find a supply is a "necessary" if it is reasonably needed in the ship's business, such as stevedoring services for cargo vessels, tourist brochures and advertising matches for cruise vessels, liquor for the crew of a fishing vessel, and containers for a ship designed to transport container cargo. *See, e.g., Foss Launch & Tug Co. v. Char Ching Shipping U.S.A., Ltd.*, 808 F.2d 697 (9th Cir. 1987). In *Motor–Services Hugo Stamp, Inc. v. M/V Regal Empress,* 2006 WL 279241 (11th Cir. 2006 unpublished) the court stated that "[i]t is unimaginable in today's world that a luxury cruise ship could be successful without a fully functioning telecommunications system. Because such a system is vital to the mission of the Regal Empress, the [court] correctly concluded that MTN's equipment was appurtenant to the ship." Thus a working system was a "necessary." Generally, one is entitled to a lien although he or she provides the repairs or supplies through third persons.

Section 31342's requirement that the necessaries be "provid[ed] ... to a vessel" imports two separate considerations. First, the supplies or services must be actually delivered to the vessel, and, secondly, the supplier must rely upon the credit of the vessel for payment. The first of these considerations has been the source of much difficulty. The landmark case is *Piedmont & George's Creek Coal Co. v. Seaboard Fisheries Co.*, 254 U.S. 1 (1920), in which the supplier of coal to a fleet of vessels was denied a lien against any of the vessels because he could not establish that any particular coal was intended for and actually did reach a particular vessel. The *Piedmont* case provided more confusion than guidance, and, as Gilmore & Black have remarked, it "is all things to all men and is regularly cited on both sides of every case in which it is relevant." Gilmore & Black, *supra*, p. 661. Where the supplies are not actually delivered to the vessel, the lienholder must be prepared to establish that they were delivered to the vessel's dock or some other convenient place and that they were in fact used aboard or were "earmarked" for the vessel. This has caused some difficulties, particularly with persons providing containers to container vessels. *See, e.g., Itel Containers International Corp. v. Atlanttrafik Express Service Ltd.*, 982 F.2d 765 (2d Cir. 1992).

Some courts hold that insurance premiums are not "necessaries" because insurance benefits the owner and not the vessel, and thus the insurer did not "provide to [a] vessel." That view probably will not survive, however. *See, e.g., Equilease Corp. v. M/V Sampson*, 793 F.2d 598 (5th Cir. 1986).

Since a contract to build a vessel is not maritime, there is no maritime lien for building a vessel or for supplying materials for the original construction.

As noted, a supplier has not "provid[ed] necessaries to a vessel" if he does not rely upon the credit of the vessel for payment. The Lien Act provides that the lienor "is not required to allege or prove ... that credit was given to the vessel." 46 U.S.C.A. § 31342(a)(3). However, this provision does not abrogate the requirement that the lienholder rely upon the credit of the vessel, but merely creates a presumption that credit was extended to the vessel. The requirement that the supplier rely upon the credit of the vessel for payment sometimes has meant that when the supplier extracts or accepts any other security for the debt, he will be denied a lien. However, cases require a showing that the supplier, in accepting the additional security, "purposefully intended to forego" the maritime lien. *Point Landing, Inc. v. Alabama Dry Dock & Shipbuilding Co.*, 261 F.2d 861 (5th Cir. 1958). Courts are hesitant to find a lien waiver from efforts aimed at collecting the debt from other sources or from taking additional security for the debt.

The necessaries must be furnished upon the order of the owner "or a person authorized by the owner." 46 U.S.C.A. § 31342(a). Thus, an essential element of a lien for necessaries is proof that the person who ordered the maritime service was in fact authorized to do so by the owner. The Lien Act eases this burden in some cases by establishing a rebuttable presumption of such authority for "(1) the owner; (2) the master; (3) a person entrusted with the management of the vessel at the port of supply; or (4) an officer or agent appointed by (A) the owner; (B) the charterer; (C) an owner pro hac vice; or (D) an agreed buyer in possession of the vessel." 46 U.S.C.A. § 31341. Cases indicate that a person "entrusted" within the meaning of the Act must have some discretion and control over the use or security of the vessel. The doctrine of apparent authority may provide sufficient authorization by the owner to support a lien chargeable to the owner.

The question of whether a charterer may impose a lien has been a difficult one. The Lien Act, 46 U.S.C.A. § 31341, provides that persons presumed to have authority to procure necessaries for a vessel include an officer or agent appointed by a charterer or owner pro hac vice. Thus some of the charterer's agents are presumed to have authority to impose liens for necessaries. This presumption should carry the day for the maritime supplier where the charter party does not prohibit the charterer from imposing a lien on the vessel. Provisions obligating the charterer to (1) discharge any liens that arise, (2) provide and pay for supplies, or (3) indemnify the owner against all lien claims do not prohibit the charterer from imposing a lien. The charter party, however, may contain a "prohibition of lien" clause, such as a provision that the charterer will "not suffer nor permit any lien" on the vessel. *Dampskibsselskabet Dannebrog v. Signal Oil & Gas Co.*, 310 U.S. 268 (1940). If such a "prohibition of lien" clause is contained in the charter party, and the marine supplier knows about it, he may not rely upon the presumption of authority contained in Section 31341. What if the maritime supplier does not know about the "prohibition of lien" clause, but could have discovered it in the exercise of reasonable diligence? Prior to 1971, the Lien Act provided that no lien arose when the supplier knew or by the exercise of reasonable diligence could have ascertained that because of the terms of a charter party, the person ordering the necessaries was without authority to bind the vessel. The supplier, under a duty to investigate, was charged with the knowledge he would have acquired from an investigation. Because a copy of the charter containing the "prohibition of lien" clause was posted on the mast of the vessel under charter, the supplier could have discovered the lack of authority by reasonable investigation. Accordingly, no lien arose if a charter contained a "prohibition of lien" clause. This result was changed by the 1971 amendment to Section 973, now 46 U.S.C.A. § 31341, deleting the provision that no lien attaches if the furnisher could have ascertained the existence of the "prohibition of lien" clause by the exercise of reasonable diligence. Now, a supplier may rely upon the presumption of authority of the charterer or his agents contained in Section 31341, unless he has actual knowledge of the existence of the charter and the "prohibition of lien" clause; the jurisprudence since the amendment supports this conclusion. *See, e.g., Stevens Shipping & Terminal Co. v. JAPAN RAINBOW II M/V*, 334 F.3d 439 (5th Cir. 2003); *Gulf Oil Trading Co. v. M/V CARIBE MAR*, 757 F.2d 743 (5th Cir. 1985). The owner's breach of a charter party will give rise to a lien on the chartered vessel.

American admiralty courts will enforce liens arising in foreign countries. The law governing maritime liens arising in foreign countries may be summarized in this fashion: American courts (1) will uphold any choice-of-law clause selected by the parties, and (2) in the absence of such a clause, will apply the law of the nation with the most significant contacts with the controversy, with special weight given to protection of an American lienholder. Where the dispute is between a lienholder and a mortgage holder, however, the Commercial Instruments and Maritime Lien Act may govern priorities. *See, e.g., Oil Shipping v. Sonmez Denizcilik Ve Ticaret A.S.*, 10 F.3d 1015 (3d Cir. 1993).

c. *Assignments and Advances*

The maritime preferred mortgage was not available prior to 1920, and maritime law did not permit assignment of liens. The need for a device by which a shipowner could pledge his vessel as security for repayment of money borrowed to satisfy liens led to the development of the doctrine of "advances." Under this doctrine, if one loans money to a ship-owner "on the credit of the vessel" and for the purpose of satisfying a lien on the vessel, or for payment of a creditor who would be entitled to a lien on the vessel, and the funds actually are used for that purpose, the lender "inherits" the lien and ranking of the creditor. Gilmore & Black observe that "[t]he rule appears to be so firmly established that it rarely surfaces in litigation." Gilmore & Black, *supra*, page 634. An advance is upheld even though the lien discharged by the funds is not in existence at the time of the advance. The doctrine now is of limited utility because of the adoption of the Ship Mortgage Act and because maritime liens now may be assigned.

A person may be denied a lien if the enforcement of the lien would present insuperable legal difficulties or would be inequitable to other claimants. Such a situation exists when the person advancing the funds is a part owner or joint venturer or has a fiduciary relationship with the vessel and its owner. A general agent of a ship may not assert a maritime lien against the vessel unless the owner expressly or impliedly agrees that he may do so. *See, e.g., Ameejee Valleejee and Sons v. M/V Victoria U*, 661 F.2d 310 (4th Cir. 1981).

d. *Liens in Custodia Legis*

A lien cannot arise while the vessel is in the custody of the court; thus liens for seamen's wages, wharfage, and similar continuing services to a vessel are limited to the period prior to seizure by judicial process. The court in which the seizure is pending, however, may authorize a continuation of such services during the seizure, and the charges for such services then may become payable as expenses of the administration of justice in the same manner and with the same ranking as costs of court. *New York Dock Co. v. Steamship Poznan*, 274 U.S. 117 (1927).

e. *Liens Created by State Law*

During the nineteenth century, implied maritime liens could not arise for services or supplies furnished in the vessel's home port. The rationale was that because the owner presumably was present at the home port, the supplier could look to the credit of the owner, making it unnecessary to pledge the credit of the vessel to assure that a voyage would be undertaken or completed. To fill the obvious need, states passed laws providing for home port liens. These state law liens at first were recognized as enforceable *in rem* in admiralty, but the Supreme Court subsequently held that such liens could not be enforced in that manner. Thereafter, the Maritime Lien Act was adopted. The Lien Act permits home port liens under admiralty law and provides that the federal lien for necessaries supersedes any state liens that otherwise would be enforceable *in rem* in admiralty. 46 U.S.C.A. § 31307. The result is that state law liens on vessels have limited utility. A state may establish a lien upon a vessel that will be enforceable *in rem* in federal admiralty court, but only if the underlying claim is maritime and is not secured by a lien under the Maritime Lien Act. Since the Maritime Lien Act provides a lien for a broad category of marine services and supplies, little room remains for operation of state law liens. A state may provide for a lien on a vessel and for enforcement of it in state court. Such liens, however, should rank below any subsequently arising maritime liens, and the judicial sale in state court does not discharge maritime liens which were not actually litigated in the proceeding.

f.   *Property to Which Liens Attach*

A maritime lien attaches to "the vessel itself and all equipment which is 'an integral part of the vessel and [is] essential to its navigation and operation,'" even though such equipment belongs to a third person. *National Western Life Insurance Co. v. Tropical Commerce Corp. (In re Steamship Tropic Breeze)*, 456 F.2d 137 (1st Cir. 1972). The lien also attaches to other equipment and chattels that belong to the vessel's owner and are placed on the vessel for its completion or ornamentation.

g.   *Enforcement of Liens in Rem*

A maritime lien may be enforced *in rem* only by a federal court sitting "in admiralty." Supplemental Rules C and E, Admiralty and Maritime Claims, provide the basic procedure. The claimant must file a verified complaint naming the vessel as defendant and describing it "with reasonable particularity."

The clerk then issues a warrant for the arrest of the vessel, and the marshal seizes the vessel.

A shipowner may avoid seizure of his vessel in a particular district by filing a general bond with the district court to secure any future lien claims against the vessel. Supp. Rule E(5)(b), Admiralty and Maritime Claims. If a general bond has not been posted, the marshal effects seizure of the vessel, and takes possession if it is practical to do so. Service is effected by affixing a copy of the writ in a conspicuous place aboard the vessel, and delivering a copy to the person in possession of the vessel or his agent.

The rules provide for a ten-day delay after seizure; during this period, the owner usually receives actual notice of the seizure. The owner then may make a special appearance, file his claim as owner, and effect a release of the vessel by providing a special bond. Supp. Rule E(5)(a), Admiralty and Maritime Claims. In lieu of a special bond, the parties may stipulate to the release of the vessel. The claimant's agreement to the stipulation usually is based upon the owner's acknowledgment that he will personally satisfy any judgment rendered against the vessel. Supp. Rule E(5)(c), Admiralty and Maritime Claims. Where the owner provides a special bond, any judgment in favor of the lien claimant in the proceeding is satisfied through the bond, and the vessel thereafter is not subject to seizure *in rem* for that debt.

If the owner fails to appear within the ten-day period after seizure, the court orders newspaper publication of the seizure and fixes an additional delay for answer. If the owner does not claim the vessel before the expiration of this additional delay, a default judgment may be taken against the vessel, which thereafter may be sold and the maritime liens satisfied out of the proceeds of the sale. The marshal's sale of a vessel must be confirmed by the court, which has the power to set aside the sale "if the price is so grossly inadequate as to shock the conscience." *Jefferson Bank & Trust Co. v. Van Niman*, 722 F.2d 251 (5th Cir. 1984).

h. *Extinction of Liens*

A lien is extinguished by judicial sale in an *in rem* proceeding either in a federal court with admiralty jurisdiction or in a comparable foreign court. Additionally, a lien is lost if the claim it secures becomes time barred. A court also may bar enforcement of the lien through laches although the underlying claim is not time barred, particularly where the lienholder foregoes reasonable opportunities to enforce the lien. Loss or destruction of the vessel also will extinguish the lien, but the lien probably would be revived in the event of salvage. A party may waive a lien, either expressly or by implication.

i. *Ranking of Liens*

Congress has not made any general provision for the ranking of maritime liens, and the Supreme Court has not spoken directly to the question since the nineteenth century. Thus the law governing the ranking of liens is found in a smattering of opinions from the lower federal courts and in a section of the Ship Mortgage Act providing for the ranking of preferred mortgages vis-a-vis other maritime liens. The following discussion reflects the present state of the law as outlined by both judges and scholars.

Liens are ranked by class and by time. Ranking first in class are the "expenses of justice"—court costs and those other expenses incurred for the care and operation of the vessel or other property while it is in the custody of the court. *New York Dock Co. v. S/S Poznan*, 274 U.S. 117 (1927). Seamen's wages rank second. However, penalties for failure to pay wages timely may not be included in this priority. Salvage, both contractual and quasi-contractual, ranks next. These liens are followed by tort liens, including those securing collision damages and those securing maritime personal injury claims. The argument that personal injury claims should rank ahead of property damage claims has found little judicial support. Contract liens, including claims for repairs, supplies and other necessaries, rank next.

This ordering scheme leaves a number of unsettled issues. There appears to be no consensus as to the ranking of the shipper's lien for the breach of the contract of affreightment or the lien for the breach of a towage contract. When the liability of the carrier or tower is based upon his negligent performance of the contract, the claim may be treated as one in tort. Pilotage may be analogized to seamen's wages and given one of the highest priorities, or it may be treated as a "necessary" and ranked nearer the bottom. Similarly, general average may be ranked with salvage, or with or below contract liens.

This order of ranking is not always followed by the courts. Decisions have ranked salvage above seamen's wages and have placed a collision lien of an innocent vessel ahead of wage claims by seamen on the offending vessel. These decisions suggest that the lower courts have tempered order with justice in distributing the proceeds of an *in rem* proceeding.

Where the claim is not secured by a maritime lien, such as a non-lien maritime claim or a state law claim, the claimant nevertheless may seek payment of his claim out of the proceeds of a sale resulting from an *in rem* proceeding brought by a maritime lienholder. The admiralty court may enforce a non-lien claim in the foreclosure, but such a claim obviously would rank behind all maritime liens.

As to claims within the same class, the general rule is that the last claim to accrue is the first to be paid. *The St. Jago de Cuba*, 22 U.S. 409 (1824). This "last on, first off" rule is based upon the notion that each maritime lienholder performs a service which contributes to the success of the voyage and thus benefits prior lienholders whose security (the previously arising lien) depends upon such success. The rationale (which is contrary to the general rule on land) does not hold in all cases, such as when it is applied to tort liens, but the "last on, first off" rule is well-settled.

However, rigid application of the "last on, first off" rule produces a totally undesirable result in the ranking of liens for necessaries. Such liens are granted to encourage suppliers to advance credit to a vessel for completion of a voyage. If the lienholder is primed by all persons subsequently furnishing supplies for the voyage, he may be inclined to enforce his lien without much delay, thus reducing the period of time within which he extends credit to the vessel. To avoid this, courts have developed rules that permit all contract liens accruing within a period of time to share equally in all proceeds from the sale of the vessel accruing to that class of liens. The original rule, and still the general rule for traditional ocean voyages, is the "voyage rule," under which all suppliers of necessaries to the vessel for a certain voyage are ranked equally, with the suppliers for each subsequent voyage priming the suppliers for prior voyages. The "voyage rule" has proved unworkable for suppliers of tugs and harbor vessels, and courts have developed other variations. In some eastern harbors, courts apply a "forty day" rule in which each lienholder shares equally with others whose liens accrue within 40 days thereafter. The probable reason for the selection of 40 days is to encourage the supplier to extend credit for 30 days, and allow the customary 10 days thereafter for settlement of accounts. In some areas, courts apply the "calendar year" rule, under which all liens accruing within a calendar year share equally.

See, e.g., National Shawmut Bank of Boston v. The Winthrop, 134 F.Supp. 370 (D. Mass. 1955).

46 U.S.C.A. § 31326(b)(1) gives the preferred mortgage a superior ranking over all claims except the preferred maritime lien. 46 U.S.C.A. § 31301(5) defines a "preferred maritime lien" as including a maritime lien arising before the preferred mortgage was filed, tort liens, certain wage liens, general average, and salvage. Thus the only significant liens which are ranked below the maritime preferred mortgage are contract liens arising after the execution of the mortgage. Contract liens accruing prior to the execution of the mortgage, which ordinarily would rank behind subsequently accruing contract liens under the "last on, first off" rule, are given preference where there is an intervening preferred mortgage. There is a "mortgage renewal rule" which provides that unless a contrary intention clearly appears, the execution and delivery of a new maritime mortgage in renewal of a former one, even though accompanied by a formal satisfaction and discharge of the initial mortgage, does not have the effect of extinguishing the priority that the initial mortgage carried. *Bank of America, NT & SA v. PENGWIN*, 175 F.3d 1109 (9th Cir. 1999). The matter is of little significance, because most pre-mortgage lien claims are satisfied before disbursement of the proceeds of the preferred mortgage.

Maritime preferred mortgages and other maritime liens may be subordinated to liens they otherwise would prime where equity dictates such a result. *See, e.g., Custom Fuel Services, Inc. v. Lombas Industries, Inc.*, 805 F.2d 561 (5th Cir.1986), and the authorities cited therein. The courts usually do not find equitable subordination in the absence of fraud, breach of a fiduciary duty or some type of misrepresentation.

j. *Maritime Liens and Bankruptcy*

Formerly, there was much uncertainty as to whether a bankruptcy court or the federal admiralty court enforcing a maritime lien against the bankrupt's property had jurisdiction over the maritime property. The matter apparently has been resolved by recognizing the bankruptcy court's jurisdiction over the bankrupt's property, including vessels seized *in rem* in an admiralty proceeding in the same or another judicial district. *See, e.g., In re Louisiana Ship Management, Inc.*, 761 F.2d 1025 (5th Cir. 1985).

CHAPTER VI

THE SEAMAN'S EMPLOYMENT CONTRACT, WAGES AND COMPROMISE OF CLAIMS

Before entering into the service of a vessel, a seaman generally signs a contract of employment ("articles"). Federal law, 46 U.S.C.A. § 10301 et seq., requires articles for seamen on American-owned vessels engaged in voyages from ports in the United States to foreign ports (with certain exceptions), and for seamen on some vessels engaged in coastwise trade (voyages between ports in the United States). 46 U.S.C.A. § 10501 et seq. The articles, which must be signed in the presence of the master or "individual in charge," specify the capacity in which the seaman is to serve aboard the vessel and obligate him to report for duty at a designated time and place, to stand by the ship, and to obey the master until the voyage is completed. By "signing on" in a specific capacity, the seaman impliedly warrants that he or she is competent to perform the duties of that position. If the master determines that the seaman is incompetent or has been guilty of misconduct, he may "disrate" the seaman. In that event, the seaman may demand discharge or accept the new position for the remainder of the voyage.

Seamen are "wards of admiralty" who must be protected from "overreaching" by a ship's owner or master. The rationale for the "wardship" principle was expressed by Justice Joseph Story in these words:

> Seamen ... are unprotected and need counsel ... they are thoughtless and require indulgence; ... they are credulous and complying, and are easily overreached.... They are considered as placed under the dominion and influence of men who have naturally acquired a mastery over them; and as they have little of the foresight and caution belonging to persons trained in other pursuits of life, the most rigid scrutiny is instituted into the terms of every contract in which they engage.

Harden v. Gordon, 11 F.Cas. 480 (C.C. Me. 1823).

The seaman's protection is reflected in federal statutes regulating his or her employment relationship with the vessel. Legislation prescribes the basic qualifications which a person must possess to "sign on" as a seaman, 46 U.S.C.A. § 7301 et seq., the hours and conditions of the seaman's employment, 46 U.S.C.A. § 8104, and the living conditions with which the seaman must be provided aboard ship, 46 U.S.C.A. § 11101 et seq.

The specific protections afforded seamen are best illustrated by the remedies available for payment of wages. The owner and master are both liable for the payment of wages. The seaman also has a lien on the vessel, usually of the highest rank, for payment of wages, and his or her claim is exempt from limitation of liability. A seaman may enforce the claim for wages in a summary proceeding in federal court, without prepayment of court costs. 46 U.S.C.A. § 603, 28 U.S.C.A. § 1916. A seamen's wages must be paid periodically upon demand and upon termination of the seaman's employment. 46 U.S.C.A. §§ 10313, 10504, 11105, 11106. The penalty of "double wages" applies if the shipowner fails to pay a seaman's wages without sufficient cause. 46 U.S.C.A. § 10504. In *Griffin v. Oceanic Contractors, Inc.*, 458 U.S. 564 (1982), the Supreme Court ruled that a court does not have discretion to limit the period during which the penalty wages accrue, even though the result was that a seaman would recover several hundred thousand dollars in penalties for nonpayment of a few hundred dollars in wages. The penalty wage provision may impose liability upon the master or owner but not upon the vessel itself, and thus the seaman's lien for penalty wages may not prime a preferred ship mortgage on the vessel. *The Governor and Company of the Bank of Scotland v. Sabay*, 211 F.3d 261 (5th Cir. 2000).

A seaman also may demand one-half of his wages earned and unpaid at any port at which cargo is loaded or discharged. 46 U.S.C.A. § 10313. The employer may not make an advance of wages to the seaman, 46 U.S.C.A. §§ 10314, 10505, and the wages are exempt from attachment (except for support of the seaman's spouse and children) or assignment. 46 U.S.C.A. § 11109.

Generally, in the absence of a contract providing to the contrary, a seaman is an "at will" employee who may be discharged for "good cause, for no cause, or even in most circumstances, for a morally reprehensible cause." *Smith v. Atlas Off–Shore Boat Service, Inc.*, 653 F.2d 1057 (5th Cir. 1981). Since the 1980s, however, the courts and Congress have imposed some important limitations on the "at will" status of a seaman. In *Smith v. Atlas Off–Shore Boat Service, Inc.*, 653 F.2d 1057 (5th Cir. 1981), the Fifth Circuit found that a seaman may have an action for the tort of wrongful discharge if his or her termination is in violation of an important public policy, such as in retaliation for the seaman's filing of a personal injury action against the employer. This remedy is available to a worker whose seaman status arises after his injury but before his termination. *Hyman v. Transocean Offshore U.S.A., Inc.*, 2006 WL 3497286 (5th Cir. 2006). Two years after *Smith*, the Fifth Circuit held in *Donovan v. Texaco, Inc.*, 720 F.2d 825 (5th Cir. 1983), that a seaman who was terminated subsequent to reporting safety violations to the Coast Guard had no cause of action against his employer. In response, Congress passed the Seaman's Protection Act, 46 U.S.C.A. § 2114. Under the Act, a seaman may bring suit against his employer for discharge or other discriminatory acts based on (1) the seaman's report or plan to report a violation of a federal maritime safety law or regulation, and (2) the seaman's refusal to perform duties ordered by the employer based on the seaman's reasonable apprehension or expectation that performing such duties would result in serious injury to the seaman, other seamen, or the public. In the case of the latter, the seaman must seek unsuccessfully the correction of the unsafe condition from his employer in order to maintain an action under the statute. Where the seaman is successful in establishing his claim, a court may order restraining violations, reinstatement with back pay, and costs and attorney's fees. The Seaman's Protection Act does not preempt traditional state whistleblower laws or other state law claims for wrongful discharge. *See Robinson v. Alter Barge Line, Inc.*, 513 F.3d 668 (7th Cir. 2008).

The protections afforded a seaman also extend to a seaman's compromise of his claims. *See Steverson v. GlobalSantaFe Corp.*, 508 F.3d 300 (5th Cir. 2007). A settlement with a seaman is liberally construed to protect the seaman. *Miles v. American Seafoods Co.*, 197 F.3d 1032 (9th Cir. 1999). "One who claims that a seaman has signed away his rights to what in law is due him must be prepared to take the burden of sustaining the release as fairly made with and fully comprehended by the seaman." *Harmon v. United States*, 59 F.2d 372 (5th Cir. 1932) (quoted with approval by the Supreme Court in *Garrett v. Moore–McCormack Co.*, 317 U.S. 239 (1942)). This burden of proof is an integral part of substantive admiralty law and must be applied even when the release is pleaded as a defense in state court. The operative test for determining the validity of the seaman's release appears to be whether under all of the circumstances the seaman made an intelligent choice to effect the settlement and forego litigation. Adequacy of consideration, although relevant, is not controlling. However, a seaman's release may be invalid as a matter of law if the consideration is "grossly inadequate," *Orsini v. O/S Seabrooke O.N.*, 247 F.3d 953 (9th Cir. 2001), and when a seaman is signing a release without benefit of counsel, "(a)t the very least" the seaman should be told that he or she has "an unbeatable right of action under the maritime law for maintenance and cure." *Richards v. Relentless, Inc.*, 341 F.3d 35 (1st Cir. 2003). The fact that the seaman was advised to execute the release by counsel of his own choosing will not validate the release, if counsel was not aware of the seaman's rights. Conversely, a release granted without advice of any counsel other than the shipowner's attorney may be upheld if the circumstances indicate that the seaman made a "knowing choice."

An agreement by which the settling defendant retains an interest in the plaintiff's claim against the nonsettling defendant—sometimes called a "Mary Carter" agreement—is common in admiralty. Since such an agreement may provide a seaman with funds with which to pursue his claim against other defendants, maritime courts permit the use of a "Mary Carter" agreement in a seaman's claim. However, full disclosure of the agreement is required, and the court has the power to refuse to enforce an agreement which abuses the seaman's rights. *Bass v. Phoenix Seadrill/78, Ltd.*, 749 F.2d 1154 (5th Cir. 1985).

A seaman's employment contract is exempt from the coverage of the Federal Arbitration Act. 9

U.S.C. Sec. 1, et seq. However, the exemption may not apply where the contract is governed by the Convention on the Recognition and Enforcement of Foreign Arbitral Awards, 9 U.S.C. Sec. 202, et seq.; *Bautista v. Star Cruises*, 396 F.3d 1289 (11th Cir. 2005).

CHAPTER VII

MARINE INSURANCE

In the United States, the question of what law governs the validity or interpretation of a marine insurance contract is not easily answered. An agreement insuring maritime property or a maritime risk is a maritime contract, and ordinarily would be governed by admiralty law. However, in *Wilburn Boat Company v. Fireman's Fund Insurance Co.*, 348 U.S. 310 (1955), the Supreme Court ruled that the marine insurance contract in that case was governed by state law because there was no applicable federal statute or settled maritime common-law rule governing the issue and no need to articulate a uniform maritime rule. The insurance policy in *Wilburn Boat Company* insured a houseboat used to carry passengers on a lake between Texas and Oklahoma. Despite harsh criticism (*see, e.g.,* Gilmore & Black, *supra*, pages 68–71), *Wilburn Boat Company* has not been limited, expanded, or explained by the Supreme Court. The lower courts also have been faithful to *Wilburn Boat Company*. *See, e.g., Littlefield v. Acadia Ins. Co.*, 392 F.3d 1 (1st Cir. 2004); *Certain Underwriters at Lloyd's, London v. Inlet Fisheries, Inc.*, 518 F.3d 645 (9th Cir. 2008); *Royal Ins. Co. of America v. KSI Trading Corp.*, 563 F.3d 68 (3d Cir. 2009); *Sea Byte, Inc. v. Hudson Marine*

Management Services, Inc., 565 F.3d 1293 (11th Cir. 2009). Although the lower courts have found and applied some "judicially fashioned" federal rules, they have disposed of most marine insurance questions by applying state law. *See, e.g., Suydam v. Reed Stenhouse of Washington, Inc.*, 820 F.2d 1506 (9th Cir. 1987); *Taylor v. Lloyd's Underwriters of London*, 972 F.2d 666 (5th Cir. 1992) (no established maritime rule on insurability of liability for punitive damages). Some courts recognize a presumption against creating a federal admiralty rule. Whether the Court would adhere to *Wilburn Boat* on insurance policies covering vessels engaged in international trade, or even those regularly utilized in significant domestic maritime commerce, is questionable because there may be a significant need for uniformity of laws governing the validity and interpretation of such policies.

Many post–*Wilburn* "domestic" maritime insurance cases focus upon which state's law applies in a marine insurance dispute in which there are multistate contracts. This federal maritime "choice-of-law" rule apparently differs little from the traditional choice-of-law rule for contracts, i.e., the governing law is that of the state with the "most significant relationship" to the insurance dispute. Emphasis is placed upon such contacts as the place of making (where the policy was issued and delivered), the place of performance (where the vessel is employed and the premiums are paid), and the domiciles or places of business of the parties. *See, e.g., Albany Ins. Co. v. Anh Thi Kieu*, 927 F.2d 882 (5th Cir. 1991).

Where there is an established admiralty common-law rule, its roots usually are in British law. The development of insurance in England was closely related to maritime shipping and commerce, and marine insurance was in full use there by the sixteenth century. The American marine insurance industry developed slowly, and at first, British insurers dominated the American market. Although the British dominance has waned, English marine insurers and English law (particularly the Insurance Act of 1906) still are significant factors in American marine insurance.

In a marine policy, the "assured" pays a premium and makes certain warranties to the "assurer," who agrees to pay certain losses caused by certain events. The two most common policies are those which insure the vessel, called hull policies, and those which insure the owner against liability to others for damages caused by the vessel or its crew, called protection and indemnity (P & I) policies.

An express warranty may arise from words in any form from which one may infer the intention to warrant. In addition, maritime law implies warranties in different types of insurance policies. A breach of a warranty usually will void the policy.

A hull policy may insure the vessel for a particular voyage or for a period of time. Under a hull policy, the assured usually warrants that he has an "insurable interest" in the vessel. This does not require ownership, but only an expectation of benefit from the preservation of the property or the avoidance of the risk insured against. As the Supreme Court observed, one has an insurable interest in maritime property if one may sustain "injury from its loss or benefit from its preservation." *Hooper v. Robinson*, 98 U.S. 528 (1878). The assurer may issue an "honor" policy, in which it agrees not to raise the defense of lack of insurable interest.

There is some confusion about the extent of the assured's warranty of seaworthiness of the insured vessel. In voyage policies, the rule appears to be that there is an implied warranty of seaworthiness at the beginning of the voyage or at the time at which the policy attaches. In time policies, the English rule is that the assured does not warrant seaworthiness, but he may not recover any loss attributable to unseaworthiness if, "with the privity of the assured," the vessel is sent to sea in an unseaworthy condition. The American law is probably the same, although there is some authority to support an "American Rule" that in a time policy the assured impliedly warrants both the seaworthiness of the vessel at the time the insurance attaches, and that the owner thereafter will not knowingly permit the vessel to "break ground"—embark on a voyage—in an unseaworthy condition. *See, e.g., Saskatchewan Government Ins. Office v. Spot Pack, Inc.*, 242 F.2d 385 (5th Cir. 1957).

The warranty of seaworthiness in a marine insurance policy generally is absolute and extends to equipment and working procedures as well as the integrity of the vessel's physical structure. If a vessel sinks in calm waters, a presumption of unseaworthiness may arise. *Thanh Long Partnership v. Highlands Ins. Co.*, 32 F.3d 189 (5th Cir. 1994); *Underwriters at Lloyd's v. Labarca*, 260 F.3d 3 (1st Cir. 2001). A policy may contain a "Captain Warranty" through which the insurer has the right to approve the vessel captain. *Yu v. Albany Ins. Co.*, 281 F.3d 803 (9th Cir. 2002).

A party seeking marine insurance is required to disclose all circumstances known to him which materially affect the risk. A failure to make such a disclosure, or an incorrect assertion of a material fact by the assured, will void the policy. It is not clear whether this rule ("utmost good faith," or *uberrimae fidei)* is an established admiralty rule or whether a less demanding state rule may apply. *Compare Albany Ins. Co. v. Anh Thi Kieu*, page 127; *New York Marine & General Ins. Co. v. Tradeline*, 266 F.3d 112 (2d Cir. 2001); and *Certain Underwriters at Lloyds, London v. Inlet Fisheries, Inc.*, 518 F.3d 645 (9th Cir. 2008). A fact is material if it would influence a prudent insurer in fixing the premium or in deciding to insure the risk. Formerly, deviation in the voyage (including operating the vessel outside the trading limits specified in the policy) voided the policy. However, policies now provide (through the "held covered" clause) that deviation will not defeat coverage, except, perhaps, if the deviation is willful or intentional. Deviation should result, at the least, in an adjustment of the premium.

Hull policies usually provide for payment of repairs or payment of the stipulated value of the vessel when it is a total loss. The American rule is that if the vessel is not a total loss but the cost of repairs exceeds one half the value of the vessel, the assured may elect to "abandon" the vessel to the assurer and recover the insured value under the theory of "constructive total loss"; however, the policy may provide that the vessel is a total loss only if the repairs equal the value or agreed value of the vessel. In a "value policy," the policy recites the value of the insured property and the insurer agrees to pay that amount for a total loss.

The hull policy will specify the risks against which it insures. A "marine risks" hull policy protects against loss from accidents in navigation or loss caused by extraordinary action of elements of the sea, fire, theft, or battery. "War risk" insurance may be written separately, or the "marine" and "war" risks may be combined in an "all risks" policy. Since the insurer is liable only if the loss is "proximately caused" by the risk insured against, troublesome questions can arise if the "marine" and "war" risks are covered by different insurers.

In addition to covering the owner's interest in the vessel, the hull policy may provide him with protection against other losses through "specially to cover" clauses. Common special coverages include (1) the "collision and running down" clause, which provides indemnity against liability for collision damages to vessels and the property carried on such vessels; (2) "disbursements" coverage, which permits the assured to recoup money spent on the voyage; and (3) insurance against loss of freight. Two of the more interesting special coverages are the "sue and labor" clause and the "Inchmaree" clause. The "sue and labor" clause makes the assurer liable, in addition to his liability for loss or damage to the vessel, for expenses reasonably incurred by the assured in attempting to recover or preserve the insured property. The "Inchmaree" clause covers accidents in handling cargo or in bunkering (fueling) caused by negligence of the master or crew, and damage from explosion or from a "latent defect" in the vessel or its machinery. Coverage under this clause does not attach if the loss results from "want of due diligence" by the assured or the owner or manager of the vessel, or, in some policies, by any person.

The P & I policy is an outgrowth of and complements the coverage of the hull policy. Hull insurers initially were unwilling to extend full protection to a vessel owner under the theory that a fully-insured owner would not take available precautions for the safety of the ship. Thus, the hull policy provided the owner with limited public liability protection, including insurance against only three-fourths of the damage caused by "running down" another vessel. To meet the need for full coverage, the owners banded together in "Protection and Indemnity Societies" to provide mutual insurance against risks and losses not covered by hull policies. Some P & I associations are still active, although much of the P & I insurance today is written by commercial insurers.

The primary purpose of modern P & I insurance is to provide public liability coverage to the shipowner by insuring him against claims for personal injury or wrongful death and claims for non-collision loss or damage to other vessels or property. The P & I policy also provides "excess" insurance over the hull policy for damages to other vessels caused by collision and insures against the cost of removal of a wrecked vessel when such removal is "compulsory by (under) law." A P & I policy also insures against a number of other risks, including salvage, pollution and liability for cargo. The policy also may contain an "omnibus clause" extending coverage to other unspecified but exceptional risks.

The P & I policy insures the vessel owner against personal injury and wrongful death claims by seamen, including claims for maintenance and cure. The policy, however, ordinarily excludes liability "under any compensation act to any employee of the assured" other than a seaman; hence claims under the Longshore and Harbor Workers' Compensation Act or a state worker compensation program are not covered. The prudent shipowner will obtain protection for these risks by obtaining an "Employer's Liability Policy" or by securing the deletion of the Compensation Act exclusion from the P & I policy.

Several other aspects of the P & I policy should be mentioned. The policy affords protection only for an "act or omission of a vessel." Since that phrase is a term of art subject to judicial interpretation, a shipowner runs the risk that his liability arising out of the activities of his vessel or its employees may not be deemed to have been caused by an "act or omission" of the vessel, and will not be covered by the P & I policy. To protect against claims that do not fall within the P & I policy, a shipowner may purchase a "general liability" policy which does not contain a "watercraft exclusion."

The P & I policy also may exclude liability assumed by the shipowner through contract. A shipowner whose vessel performs a maritime service often makes warranties—express or implied—to the customer. The shipowner may obtain coverage for these obligations from some other source, usually a general liability policy.

Maritime liability insurance may clearly be excess, as when coverage only begins above a specified amount of loss. In some cases, however, two or more policies may cover the same loss. In such cases, the ranking of policies is made by interpretation of the "other insurance" clauses in the policies, and perhaps by applying state law rules of interpretation.

The P & I policy may provide that the insurer is not liable to any greater extent than the assured would have been had the assured been the owner of the vessel and entitled to all rights of limitation of liability to which a shipowner is entitled. When a policy so provides, the time charterer, who is not entitled to limitation, either must obtain additional insurance or must secure deletion of that clause from the P & I policy.

Cargo insurance covers those risks which maritime law imposes upon the shipper or consignee. (*See* Chapter IV, *supra*). In addition to the normal perils of the sea, cargo insurance may extend to consequential losses resulting from some commercial happenings, such as delays in production and diversion of shipments.

Generally, the insurance policy provides coverage only if the covered peril was the "proximate cause" of the loss.

The general rule in admiralty is that attorney's fees are not recoverable in the absence of statute or contract. *Alyeska Pipeline Serv. Co. v. Wilderness Soc'y*, 421 U.S. 240 (1975). However, it is not clear whether a court may apply against a marine insurer a state statute subjecting an insurer to an award of attorney's fees. *Compare All Underwriters v. Weisberg*, 222 F.3d 1309 (11th Cir. 2000), with *Flores v. American Seafoods Co.*, 335 F.3d 904 (9th Cir. 2003).

Maritime common law provides that an insurer which pays a covered loss is subrogated to the assured's claim against third persons. The LHWCA specifically provides for subrogation to an insurer for benefits which it pays to a maritime worker under the Act. 33 U.S.C.A. § 933(h). A marine policy may specifically provide for a waiver of subrogation against a designated third person, which is a method of making that person an assured under the policy to the extent of any loss that person causes to the named assured.

CHAPTER VIII

TOWAGE AND PILOTAGE

A. TOWAGE

An important part of American maritime commerce is transportation of goods by barges that lack motive power but are propelled by tugboats or towboats. A boat which pushes a barge is a towboat, and one which pulls a barge is a tugboat; in common parlance, however, the barge is referred to as the tow, and both the towboat and the tugboat are called the tug. A contract by which the owner of a tug (towboat or tugboat) agrees to expedite the voyage of a tow (barge) belonging to another is a contract of towage, governed by special maritime contract rules.

The contract of towage must be distinguished from similar contracts governed by different rules. *See, e.g., Sacramento Navigation Co. v. Salz*, 273 U.S. 326 (1927). Where one person owns both tug and tow and agrees to carry the goods of another, the contract is one of affreightment, governed by the rules applicable to charters or bills of lading. *See* Chapter IV, *supra*. Where the owner of a tug obtains a tow from another for use in the business of the tug or its owner, the contract is one of charter, and not of towage.

The towage contract need not be in writing. In the absence of express contractual provisions, the tower warrants that it will furnish a seaworthy vessel and crew and that it possesses sufficient skill and knowledge to perform the contract safely. The owner of the tow must furnish a seaworthy vessel, with proper equipment and lighting; where the tow is manned, the crew of the tow must be competent and sufficient in number.

The duty which the tug owes to the tow is couched in negligence terms: the tug must exercise reasonable care in towing and in mooring the tow. There have been some cases in which the towing contract has been held to include an implied warranty of workmanlike performance by the tug, but the theory typically is used only to provide indemnification to the tow. *See* Chapter XVII.

Attempts by tug owners to contract away their liability to tows for negligent performance of towage contracts have been thwarted by the Supreme Court as violative of public policy. In the first decision invalidating such an exculpatory clause, the Court found an absence of equal bargaining power. *Bisso v. Inland Waterways Corp.*, 349 U.S. 85 (1955). In a subsequent case, however, the Court struck down the contract even though the evidence indicated that the parties enjoyed relatively equal bargaining positions. *Dixilyn Drilling Corp. v. Crescent Towing & Salvage Co.*, 372 U.S. 697 (1963). The Supreme Court also has refused to enforce a contract provision through which the tug attempts to escape liability for its own negligence by desig-

nating the officers and crew of the tug as agents of
the tow for the voyage. *Boston Metals Co. v. The
Winding Gulf*, 349 U.S. 122 (1955).

The effect of *Bisso* has been weakened by a
Supreme Court decision validating an exculpatory
clause which was part of a tariff filed with the
Interstate Commerce Commission, *Southwestern
Sugar & Molasses Co. v. River Terminals Corp.*, 360
U.S. 411 (1959), and another upholding the validity
of a clause in a towage contract requiring that all
disputes be resolved by a designated foreign court.
M/S Bremen v. Zapata Off–Shore Co., 407 U.S. 1
(1972). An appeals court also has upheld the validity of a provision requiring the tow to insure against
its loss and to obtain a waiver by its insurer of
subrogation rights against the tug, a device which
has the same practical effect as a contractual provision relieving the tug from liability to the tow for
negligent performance of the towage contract.
*Twenty Grand Offshore, Inc. v. West India Carriers,
Inc.*, 492 F.2d 679 (5th Cir. 1974). Another appeals
court further weakened *Bisso* when it held that for
an exculpatory clause to be rendered void based on
unfair bargaining power, there "must be some evidence that the party holding the superior bargaining power exerted that power in overreaching the
less sophisticated party by, for example, engaging in
fraud or coercion or by insisting on an unconsciona-
ble clause." *Sander v. Alexander Richardson Investments*, 334 F.3d 712 (8th Cir. 2003).

The towage contract is not one of bailment. *Stevens v. The White City*, 285 U.S. 195 (1932). Thus,

proof by the plaintiff of delivery of the tow in good condition and redelivery in a damaged condition does not give rise to a presumption that the tug was at fault. The finder of fact, however, may infer negligence on the part of the tug when the evidence shows (1) the damage occurred while the tow was in the exclusive control of the tug (such as where the tow is unmanned), and (2) the most probable cause of the damage was the tug's negligence. In making this common-sense evaluation of circumstantial evidence, the courts frequently invoke the Latin phrase *res ipsa loquitur.*

If the tug performs additional services beyond those set forth in the contract, such as regaining control after the tow breaks away without fault of the tug, courts may award compensation beyond that provided by the contract. If the contract does not specify the compensation, the tower is entitled to reasonable compensation for the services rendered. A tug also may be entitled to a salvage award if it incurs risks and performs duties on behalf of the tow which are not within the contemplation of the towage contract.

The collision rules make special provisions for tug and tow, including a requirement of distinctive lights. Liability to third persons for collision damages depends upon the nature of the towage. If the tow is a "dumb" (unmanned) barge, or is otherwise under the control of the tug, liability for negligence will be imposed upon the tug (the "dominant mind" in the venture), but not upon the tow. Even if the tow is manned, liability may rest solely upon the tug if that vessel's mariners can be said to be the "dominant mind" in the relationship. If both tug and tow are negligent, they are jointly and severally (solidarily) liable for damages caused to others.

Under the "flotilla doctrine," the owner of a "fleet" (two or more tugs or a tug and tow) involved in a marine disaster may be required to surrender both vessels in seeking limitation of liability. *See* Chapter XVIII, *infra*.

Claims between the tug and tow arising out of the towage contract are secured by liens on the offending vessels.

B. PILOTAGE

Generically, a pilot is the person aboard ship who is in charge of the helm and the vessel's route. However, "pilot" is used more frequently to describe a person with specialized knowledge of conditions in a specific geographic area, such as a harbor or an inland stream, and who goes aboard the vessel to direct it to safety in those conditions.

Federal law requires the use of federally licensed pilots during certain coastwise voyages. 46 U.S.C.A. § 8502. In other cases, the use and licensing of pilots is left to the states. 46 U.S.C.A. § 8501; *see also* 46 U.S.C.A. § 8502(g) (requiring that pilots on vessels navigating Alaska's Prince William Sound be licensed by the state of Alaska) and 46 U.S.C.A. § 8502(I) (exempting dredges from the federal license requirement). A shipowner is not vicariously liable for damages caused by the fault of a pilot he is compelled by law to employ. However, the vessel is liable *in rem* for the torts of the compulsory pilot. In addition, maritime law does not permit the ship's master to abdicate his authority and responsibility to a pilot. *See The China*, 74 U.S. 53 (1868). Consequently, the shipowner may become personally liable, through respondeat superior, for the master's negligence in failing to assert command when the compulsory pilot's conduct is obviously improper.

The unincorporated association or nonprofit corporation through which some pilots operate generally is not liable for the pilot's tort. *See, e.g., In Re Moran Towing Corp.*, 497 F.3d 375 (3d Cir. 2007). A commercial venture may be vicariously liable for the tort of its employee pilot, but such liability often is negated by a provision (a "Pilotage Clause") in the pilotage contract which makes the vessel solely liable for the torts of the pilot. *See, e.g., Sun Oil Co. v. Dalzell Towing Co.*, 287 U.S. 291 (1932).

CHAPTER IX

SALVAGE

Salvage, the provision of a financial reward for the rescue of property from a maritime peril, dates back to Roman times. The rescue may occur pursuant to an express contract (contract salvage) between the owner and the salvor. In many cases, however, the salvor acts to save maritime property without any pre-existing agreement as to the compensation to be paid by the owner. In such cases of voluntary or "pure" salvage, maritime law imposes a quasi-contractual obligation upon the property and its owner to compensate the salvor for his efforts. The salvage claim is secured by a maritime lien on the property salvaged. This general maritime law right to recover for rescue is markedly different from the common law where, at best, a "thanks" is the most the rescuer can legally expect.

During the twentieth century, much of the law of salvage was governed by the Salvage Convention of 1910, to which the United States was a party. That convention generally restated American salvage law, however, and several of its provisions were found in the Salvage Act (former 46 U.S.C. §§ 727–31, now codified at 46 U.S.C.A. § 80107). As a result, the convention rarely was cited in American courts. The United States ratified the 1989 Interna-

142

tional Convention on Salvage, which became effective in 1996. That convention (hereinafter "the Convention") parallels American maritime law in many important particulars. In addition, the Convention is limited in its application, relegating many matters to local control by state members, and excepting certain property from its reach. Thus the adoption of the Convention by the United States has not effected broad changes in American salvage law.

A. CONTRACT SALVAGE

Salvage contracts present few uniquely maritime issues for litigation. The property which is the object of the contract must be maritime property, or the contract will not be treated as one of salvage within admiralty jurisdiction. The Convention applies to contract salvage unless the contract "otherwise provides expressly or by implication." Article 6. The agreement between the parties to enter into a salvage contract must be clear. The contract may provide that the salvor will be reimbursed at a temporal rate, regardless of the outcome of the salvage attempt. Frequently, however, the contract salvor is engaged on a "no cure, no pay" basis and is entitled to compensation only if successful. This type of contract often provides for substantial recovery in the event of success. When the property is saved quickly, the owner may attempt to avoid payment of the full contract price by contending that the contract was induced by fraud or that the owner's consent was given under duress. If a salvor has in fact taken unfair advantage of an owner who was *in extremis,* courts will set aside the contract and will reduce or deny any salvage award. However, the courts are unwilling to relieve the owner simply because it made a bad bargain. The Supreme Court has held that a court may set aside the contract only if it determines that, under the circumstances which existed at the time the contract was entered into, the compensation stipulated in the contract was "grossly exorbitant." *The Elfrida,* 172 U.S. 186 (1898). Article 7 of the Convention provides that a salvage contract may be annulled or modified if entered into "under undue influence or the influence of danger and its terms are inequitable," or if the payment under the contract "is an excessive degree too large or too small for services actually rendered."

B. QUASI–CONTRACT SALVAGE

Quasi-contractual or "pure" salvage has generated much more litigation than contract salvage. The premise underlying an award of quasi-contractual salvage is that when property is in a position of maritime peril, the potential rescuers are few, the risks in rescue are great, and the temptation to the rescuer to appropriate the property as his or her own is strong. Accordingly, the seagoing potential "Good Samaritan" must be given added incentive to undertake rescue efforts and to return the rescued property to its owner. The operative principle under American maritime law is that one who directly and voluntarily rescues maritime property which is derelict, or is in a position of "peril," is entitled to an award, determined by the court, which is commensurate with the value of the property; the risk involved; and the effort expended. Under the Convention, salvage is "an act or activity undertaken to assist a vessel or any other property in danger" in water, Article 1(a), and which has a "useful result." Article 12.

Only maritime property may be the object of salvage, but there is no standard definition of maritime property for these purposes. In *Cope v. Vallette Dry–Dock Co.*, 119 U.S. 625 (1887), the Supreme Court held that a floating drydock was not subject to salvage because it was neither a ship, ship's furnishings, nor cargo. Similar reasoning would preclude salvage claims for the rescue of offshore mineral production platforms and similar structures which maritime law treats as extensions of land. Since the purpose of rewarding a salvor is to encourage the limited number of potential rescuers, one important inquiry should be whether the rescuer necessarily is subjected to maritime peril in effecting the rescue. Under that approach, some offshore platforms and dry docks could be treated as maritime property for salvage purposes. However, the application of the Convention may produce a different result. The Convention describes "property" for salvage purposes as "any property not permanently and intentionally attached to the shoreline," Article 1(a), but specifically excludes fixed or floating platforms or mobile offshore drilling units on location engaged in the exploration for or production of mineral resources. Article 3.

Under the jurisprudence, mail and bills of exchange are not subject to salvage. The rationale is that a salvor must receive his reward from the proceeds of a judicial sale of the salvaged property, but since the mail (and nonnegotiable commercial paper) may not be sold effectively at public auction, no salvage award can be made. That rule may not survive the broad definition of salvageable property contained in the Convention.

The theory that salvage does not extend to things which may not be sold through judicial process may also have underlain the common-law rule that one is not entitled to a salvage award for rescue of human life. Since that rule could produce the unacceptable scenario of salvors rescuing cargo while permitting passengers and crew to perish, Congress modified it by providing that: "A salvor of human life, who gave aid following an accident giving rise to salvage is entitled to a fair share of the payment awarded to the salvor for salvaging the vessel or other property or preventing or minimizing damage to the environment." 46 U.S.C.A. § 80107(a). The Convention also articulates this principle. Article 16. If there is no concurrent property salvage (thus a "pure life" salvage), a rescuer of persons at sea may *not* recover *or* possibly may recover the expense of the rescue from the vessel on which the imperiled person served or was a passenger, either under the doctrine of unjust enrichment or under the theory that a person who incurs expenses in performing a maritime duty owed by a third person may recoup from that third person the expenses incurred in performing the duty. *See, e.g.*, *Peninsular & Oriental Steam Navigation Co. v. Overseas Oil Carriers, Inc.*, 553 F.2d 830 (2d Cir. 1977). Both the Convention and federal statutes limit salvage claims against warships and other public vessels. *See, e.g.*, Article 4 of the Convention and 46 U.S.C. § 80107(d).

Under the general maritime jurisprudence, salvage efforts qualify for an award only if direct and voluntary. The Convention apparently does not continue such a "direct" requirement. Persons who are under a duty to aid a vessel or other property in peril may not recover salvage, since their efforts are not "voluntary." This jurisprudential rule usually precludes salvage awards to the master, crew, and passengers of the salvaged vessel. However, if the crew member's obligation to serve the vessel has terminated, as when the ship has been abandoned, his subsequent efforts may be "voluntary" and may qualify for a salvage award.

Generally neither the owner nor the crew of a vessel which negligently causes a collision is entitled to salvage for saving other vessels from the peril created by the collision. Two statutes impose upon the master of a vessel the duty to assist other vessels which are in positions of peril in navigable waters. The "Standby Act," now Title 46 U.S.C.A. Section 2303, requires that the master of a vessel involved in a marine casualty identify himself and his vessel and render assistance to persons endangered by the casualty, "so far as [he] ... can do so without serious danger" to his own vessel or persons on board. 46 U.S.C.A. § 2304 imposes upon a master the duty to render assistance "to any individual found at sea in danger of being lost, so far as the master ... can do so without serious danger" to his own vessel or persons on board. Article 10 of the Convention echoes that same concept. The Standby Act supports the argument that the master's aid to a vessel in peril is not "voluntary," and thus he is not entitled to salvage. However, it is doubtful that the master would be deprived of salvage through the application of either of these statutes unless his fault placed the salvaged property in the position of peril. Under Article 10(3) of the Convention, the owner is not liable for the master's violation of the "standby" provision.

Under the general maritime law, public employees engaged in salvage efforts, such as harbor firemen, ordinarily are not entitled to salvage awards. Since their employment duties encompass salvage attempts, their efforts are not "voluntary." However, if their efforts are extraordinary, a court may award salvage. Members of the crew of a vessel regularly employed in contract salvage may not be entitled to salvage awards, particularly if their normal pay reflects an allowance for the dangerous nature of salvage work. A tug may not recover a salvage award from its tow, unless it rescues the tow from an extraordinary peril.

The United States engages in numerous salvage efforts. The Navy often claims salvage awards. *See, e.g.*, 10 U.S.C.A. §§ 7361–67. The Coast Guard, however, is charged by statute, 14 U.S.C.A. § 88, with the duty of engaging in rescue efforts; thus its services may not be "voluntary," and it may not be entitled to a salvage award. Article 5 of the Convention provides quite cryptically that the Convention "shall not affect any provision of national law ... relating to salvage ... by ... public authorities," but "[n]evertheless, salvors carrying out ... salvage operations shall be entitled to avail themselves of the rights and remedies provided for in this Convention...."

Under American maritime law developed prior to the Convention, property either must be in a position of peril from which it would not otherwise escape or, at least, subject to a high probability of loss or destruction unless it receives aid. Article 1(a) of the Convention requires only that the property be "in danger in navigable waters." The American jurisprudence holds that if the property is "derelict," *i.e.*, abandoned at sea by its owner or his agents without hope of recovery or intention to return, the salvor may effect salvage without the permission of the owner or his agents. The salvor may thereafter continue his efforts without regard to the owner's wishes, and usually may bring the property to the port of his choice. Even when the owner or his agent remains aboard the imperiled vessel, the vessel is subject to salvage if there is a reasonable apprehension that the vessel will be lost or damaged unless salvage services are provided. If the owner or his agent remains aboard the imperiled vessel, however, he may refuse a proffered rescue, even if a reasonable person would not have done so under similar circumstances. If the owner or agent remains on board and accepts the tender of salvage, he nevertheless may retain the right to direct the port to which the vessel will be delivered. These rules indicate that something more than romanticism impels a master to remain aboard a vessel in distress after the crew abandons ship. Under Article 19 of the Convention, a salvage award is not payable if the owner or master makes an "express and reasonable prohibition" of salvage operations.

Formerly, if the salvaging and salvaged vessels were under common ownership, the salvaging vessel was not entitled to an award, under the theory that it did not save the property of another. This rule also barred members of the crew of the salvaging vessel from any award; however, that result was changed by statute. 46 U.S.C.A. § 80107(b). Article 12(3) of the Convention also allows a salvage award although the salvaged vessel and the vessel undertaking the salvage operations belong to the same owner.

American admiralty law sanctions a "pure" salvage award only if the salvage efforts are successful; if the property ultimately perishes in the peril, salvage is not owed. The Convention apparently would not change the result, except where the salvage operations avert threatened damage to the environment. Articles 12, 14. A person claiming the salvage award need not effect the rescue, if the property is saved and he or she has performed an act which contributed to its ultimate safety. Thus a salvor who aids a vessel by transmitting a radio message, by warning of impending peril, or even by simply standing by, may be entitled to an award.

Where one aids in salvage efforts but is not the ultimate rescuer, the vessel owner or the last rescuer may assert that that earlier salvor abandoned his or her efforts and thus forfeited any right to a salvage award. The courts ordinarily will not find an abandonment that defeats the first rescuer's right to an award unless that rescuer ceased efforts under circumstances which established that he or she had no further interest in the property or was indifferent to whether it was saved. *Saint Paul Marine Transp. Corp. v. Cerro Sales Corp.*, 505 F.2d 1115 (9th Cir. 1974). The Convention does not speak expressly to the issue but requires a salvor to seek and accept assistance from other salvors under appropriate circumstances. Article 8(1)(c), (d).

Rescue frequently is effected by towing the imperiled vessel, and persons opposing the salvage award may contend that the rescuer is entitled only to a towage fee and not to the usually larger salvage award. If the towage did not merely expedite the ship's voyage but relieved it from either present or reasonably apprehended danger, the court may treat it as "salvage towage" and make a salvage award. The Convention apparently would not affect the rule, since it permits a salvage award only when the vessel is "in danger." Article 1(a).

In *The Blackwall*, 77 U.S. 1 (1869), the Court provided these factors for fixing a "pure" salvage award:

1.   the value of the property saved, and the degree of danger from which it was rescued;

2.   the value of the property utilized by the salvor in its rescue efforts;

3.   the skill and labor utilized; and

4.   the risks involved.

Article 13 of the Convention basically codifies those factors, but adds an additional one—the skill and effort expended in preventing or minimizing damage to the environment. Article 13(1)(b).

The salvage award rarely will exceed one-half of the value of the property saved, although there is no hard and fast rule. The court also may award an additional sum to reimburse the salvor for out of pocket expenses. A costly salvage effort that rescues items of historical and archeological value may justify an award approaching 100% of the value. *See, e.g.*, *Columbus–America Discovery Group v. Atlantic Mut. Ins. Co.*, 56 F.3d 556 (4th Cir. 1995). Article 14 of the Convention contemplates an award in excess of the value of the saved property where the salvor has prevented or minimized damage to the environment.

The American maritime law rule is that if the salvage is effected by a vessel, the owner of the salvaging ship and that ship's cargo share the award with the master and crew. The portion allotted to the master and crew usually is divided in this manner: the master and each member of the crew receive a basic share, and additional shares are allotted to those among them who directly participated in the rescue operations. The Convention relegates the allocation among salvors to the law of the appropriate nation. Article 15.

General maritime law makes the salvaged vessel liable *in rem* for the salvage award. A person with a direct pecuniary interest in the salvaged property who asserts a claim to the property may be liable *in personam* for the award. The Convention retains the salvor's maritime lien but conditions enforcement upon the failure of the owner to provide satisfactory security for the claim. Articles 20, 21. The Court also may order the owner to make an interim payment on the award to the salvor. Article 22.

Generally, the salvor is held to a duty of reasonable care under the circumstances and any breach of that duty will diminish the salvage award. Article 8(1)(a) of the Convention requires that the salvor carry out the salvage operations "with due care." What if the damage from the salvor's negligence exceeds the salvage award, or there is no award because the rescue was unsuccessful? Some jurisprudence sanctions an affirmative award of damages against the salvor if he has been guilty of gross negligence in his salvage efforts. That jurisprudence may have been altered by 46 U.S.C.A. § 2303(c), which provides in part:

> An individual ... gratuitously and in good faith rendering assistance at the scene of a marine casualty without objection by an individual assisted, is not liable for damages as a result of rendering assistance ... or arranging salvage ... when the individual acts as an ordinary, reasonable, and prudent individual would have acted under the circumstances.

The Convention does not indicate that an affirmative award against the salvor would be appropriate for negligent performance of the salvage.

American maritime law requires that the salvor maintain "the most scrupulous fidelity," *Cromwell v. The Island City*, 66 U.S. 121 (1861), and a salvor who breaches that trust forfeits the right to a salvage award and to compensation on a *quantum meruit* basis. Examples of conduct which may justify forfeiture of any award include embezzlement of the salvaged property, unreasonable refusal of salvage assistance from another, and misrepresentation designed to secure salvage work or to obtain a higher compensation for salvage services. Article 18 of the Convention provides that the salvor may be deprived of the whole or part of his award if the salvor has been guilty of "fraud or other dishonest conduct."

Congress has provided a two-year statute of limitations on salvage claims, with a proviso that suit may be brought after that period has elapsed if, during the two-year period, the salvor has not had a reasonable opportunity to arrest the salvaged vessel within the jurisdiction of the court or within the territorial waters of the country where the salvor resides or has his principal place of business. 46 U.S.C.A. § 80107(c). Article 23 of the Convention provides a two-year limitation period and permits extension through acknowledgment by the debtor. Additionally, the article apparently allows the application of any longer limitation period provided by the law of the nation in which the salvage proceedings are instituted.

C. FINDS

If the owner expressly disclaims ownership, or the property has been abandoned at sea for a long period of time, it may be unreasonable to allow the owner to assert a claim in opposition to the salvor. Under such circumstances, maritime law may classify the property as "found" and not "salvaged," and, under the doctrine of "finds," may reward the rescuer with the ownership of the property rather than with a lesser award for salvage. There appears to be no clear line of demarcation between property that is "salvaged" and property that is a "find." Courts generally favor salvage over "finds," which eliminates the former owner's claim to all or part of the property. Regardless of which doctrine is applied, the result may be the same when no owner comes forward to claim the property or the salvage award equals or nears the value of the property.

"Finds" has been applied in some cases of "treasure salvage," eliminating the former owner and generating an ownership battle between the "finder" and the sovereign.

The federal sovereign has asserted title to all abandoned shipwrecks which are imbedded ("firmly affixed ... such that the use of tools of excavation is required ... to move the bottom sediments to gain access to the shipwreck") within American waters, and has transferred to each state title to the abandoned shipwrecks located within that state. The Abandoned Shipwreck Act of 1987, 43 U.S.C.A. § 2101 et seq. The act provides that the law of salvage and the law of finds do not apply to abandoned shipwrecks within its coverage. 43 U.S.C.A. § 2106.

Interesting issues may arise when the state desires to establish ownership of a shipwreck under the Abandoned Shipwreck Act and the finder wants to shield the state and others from the location of the wreck until some key issues are resolved. *Great Lakes Exploration Group, LLC v. Unidentified Wrecked and Abandoned Sailing Vessel*, 522 F.3d 682 (6th Cir. 2008).

D. PRIZE

Prize is a sovereign's capture at sea of a vessel or other property of an enemy belligerent during time of war. The captor takes the vessel to a prize court, where the issue of "prize or no prize" is adjudicated in an *in rem* proceeding. If the decision is "prize," the vessel is sold and the proceeds are paid to the captor. 28 U.S.C.A. § 1333 grants federal district courts exclusive jurisdiction over "[a]ny prize brought into the United States and all proceedings for the condemnation of property taken as prize." The United States law on prize is set forth in 10 U.S.C.A. § 7651–81; 10 U.S.C.A. § 7668 provides that "[t]he net proceeds of all property condemned as prize shall be decreed to the United States." Prize has not played a significant role in American admiralty law in the twentieth or twenty-first centuries.

CHAPTER X

GENERAL AVERAGE

In the typical maritime voyage, a vessel, its cargo and the freight (the vessel's fee for carrying the cargo) may be said to be "at risk"; if the voyage is unsuccessful, the owner of one or more of these interests may suffer loss. Ordinarily, the damages will be borne by the owner of the interest which is lost or damaged, the owner's insurer, or a third party (or its insurer) whose fault caused the damages. The allocation of loss in such a maritime case is called "particular average" although it is merely a simple allocation of risk with a fancy maritime name.

In some cases, damage to one or more of these three interests—vessel, cargo, and freight—may be inflicted deliberately by the master or operator of the vessel in an effort to save the entire voyage (and thus the other interests) from loss or damage from an impending maritime peril, or at least a real and substantial danger. *See, e.g., Navigazione Generale Italiana v. Spencer Kellogg & Sons, Inc.*, 92 F.2d 41 (2d Cir. 1937). If the vessel was at fault in incurring the peril, it may be liable to the owner of the property lost in the peril. But such is often not the case; the "perils of the sea" may endanger a vessel whose master and crew are free from fault. When these circumstances exist—a maritime peril, a lack of vessel fault, and a voluntary "sacrifice" of one interest to save the voyage—maritime law dictates that "the loss occasioned for the benefit of all must be made good by the contribution of all." 2 The Digest of Justinian 385 Monro transl. 1909, Digest 14.2.1. This principle is called "general average," as distinguished from "particular average." General average, which is unique to maritime law, applies only when (1) there is a danger to which both vessel and cargo are exposed; (2) the danger is imminent and apparently "inevitable," which means that there is no probable escape except by inflicting loss upon one of the interests; (3) there is a voluntary sacrifice, such as jettisoning cargo or stranding the vessel; (4) the attempt to avoid the common peril is successful; and (5) the party seeking contribution from the owners of the other interests is free from fault.

The "sacrifice" need not be destruction or damage to property. As the Supreme Court has observed:

Losses which give a claim to general average are usually divided into two great classes: (1) Those which arise from sacrifices of part of the ship or part of the cargo, purposely made in order to save the whole adventure from perishing. (2) Those which arise out of extraordinary expenses incurred for the joint benefit of ship and cargo.

The Star of Hope, 76 U.S. 203 (1869).

When the requirements for general average are met, the loss is transferred from the owner of the interest which is sacrificed to the owners of all of the interests at risk; the owners of the "saved" interests pay to the owner of the "sacrificed" interest their pro rata share of his loss. While the calculations may be much more complicated, a simple illustration captures the basic idea. Assume that a vessel valued at $800,000 is carrying cargo worth $150,000, for a freight charge of $50,000. Assume further that two-thirds of the cargo (valued at $100,000) is jettisoned, and the sacrifice qualifies for general average. The total of the interests at risk is $1,000,000, the cargo loss is $100,000, and the vessel owner represents 85% (the vessel plus the freight) of the marine venture which was saved from the peril. The vessel owner must reimburse the cargo owner for 85% of the latter's loss, or a total of $85,000; the cargo owner bears the remainder of his loss ($15,000), which is the percentage of the total loss (15%) equal to his percentage in the maritime venture.

A claim for general average may be brought in admiralty and is secured by a maritime lien on the property saved. In the overwhelming number of cases, the interests at risk are insured against, and general average is computed and paid through informal proceedings among insurers. Thus the resolution is private and there is little resulting recent "law." The basis for most settlements is the decision of a "general average adjuster," who investigates the occurrence and the values involved and makes a determination of the adjustment that should be made between the interests at risk in the maritime venture. Some cases do reach the courts, however. Many of these raise questions of whether the voyage actually was in peril or whether the sacrifice was "voluntary" and was for the purpose of saving the voyage. Some courts have required some imminent peril, whereas more modern courts have required less. Most of the precise issues in both adjustment and litigation of general average cases are resolved by the application of the York–Antwerp Rules, which are incorporated into virtually all commercial voyages by the terms of the charter or bill of lading.

Under maritime common law, a carrier who is guilty of fault cannot claim general average. However, federal legislation (The Harter Act and COGSA) relieves the carrier from liability to the cargo owner for some of the consequences of his fault, such as that incurred in the navigation and management of the vessel. Carriers initially contended that the Harter Act automatically removed the bar to the recovery of general average when their negligence was that from which a carrier is relieved by the Act. After the Supreme Court rejected this contention, carriers began inserting clauses in bills of lading providing that general average is payable if it arises through negligence of the carrier for which he is exculpated by the Harter Act. The enforceability of these clauses was upheld by the Supreme Court; they were termed "Jason clauses," from the case in which the Court sanctioned their use. *The Jason*, 225 U.S. 32 (1912). A similar clause (the New Jason Clause) generally has been in use since the adoption of COGSA.

CHAPTER XI

MARITIME TORT LAW

A. GENERAL MARITIME TORT LAW

Where a tort is "in admiralty" (i.e., there is maritime tort jurisdiction), federal maritime law provides the rules of decision, unless the controversy is deemed "maritime but local,"—i.e., there is no need for a uniform maritime rule—and state law is applied. *See Yamaha Motor Corp., U.S.A. v. Calhoun*, 516 U.S. 199 (1996). Among the more frequently occurring maritime torts are those arising out of collisions between vessels, injuries to seamen resulting from conditions of the vessels on which they are serving, and claims by maritime workers against vessels and their operators pursuant to section 905(b) of the Longshore and Harbor Workers' Compensation Act. Each of these kinds of maritime tort, and the seamen's negligence action against his employer (the Jones Act claim), are regulated by distinct and fairly comprehensive bodies of law which are the subject of independent treatment in this work. (*See* Chapters XII and XIII). However, in collision, Jones Act, and 905(b) cases, some issues arise in which those special bodies of law do not provide a dispositive rule. In those situations, and in *all other* tort cases in which federal maritime law furnishes the rule of decision but there is no federal statute on point, the applicable substantive law is what properly may be called general maritime tort law. This law basically is a product of the federal judiciary. Since the Supreme Court infrequently speaks to maritime matters, general maritime tort law has been fashioned for the most part by the lower federal courts. As a result, some of the discussion which follows is supported by scant authority.

There are few reported intentional tort cases in maritime law. *See, e.g., Furness Withy (Chartering), Inc., Panama v. World Energy Systems Associates, Inc.*, 772 F.2d 802 (11th Cir.1985). In most cases it is probably safe to assume that maritime law will follow the general common law governing intentional torts. *See, e.g., Wallis v. Princess Cruises, Inc.*, 306 F.3d 827 (9th Cir.2002) (holding that general maritime law recognizes tort of intentional infliction of emotional distress). As new claims develop at common law, courts applying maritime law will be required to decide those claims. *Smith v. Atlas Offshore Boat, Inc.*, 653 F.2d 1057 (5th Cir.1981). For example, in a seaman's suit against his employer, a court will have to decide whether the Jones Act's provision of a negligence claim against the employer pretermits or preempts the particular intentional tort alleged. *Wiora v. Harrah's Illinois Corp.*, 68 F.Supp.2d 988 (N.D. Ill. 1999).

Maritime tort law, probably utilizing a test similar to that found at common law, recognizes vicarious liability for intentional torts. *See, e.g., Jackson Marine Corp. v. Blue Fox*, 845 F.2d 1307 (5th Cir.

1988); *Doe v. Celebrity Cruises, Inc.*, 394 F.3d 891 (11th Cir. 2004) (cruise line strictly liable for crew member assaults on passengers on cruise, including assault on shore in port of call where encounter would not have occurred but for shipboard events). The Supreme Court's decision in *Miles v. Apex Marine Corp.*, 498 U.S. 19 (1990), cast some doubt on whether punitive damages can be recovered in any action under the general maritime law, but the Court's subsequent decision in *Atlantic Sounding Co., Inc. v. Townsend*, 129 S.Ct. 2561 (2009) reaffirmed the traditional rule regarding the availability of punitive damages for "tortious acts of a particularly egregious nature." The employer's vicarious liability for punitive damages based on the wrongful conduct of his employee was addressed by the Supreme Court in *Exxon Shipping Co. v. Baker*, 128 S.Ct. 2605 (2008), in which the Court found that a corporation could be liable for punitive damages based upon the reckless acts of one of its employees acting in a managerial capacity.

Most general maritime tort cases, however, involve theories of negligence and strict liability. The maritime common law has borrowed from and has supplied the general common law of torts. Indeed, the famous "Learned Hand" formula defining negligence was first crafted in a maritime case. *United States v. Carroll Towing Co.*, 159 F.2d 169 (2d Cir. 1947). Duty in maritime negligence, as in land torts, turns primarily upon the "foreseeability" of the risk. *See, e.g., Consolidated Aluminum Corp. v. C.F. Bean Corp.*, 833 F.2d 65 (5th Cir. 1987). One important aspect of maritime common law is the duty that the owner or operator owes to passengers and guests aboard his or her vessel. (The special duties which are owed to seamen and to other maritime workers are discussed in Chapter XIII). Maritime law rejects the "trespasser," "licensee," and "invitee" distinctions drawn in many common law jurisdictions and imposes upon the owner or operator a duty of reasonable care to all persons who come aboard the vessel for purposes not inimical to the interests of the owner or operator. *Kermarec v. Compagnie Generale Transatlantique*, 358 U.S. 625 (1959). This is similar to the duty owed by an employer to his seaman, according to at least one court that has addressed the issue; that court rejected a higher standard of care adopted by other courts and that the court itself had adopted earlier. *See Gautreaux v. Scurlock Marine, Inc.*, 107 F.3d 331 (5th Cir. 1997).

Does a maritime common carrier owe its passenger a "high degree of care" instead of merely "reasonable care under the circumstances?" The question arises in maritime common law as well as in the general common law. The dispute perhaps is largely semantic, since "reasonable care" in such cases usually translates into "extreme caution." *See, e.g., Smith v. Southern Gulf Marine Co. No. 2*, 791 F.2d 416 (5th Cir. 1986). Attempts by carriers to limit liability to passengers by contract (such as by a provision in the passenger's ticket) may run afoul of statutory safeguards. *See, e.g.*, Title 46 U.S.C.A. section 30505, which invalidates a contract limiting the shipowner's liability to passengers for negligence.

A contract for the rendering of maritime services includes an implied warranty of workmanlike performance. *Vierling v. Celebrity Cruises, Inc.*, 339 F.3d 1309 (11th Cir. 2003). Depending upon the standard applied, the warranty could equate to strict liability or simple negligence. Maritime law probably provides recovery for negligent selection of an independent contractor, *see Becker v. Poling Transp. Corp.*, 356 F.3d 381 (2d Cir. 2004), and negligent misrepresentation. *See Otto Candies, L.L.C. v. Nippon Kaiji Kyokai Corp.*, 346 F.3d 530 (5th Cir. 2003).

Maritime and common-law conceptual approaches to the question of "breach"—whether the defendant failed to act reasonably—generally coincide. *See Complaint of Paducah Towing*, 692 F.2d 412 (6th Cir. 1982) (custom may be considered, but is not conclusive, on the issue of negligence). The "substantial factor" test generally is applied in determining "cause in fact" in general maritime tort law. In Jones Act cases, the "scintilla" (or "slight") standard applies to some issues, such as causation (*see* Chapter XIII), and some courts have erroneously applied that standard to unseaworthiness cases joined with Jones Act claims. Some courts have also applied the *Pennsylvania* rule, a collision rule governing the burden of proof, *see* Chapter XII, *infra*, to non-collision cases. *But see Mawari v. Interocean Ugland Management Corp.*, 1999 WL 820454 (E.D. Pa. 1999). The doctrine of *res ipsa loquitur* generally applies in maritime cases. *Ashland v. Ling–Tem-co–Vought, Inc.*, 711 F.2d 1431 (9th Cir. 1983).

There appears to be no general consensus of the proper test for determining whether conduct is a legal (proximate) cause of injury. Some courts use traditional "proximate cause" language, while others use the "legal cause" language from Restatement (Second) of Torts, section 9. The difference between the two is largely semantic.

The traditional common law and maritime law rule is that a claimant may not recover damages for economic harm, such as loss of income or profits, unless there has been some injury to the claimant or his property. This general common law rule arises from the seminal admiralty case of *Robins Dry Dock & Repair Co. v. Flint*, 275 U.S. 303 (1927). Although admiralty courts generally adhere to the *Robins'* "bright line" test, *see Nautilus Marine, Inc. v. Niemela*, 170 F.3d 1195 (9th Cir.1999), there is some indication that there will be exceptions to the rule, such as in a case where the damaged party is a seaman whose compensation is dependent upon the earnings of his employer's vessel, or where the damaged party is a demise charterer whose liability for charter hire continues while the damaged vessel is out of service. *See, e.g.*, *State of La. ex rel. Guste v. M/V Testbank*, 752 F.2d 1019 (5th Cir. 1985). *See, also*, *Arnold M. Diamond, Inc. v. Gulf Coast Trailing Co.*, 180 F.3d 518 (3d Cir. 1999); *In re Taira Lynn Marine Ltd. No. 5, LLC*, 444 F.3d 371 (5th Cir. 2006).

In general maritime tort law, an employer is vicariously liable, through the doctrine of *respondeat superior*, for the tortious acts of an employee committed in the course and scope of the employment. In a number of general maritime tort cases the courts have been required to determine whether the direct (payroll) employee of one employer should be treated as the "borrowed servant" of another employer for the purpose of imposing vicarious liability upon the second, borrowing employer for a tort of the allegedly borrowed servant. These cases indicate that the major factor in determining whether a "borrowing employer" will be charged with the injuring employee's negligence is the extent to which he exercises control over the injuring employee. These cases should be distinguished from others in which the issue is whether an injured employee is a "borrowed employee" for the purpose of imposing liability upon the borrowing employer for claims by that employee under the Jones Act or the Longshore and Harbor Workers' Compensation Act (*see* Chapter XIII), because the underlying policy issues differ. However, courts frequently fail to make any distinction and apply the cases interchangeably to the two issues.

One important but unresolved issue is whether a cruise line is vicariously liable for the negligence of its doctor in treating a passenger. *Compare Barbetta v. S/S Bermuda Star*, 848 F.2d 1364 (5th Cir.1988), *Huntley v. Carnival Corp.*, 307 F.Supp.2d 1372 (S.D. Fla. 2004), and *Hesterly v. Royal Caribbean Cruises, Ltd.*, 515 F. Supp. 2d 1278 (S.D. Fla. 2007).

The general maritime tort law provides recovery, under negligence and strict liability theories, for personal injury and some property damage caused by a defectively made product. However, damage to the product itself or for consequential economic loss arising out of damage to the product is not recoverable in maritime tort but only in contract (*see East River S.S. Corp. v. Transamerica Delaval, Inc.*, page 48 *supra*), and thus may be governed by state contract law (frequently the Uniform Commercial Code). The *East River* bar includes all claims for economic loss arising from damage to the product, including claims arising out of a post-sale failure to warn of a pre-sale defect. *Turbomeca S.A. v. Era Helicopters LLC*, 536 F.3d 351 (5th Cir. 2008) Recovery for personal injury or damage to other property is recoverable in a maritime tort product liability action. What constitutes "other property" is not always clear. The Supreme Court has held that in determining whether property was the product itself or was other property was determined by reference to the product that the manufacturer initially sold. Property added to that initial product by a prior buyer would be other property to a downstream buyer. *Saratoga Fishing Co. v. J.M. Martinac & Co.*, 520 U.S. 875 (1997); *All Alaskan Seafoods, Inc. v. Raychem Corp.*, 197 F.3d 992 (9th Cir.1999). *Cf. Sea–Land Service, Inc. v. General Electric Co.*, 134 F.3d 149 (3d Cir.1998).

Maritime product liability theory is not fully developed in itself and thus maritime law in this area will likely follow the general common law. *See, e.g.*,

Krummel v. Bombardier Corp., 206 F.3d 548 (5th Cir.2000) (plaintiff in failure to warn maritime products liability case must establish that the product was unreasonably dangerous under a risk/utility test); *Vickers v. Chiles Drilling Co.*, 822 F.2d 535 (5th Cir.1987) (holding manufacturer liable if product is unreasonably dangerous to normal use, which includes foreseeable misuse). *See also*, *Saratoga Fishing Co. v. Marco Seattle Inc.*, 53 F.3d 984 (9th Cir.1995) (in a maritime design defect strict products liability case, the plaintiff may show the defect under either the "risk/utility" test or the "consumer expectation" test).

Joint tortfeasors are jointly and severally liable in maritime common law. (*See* Chapter XVII, *infra*). A victim may recover his damages (decreased by his comparative negligence) from any joint tortfeasor, leaving that tortfeasor to seek contribution or indemnity from its co-tortfeasor. *See, e.g., Coats v. Penrod Drilling Corp.*, 61 F.3d 1113 (5th Cir.1995); *Simeon v. T. Smith & Son, Inc.*, 852 F.2d 1421 (5th Cir.1988); *see also* Chapter XVII, *infra*.

The general maritime common law rejects contributory negligence as a bar to recovery and applies the doctrine of "pure" comparative negligence. Comparative negligence applies to reduce recovery against another negligent party and against the manufacturer in a strict products liability case governed by maritime law. *See, e.g., Miller v. American President Lines, Ltd.*, 989 F.2d 1450 (6th Cir.1993); *Lewis v. Timco, Inc.*, 716 F.2d 1425 (5th Cir.1983).

The doctrine of assumption of risk has had little impact on maritime law. One of the issues in *Kermarec*, (page 166, *supra*), was the validity of a provision in the "boarding pass" issued to the plaintiff which purported to relieve the defendant shipowner from the consequences of his negligence, i.e., express assumption of risk. The Supreme Court held that since the terms of the agreement had not been called to plaintiff's attention, his recovery could not be defeated thereby. The Court reserved decision on what the result would be if the terms of the agreement had been made known to the plaintiff before he encountered the risk. Courts generally enforce one kind of indemnitee-negligence contract, the "red letter clause" (a stipulation in an agreement between a maritime contractor and its customer that the contractor shall not be liable for its negligent performance of the contract, or that its liability shall be limited to a fixed sum). *See, e.g., Diesel "Repower", Inc. v. Islander Investments*, 271 F.3d 1318 (11th Cir.2001); *Panaconti Shipping Co., S.A. v. M/V Ypapanti*, 865 F.2d 705 (5th Cir.1989). Implied assumption of risk, at least where it overlaps with contributory negligence, does not bar recovery. It does, however, reduce damages through a comparison with the defendant's fault, as with contributory negligence. *Socony–Vacuum Oil Co. v. Smith*, 305 U.S. 424 (1939).

The U.S. Supreme Court has held that a plaintiff's misconduct could be the superseding cause of its injury that breaks the chain of legal or proximate causation, thereby relieving the defendant of liability. *Exxon Co., U.S.A. v. Sofec, Inc.*, 517 U.S. 830 (1996). Thus one may argue that the plaintiff's fault rose to the level of a superseding cause, and thereby he or she should not recover. This position is logically defensible but somewhat inconsistent with the maritime law preference for comparative fault and thus should be carefully applied. *See, e.g., Farr v. NC Machinery Co.*, 186 F.3d 1165 (9th Cir.1999).

The doctrine of "avoidable consequences" (duty to mitigate) predictably and logically applies in admiralty. *See, e.g., Pennzoil Producing Co. v. Offshore Express, Inc.*, 943 F.2d 1465 (5th Cir.1991).

Prior to 1980, there was no general statute of limitations governing general maritime tort claims; laches was applied to bar stale claims. In 1980, Congress enacted a statute of limitations, now codified at Title 46 U.S.C.A. section 30106, which provides:

Except as otherwise provided by law, a civil action for damages for personal injury or death arising out of a maritime tort must be brought within 3 years after the cause of action arose.

In cases not covered by the statute, most notably property damage claims, the doctrine of laches still applies. Generally, laches bars a claim when there has been an unreasonable delay in prosecuting the claim, and the defendant has been prejudiced by the delay. *See, e.g., Sandvik v. Alaska Packers Association*, 609 F.2d 969 (9th Cir.1979). In determining whether the delay was unreasonable, the courts will look to the analogous federal or state statute of limitations. Where the claim is filed beyond the period prescribed by the analogous statute, the plaintiff may bear the burden of proving both the reasonableness of the delay and the lack of prejudice to defendant. Where the claim is filed within the time period provided by the analogous statute, the defendant may bear the burden of proving unreasonableness of delay, or prejudice, or both. *See, e.g., TAG/ICIB Services v. Pan American Grain Co.*, 215 F.3d 172 (1st Cir.2000).

A contract of carriage of a passenger may provide that a claim against the vessel owner is barred unless notice is given, or an action is instituted, within a designated time period. Maritime law generally upholds these contractual agreements, but a special statute, 46 U.S.C.A. § 30508, weakens any requirement of notice and invalidates any provision requiring that an action be commenced in less than one year. Passenger contracts may also attempt to limit the carrier's liability for certain types of damages, such as emotional distress. The amount of damages a passenger may recover for injury on a cruise that calls only on foreign ports may be limited by the 1974 Athens Convention, to which the United States is not a party. The contract also may include a forum selection or choice of law clause that generally will be interpreted under normal rules of contract law.

General maritime law recognizes a right of action for survival and wrongful death benefits if the victim of a maritime tort dies. (*See* Chapter XIV). In

American Export Lines, Inc. v. Alvez, 446 U.S. 274 (1980), the Supreme Court held that under maritime common law, the spouse of an injured maritime worker (a longshore worker) could maintain a cause of action for the spouse's loss of society resulting from the injury. The lower federal courts generally have not expanded this consortium remedy beyond spouses to parents and children or to the family members of nonseafarers. *See, e.g., In re Maryland Marine*, 641 F.Supp.2d 579 (E.D.La. 2009). The subsequent Supreme Court decision in *Miles v. Apex Marine Corporation*, page 165, *supra*, cast some doubt upon the continuing vitality of *Alvez. See, e.g., Horsley v. Mobil Oil Corp.*, 15 F.3d 200 (1st Cir.1994). However, the better view may be that the preclusive effect of *Miles* is limited to claims filed by Jones Act seamen and their spouses or survivors against their employers. This view is supported in some part by dicta from the Supreme Court's recent decision in *Townsend*, page 165, *supra*.

In *Consolidated Rail Corp. v. Gottshall*, 512 U.S. 532 (1994), the court ruled that the proper standard for evaluating claims for negligent infliction of emotional distress brought under the Federal Employers' Liability Act is the "zone of danger" test, i.e., recovery is limited to plaintiffs who sustain a physical impact as a result of the defendant's negligent conduct, or are placed in immediate risk of physical impact by that conduct. That rule also should apply to a seaman's claim against his employer and may apply to all maritime tort claims. Subsequently in

Metro–North Commuter R. Co. v. Buckley, 521 U.S. 424 (1997), the Supreme Court held that even where there is exposure to or impact by a toxic substance, recovery for fear of developing a disease as a result of the exposure is not recoverable until the disease manifests itself. Thereafter, in *Norfolk & Western Rwy. Co. v. Ayers*, 538 U.S. 135 (2003), the Court held that one who is suffering from an asbestos-related disease may be entitled to recover for the fear of cancer stemming from the disease.

When punitive damages are recoverable in admiralty, the standards for such recovery, and the imposition of vicarious liability for punitive damages, all remain unsettled. The Supreme Court's decision in *Miles* (page 165, *supra*) left open the question of when and whether non-pecuniary damages, and by implication, punitive damages, were available for seaman and non-seaman claims. *See, e.g., Scarborough v. Clemco Industries*, 391 F.3d 660 (5th Cir.2004). Subsequent Supreme Court decisions in *Baker*, page 165, *supra* (a corporation may be liable for punitive damages for the reckless conduct of an agent while performing in his managerial capacity) and *Townsend*, page 165, *supra*, (allowing punitive damages for the willful and wanton failure to pay maintenance and cure) make clear that punitive damages are recoverable under general maritime law at least in instances where such damages were traditionally available. Given the recent decisions on the recovery of punitive damages in maritime law, more cases addressing the availability of such damages should follow.

An important element of damages in maritime tort claims is recovery for loss of future earnings or, when the victim dies, recovery by his beneficiaries for the loss of the support that they would have received from the victim. Two important issues arising in the determination of such damages are whether the trier of fact may consider (1) the amount of income tax that the worker would have paid on his future earnings, and (2) whether and how to reduce the lost future earnings stream to present value. In earlier days, federal courts generally excluded consideration of income tax effects and employed market interest rates in reducing to present value. However, in *Norfolk & Western Railway Co. v. Liepelt*, 444 U.S. 490 (1980), the Supreme Court held that under the federal common law of admiralty, the trier of fact in fixing damages for loss of future earnings may consider that the worker would have paid taxes on the income he would have earned. The Court also ruled that a jury may be instructed that its award for loss of earning capacity or future earnings is not subject to federal income taxation. Dicta in *Liepelt* indicated that inflationary trends should not be ignored in determining loss of future earnings; that dicta became law in *Jones & Laughlin Steel Corp. v. Pfeifer*, 462 U.S. 523 (1983), in which the Court ruled that inflation cannot be ignored in determining loss of future earnings in an action by a maritime worker against the vessel on which he is injured—the 905(b) case (*see* Chapter XIII)—and examined the entire reduction to present value in great detail.

The interjection of inflation into the calculation of loss of future earnings in maritime cases has necessitated closer judicial scrutiny of the method of calculating that element of damages. In making an award for loss of future earnings (or, in a death action, loss of future support), the trier of fact must determine the amount a victim would have earned if he had not been injured or killed. This usually involves a calculation of after-tax income the victim would have received in each working year after injury or death. The starting point for such a calculation is the victim's post-tax wages at the time of injury or death. This amount may be increased over the victim's projected work-life to reflect increases for "productivity," including (1) increases the victim would have received for merit or promotions (the "individualized" productivity factor) and (2) increases or decreases that all workers in his industry would have received because of the productivity growth or decline within that particular industry (the "societal" factor). The victim's after-tax income also may be decreased to reflect the unreimbursed expenses that the victim would have incurred in earning his wages, such as travel, uniform and equipment costs, and, in the case of death, the living expenses ("personal consumption") that would have been incurred by the deceased.

Since the victim (or his beneficiaries) will receive the total amount in a lump sum when judgment becomes final, but the victim would have received the money over the years of his work-life if the accident had not occurred, the victim (or his beneficiaries) will receive a "windfall" if adjustment is not made for the present receipt of future damages. This adjustment is made by "discounting" the victim's future earnings to present value, i.e., by deducting from the total amount of lost earnings the amount of interest the victim may earn on the portion of the funds paid to him at judgment, which represents future earnings. The standard method is to deduct the "market-interest" rate, the amount of interest the victim could earn on a "risk-free" investment of the future earnings, minus the income tax he would pay on that interest.

The decision in *Pfeifer*, confirming that inflation cannot be ignored in calculating loss of future earnings, forced the Court to determine the acceptable methods of integrating the inflationary factor with the other variables used in calculating lost wages—the productivity factors and the discount to present value. In *Pfeifer*, the Court gave its approval to certain methods, at least in 905(b) actions and other actions, where Congress had provided generally for an award of damages but had not given specific guidance regarding how to calculate the damages. One method that the Court sanctions is permitting the litigants to offer specific proof of the inflation rate, like any other fact. If this is done, and the calculation of the victim's future earnings includes both inflation and the societal and individualized productivity factors, the discount rate that should be applied is the after-tax "market interest" rate. However, the Court discourages the use of that method as both "unreliable and costly." It appears to find more favor with the use of the "real interest rate" method in which the inflationary factor is omitted from calculation of lost earnings and the total lost earnings is discounted only by the "real interest rate," an amount reflecting the average difference between the market-interest rate and the inflation rate. The Court observed that a trial court should not be reversed if it adopts a "real interest rate" between one and three per cent and "explains its choice." A third method which has been applied by some lower courts is the "total offset" method in which the estimate of the loss of future earnings is neither increased to reflect the inflationary and productivity factors nor "discounted" to present value. A major criticism of this approach is that it assumes the "real interest rate" will always offset the productivity factors, an assumption which may not prove true. One variation of the "offset" method is an approach which assumes the market-interest rate normally will equal both the inflationary factor and the societal productivity factor; thus the victim's future wages should be increased by his individual productivity factor, but the societal productivity factor and the inflationary factor should be disregarded and no discount to present value should be made. The Court's decision, while not specifically adopting that method, suggests that parties stipulate to its use.

Post-judgment interest on maritime claims is governed by the law of the forum. When the admiralty claim is brought in federal court, post-judgment interest accrues from the date of entry of judgment.

The amount of the interest is governed by Title 28 U.S.C.A. section 1961, which provides for interest at a rate equal to the "weekly average 1–year constant maturity Treasury yield," as published by the Federal Reserve System for the week preceding the date of judgment. The Director of the Administrative Office of the United States Courts is required to distribute to all federal judges notice of the rate and any changes in it.

The time-honored rule is that pre-judgment interest on maritime tort claims is discretionary with the court; however, recent cases establish that such interest must be awarded unless circumstances exist that make it inequitable to do so. Those circumstances usually are found where the plaintiff's action, such as a late filing of suit or an unreasonable settlement demand, is the major cause of the delay in his receiving from the defendant compensation for the injury. Indeed, the Supreme Court has held that in a collision case, pre-judgment interest should be awarded except in "peculiar" or "exceptional" circumstances, and that neither the existence of a genuine dispute over liability nor the fact that the plaintiff's loss is primarily attributable to his own negligence justifies denial of such interest. *City of Milwaukee v. National Gypsum Co.*, 515 U.S. 189 (1995). The maritime pre-judgment interest rule probably will apply when the maritime claim is brought in state court.

Special rules have developed for choice of law in claims by seamen against their employers or the vessels on which they are working. (*See* page 261, *infra*). These special rules may not apply in other maritime tort cases, however. Thus where the claim is for a tort allegedly committed by a third person on the high seas, the controlling law may be that of the forum, as the forum interprets the general maritime law. *See The Belgenland*, 114 U.S. 355 (1885).

Indemnity and contribution in general maritime common law claims are discussed in Chapter XVII.

CHAPTER XII

COLLISION LAW

A. LIABILITY

Collision law regulates the navigation of vessels and imposes liability for negligent navigation which causes injury or damage. Collision law is perhaps most analogous to land-based automobile accident law; some of the same general principles apply, and there is much statutory regulation.

Collision law also may provide the rules by which all of the damages arising out of a collision—including those of crew, passengers and cargo—are apportioned among the vessels involved. A brief explanation of this latter function is necessary. Maritime law imposes a duty upon the vessel and its operator to protect the vessel's seamen and passengers from harm. Often, crew and passengers injured in a collision of two or more vessels are likely to find it simpler to proceed first against the vessel on which they were serving or being carried. That vessel, if at fault, may be a joint tortfeasor with the other vessels and will be liable to its passengers and crew for the full amount of their damages. This joint and several liability may make it expedient for the victim to proceed first and most aggressively against the easiest defendant to identify and prove at fault.

When a vessel owner makes his claim for the damages to his vessel against the other vessels involved in the collision, he will join with it his claims for contribution for the damages he has paid to his crew and passengers. Since contribution is permitted, on the basis of percentage of fault (*see* Chapter XVII, *infra*), the collision suit is a means of allocating among all negligent vessels involved the total damages sustained by all persons in the collision.

While the usual collision case involves a collision between two moving ships, the same rules usually regulate accidents in which a moving ship collides with a stationary ship—an allision—or a fixed object, a ship runs aground, or a ship's movement causes damage to another vessel or to other property.

A vessel is liable *in rem* for its collision torts. The owner or demise charterer usually will be liable *in personam*, through the doctrine of *respondeat superior*, for the negligence of the master or crew in causing the collision. The owner is not vicariously liable for the tort of a compulsory pilot whose employment is forced upon him. However, the vessel is liable *in rem* for the torts of the compulsory pilot. *Homer Ramsdell Transportation Co. v. La Compagnie Generale Transatlantique*, 182 U.S. 406 (1901). Because the compulsory pilot rarely has sufficient assets to cover collision damages, the vessel owner (who is not personally liable) must pay the damages caused by the negligence of the compulsory pilot or lose his equity in his vessel, which is liable *in rem*.

The basis of liability in collision cases is fault; there is no recovery unless there has been negligence in the navigation or operation of the vessel. *The Java*, 81 U.S. 189 (1872). A court may reject a plaintiff's claim in a collision case by finding that the accident was "inevitable" or was caused by an Act of God. It also may deny the claim by applying the doctrine of "inscrutable fault"—there is fault, but under the circumstances it cannot be identified. *See, e.g.*, *The Grace Girdler*, 74 U.S. 196 (1868). Each of these rules, however, seems to be simply another way of saying that the plaintiff has failed to prove that the defendant was negligent.

The general test of fault is whether the person navigating the vessel acted as a "reasonably prudent mariner" at the time of the accident. However, there is a plethora of statutes and regulations designed to eliminate the risk of collision and to facilitate navigation, and violation of one of these statutes or regulations constitutes "statutory fault," the maritime equivalent of negligence *per se*. *See, e.g.*, *Union Oil Co. of California v. The San Jacinto*, 409 U.S. 140 (1972).

Vessels, because of their size and the lack of friction, may not quickly decrease speed, stop, or change course. Collision between them frequently can be avoided only if the mariners in charge of the vessels discover any risk of collision at the earliest possible time and promptly engage in a course of conduct that is designed to avoid collision and with which both mariners are familiar. The efforts that they must make to discover the risk of collision, and the actions which they must take to avoid collision after the risk is discovered, are prescribed with precision in regulations known as the Rules of the Road.

Formerly, there were four sets of Rules of the Road applicable to American maritime collision law: the International Rules, which governed conduct on the high seas, beyond American territorial waters; the Inland Rules, which governed navigation within territorial waters, except in those areas covered by the Western Rivers and Great Lakes Rules; the Western Rivers rules, which governed navigation on the Mississippi River, its tributaries and certain other rivers; and the Great Lakes Rules, which regulated navigation on the Lakes and on certain connecting waters. The International Rules were revised at a 1972 conference of seafaring nations. The revision included a procedure by which the rules could be amended by an international agency, and amendments so adopted would become effective unless one-third of the parties who previously had ratified the convention objected to the amendment. Congress balked at this provision, and after something of a stalemate between the legislative and executive branches, the new International Rules (commonly called Collision Regulations, or "COLREGS") were adopted by the United States by treaty. The COLREGS now appear at 33 C.F.R. § 81.1 et seq. and at Title 33 U.S.C.A. following Section 1602 et seq. In 1980, Congress unified the Inland, Western Rivers and Great Lakes Rules into one set of rules (the Inland Rules) which apply "to all vessels upon the inland waters of the United States, and to vessels of the United States on the Canadian waters of the Great Lakes to the extent that there is no conflict with Canadian law." 33 U.S.C.A. § 2001(a). Legislation provides for the eventual transfer of the Inland Rules to the Code of Federal Regulations.

Regulations affecting navigation have been adopted by the Coast Guard and the Corps of Engineers. *See* 33 C.F.R. Failure to comply with these regulations usually has the same effect as violation of a Rule of the Road. Violation of a state statute which does not conflict with federal regulations also may constitute "statutory fault" in collision law. The Coast Guard conducts formal investigations into major marine accidents pursuant to 33 U.S.C.A. § 1221, et seq., and Title 46 U.S.C.A. Section 6301. The result of an investigation is not admissible in the civil suit, *see, e.g.*, 46 U.S.C.A. § 6308(a), but the investigation may provide the litigants with early discovery of the surrounding circumstances.

Violation of a custom may constitute fault if the custom is "firmly established by proof," "well understood," and not in conflict with the Rules of the Road. *See, e.g.*, *Hal Antillen N.V. v. Mount Ymitos MS*, 147 F.3d 447 (5th Cir. 1998). Since the purpose of enforcing compliance with the rules is to assure certainty of mariner conduct, it would appear that a custom which is in conflict with a rule should abrogate the rule, where all persons likely to be navigating in the area can be expected to follow the custom. Such an application of custom, however, would introduce uncertainty for mariners navigating in unfamiliar waters. Perhaps this explains why there are few judicially recognized customs. One of the best known is the "point and bend" rule, prescribing that an ascending vessel on the Mississippi River must navigate to the "point" side of a river bend and the descending vessel must navigate to the opposite, or "bend" side (where the current is stronger). *See, e.g., Graham v. United States*, 112 F.Supp. 43 (E.D.La. 1953). Indeed, one influential court has said that a custom will be recognized only if it does not conflict with a statutory rule. *Hal Antillen v. Mount Ymitos MS*, 147 F.3d 447 (5th Cir. 1998).

The Rules of the Road prescribe the speed at which a vessel should proceed, the lights and shapes which it must exhibit, the sounds or signals it must emit, and the maneuvers it must take when encountering another vessel in meeting, overtaking or crossing situations. In addition, a special rule provides for vessel conduct during fog or other extremely inclement weather. The International and Inland Rules generally prescribe similar conduct in similar situations; thus a general understanding of the rules can be gleaned from a brief discussion of the key provisions of the International Rules.

Among the more important lighting regulations under the International Rules are those requiring larger vessels to maintain at night only five "running" lights, two white lights (one higher than the other) at or near the bow, another white light at the stern, a green light amidships on the starboard side, and a red light amidships on the port side. Rule 23. Where these lights are displayed, a mariner may quickly determine whether the vessel is meeting or crossing his vessel or whether it is being overtaken by his vessel. For example, a mariner observing only one white light ahead will quickly discern that he is overtaking a vessel; similarly, if he observes two white lights and a green light, he should perceive that the other vessel is crossing from the observer's left to his right.

The steering rules prescribe which vessel has the right of way in a given situation. If the vessels are meeting, neither has the right of way, but each must steer his vessel to the starboard or right side, so that the vessels will pass "port to port," that is, each to the left of the other. Rule 14. If one vessel is overtaking another, the overtaking vessel is the "burdened" or, under the revised rules, "give-way" vessel, which is charged with the duty of executing the maneuver safely. The overtaken vessel (called the "privileged" or, under the revised rules, "stand on" vessel) must maintain its course and speed, making only such changes as are fairly to be expected in the normal course of navigation. Rule 13. If vessels are in a crossing situation, the vessel on the right has the right of way, and is the "stand on" vessel; thus if a navigator observes a vessel on his right, he knows that his vessel must "give way", i.e., take the necessary maneuvers to effect the crossing safely. Rule 15.

The Vessel Bridge-to-Bridge Radio Telephone Act, 33 U.S.C.A. § 1201 et seq., requires that certain vessels operating in American waters carry radio-telephone equipment and maintain a listening watch on a designated frequency. Consequently, many of the meeting, passing and crossing maneuvers in American waters are determined by communication between the vessels through voice radio.

Rule 19, sometimes called the "Fog Rule," regulates the conduct of vessels in fog, mist, falling snow, heavy rainstorms or other conditions of restricted visibility. When confronted with such conditions, a vessel must travel at a safe speed. The prior rule prescribed "moderate speed," and the jurisprudence had established that a moderate speed, under such conditions of restricted visibility, was a speed at which a vessel could stop within one half of the distance between it and another vessel within the time after which the vessels came into view of each other. The apparent theory behind that rule was that if both vessels were traveling at the prescribed speed, and each came to a dead stop within one half of the distance, no damaging collision would occur. Under the old rule a vessel which determined the presence of another vessel in restricted visibility but could not fix its precise location was required to come to a dead stop until it could ascertain the location of the other vessel. Rule 19 now provides that except where it has been determined that a risk of collision does not exist, every vessel which hears apparently forward of her beam the fog signal of another vessel, or which cannot avoid a close quarters situation with a vessel forward of her beam, must reduce speed to the minimum at which it can be kept on its course and "if necessary take all her way off and in any event navigate with extreme caution until danger of collision is over." Vessels also are required to make periodic whistle blasts when in conditions of restricted visibility. Rule 35.

While strict adherence to the rules ordinarily is required, circumstances may arise in which a prudent mariner can avoid collision only by deviating from the precise conduct mandated by the rules. In such a case, may the mariner deviate from the rules without being guilty of "statutory fault?" Rule 2 gives a non-answer; it states that "[n]othing in these Rules shall exonerate ... the ... master ... from the consequences of any neglect to comply with these Rules or of the neglect of any precaution which may be required by the ordinary practice of seamen, or by the special circumstances of the case," and that "[i]n ... complying with these Rules due regard shall be had to ... any special circumstances ... which may make a departure from these Rules necessary to avoid immediate danger." Thus if a mariner faced with risk of collision deviates from the rules too early, or delays too long before deviating, he is guilty of statutory fault. The case law indicates that a mariner who departs from a rule should be prepared to prove that "special circumstances" mandating such departure did in fact exist. *See, e.g., Belden v. Chase*, 150 U.S. 674 (1893); *LoVuolo v. Gunning*, 925 F.2d 22 (1st Cir. 1991). A subsequent amendment to Rule 8 stresses the importance of complying with the rules to avoid collision.

There are presumptions of fault in collision cases in addition to those resulting from violations of the Rules of the Road or other regulations. One is that in a collision between a moving or drifting vessel and a stationary object, the vessel is presumed to be at fault. *The Oregon*, 158 U.S. 186 (1895); *The Louisiana*, 70 U.S. 164 (1865); *City of Chicago v. M/V Morgan*, 375 F.3d 563 (7th Cir. 2004). Another is that an unexpected and unexplained sheer by one vessel into another, causing a collision, raises a presumption of negligent steering by the sheering vessel. A third presumption is that a drifting vessel was set adrift by negligence on the part of those in control. *Hood v. Knappton Corp. Inc.*, 986 F.2d 329 (9th Cir. 1993). These are simply maritime applications of the general principle underlying *res ipsa loquitur*—sometime the incident speaks for itself, and reasonable people may conclude, given the circumstances of the incident, that negligence was the cause.

Rule 5 of the International Rules requires that every vessel "maintain a proper look-out by sight and hearing as well as by all available means appropriate in the prevailing circumstances and conditions." The lookout must be suitably experienced and properly stationed and should not be assigned other duties that would prevent performance of his primary role as a lookout. The original Inland, Western Rivers and Great Lakes Rules did not specifically require the maintenance of a proper lookout, but the failure to do so usually constituted imprudent seamanship, and thus fault, in a collision action. The Inland Rules specifically require the maintenance of a proper lookout. 33 U.S.C.A. § 2005.

The rules do not require that a vessel be equipped with radar, but mandate the proper use of radar equipment "if fitted and operational." (Rule 7b). What if a vessel is equipped with radar that subsequently becomes inoperative, and the owner or master fails to have it repaired within a reasonable time? Some courts do not impose liability in that situation, deeming it unwise to have rules that do not require a vessel owner to provide radar but impose liability upon the vessel owner who provides radar but fails to timely repair it.

Navigation in narrow and congested channels of rivers and harbors is particularly perilous, and special rules attempt to reduce the risk of collision. The International Rules apply in the inland waters of some nations; in such cases, Rule 9 of those rules prescribes conduct in narrow channels. Within inland waters, navigation in narrow channels is regulated by a special provision in the Inland Rules. 33 U.S.C.A. § 2009. That provision, concerned primarily with narrow channels in rivers, requires the ascending vessel to yield to the descending vessel, which, because of the force of the current, has much less maneuverability. *See, e.g., Burma Navigation Corp. v. Reliant Seahorse M/V*, 99 F.3d 652 (5th Cir. 1996).

If there is no statutory fault, collision liability turns upon whether the defendant acted as a reasonably prudent mariner under the circumstances. If one charged with navigation of a vessel is free from fault when an emergency arises, and his subsequent action, under the circumstances then known to him, was reasonable, he may not be found negligent even though his actions, in the absence of the emergency, would not meet the "reasonable mariner" standard. This maritime doctrine, similar to the "discovered peril" or "sudden emergency" rule in land tort law, is called the "errors in extremis" doctrine. *See, e.g., Havinga v. Crowley Towing & Transp. Co.*, 24 F.3d 1480 (1st Cir. 1994). It serves the same purpose as the "special circumstances" provision in Rule 2 and has been applied to relieve a vessel of negligence both for violation of a rule and for failure to satisfy the "reasonably prudent mariner" standard.

The breach by a vessel of its duty to others will not give rise to liability unless it is the cause in fact of the damages. In determining "cause in fact," the collision claimant often is aided by the rule in *The Pennsylvania*, 86 U.S. 125 (1873), and by the "Major/Minor Fault" rule. The *"Pennsylvania"* rule is that if a vessel's negligence is a violation of a statutory duty, the burden shifts to that vessel to prove that its conduct did not and could not have caused the accident. The *"Pennsylvania"* burden, designed to enforce compliance with the collision rules, is a heavy, but not impossible, one to meet. The offending vessel probably meets the burden if it proves by clear and convincing evidence that its conduct did not contribute to the collision. *See, e.g.,* *Trinidad Corp. v. S.S. Keiyoh Maru,* 845 F.2d 818 (9th Cir. 1988). The *Trinidad* court also said that the *"Pennsylvania"* rule only applied to statutes delineating a clear legal duty and not to regulations that required judgment and assessments of particular circumstances.

The "Major/Minor" rule provides that if the fault of a vessel is uncontradicted and sufficient in itself to account for the accident, there is a presumption that the other vessel was not at fault, or that its fault did not contribute to the collision. The obvious genesis of the rule was a desire to alleviate the harshness of the former collision rule of "divided damages," which provided that each vessel at fault was liable for its per capita share (if both vessels were at fault, each was liable for 50%) of all damages incurred in the collision, regardless of the degrees of fault of the offending vessels.

Two other rules of maritime collision law merit mention. Admiralty courts have recognized a doctrine of "last clear chance." *See, e.g., Chemical Transporter, Inc. v. M. Turecamo, Inc.,* 290 F.2d 496 (2d Cir. 1961). However, the doctrine is sparingly applied. Another doctrine much akin to "last clear chance" is the "condition, not cause" rule: if one vessel is initially at fault, but the second vessel could thereafter have avoided the accident, the initial fault of the first vessel is said to be a "condition" of the accident but not a "cause." *See, e.g., Crawford v. Indian Towing Co.,* 240 F.2d 308 (5th

Cir. 1957). These rules probably do not survive the general adoption of comparative fault in maritime law, and their passing should mean a simpler, more cohesive body of law.

For over a hundred years, admiralty law embraced the rule of "divided damages" in collision cases. In 1975, in *United States v. Reliable Transfer Co.*, 421 U.S. 397 (1975), the Supreme Court jettisoned that sometimes inequitable and often illogical rule in favor of proportionate allocation of fault among joint tortfeasors in collision cases. Each vessel now is liable to the other offending vessel in contribution for that part of the total damages proportionate to its fault, and is liable for its per capita (virile) share only when the respective faults of the vessels are equal, or when proportionate fault cannot be determined.

The adoption of comparative contribution in maritime collision cases has brought into question the future of the *"Pennsylvania,"* "Major/Minor" and "last clear chance" doctrines. The "Major/Minor" rule, designed solely to avoid the "all or nothing" approach of the "divided damages" rule, apparently has not survived. *See, e.g., Acacia Vera Navig. Co., Ltd. v. Kezia, Ltd.*, 78 F.3d 211 (5th Cir. 1996). The "last clear chance" rule probably has suffered the same fate, but the answer does not appear as certain. *See Cenac Towing Co. v. Richmond*, 265 F.2d 466 (5th Cir. 1959). The *"Pennsylvania"* rule, aimed primarily at encouraging compliance with the Rules of the Road, has survived the advent of comparative contribution in maritime collision law.

A discussion of collision law deserves one post-script. Since the standard of conduct when there is no applicable Rule of the Road is that of a "reasonably prudent mariner," and since Rule 2 may be read to require the same conduct—"the ordinary practice of seamen"—it is arguable that the rules, and thus "statutory fault," have swallowed up the whole of collision law. There apparently are no decisions on this point, however.

B. DAMAGES

When a vessel is lost as a result of a collision or other tort (or is a "constructive total loss" because the cost of repairs exceeds the value), the owner may recover the fair market value of the vessel, together with net freight (gross freight, less the expenses of the voyage). *The Umbria*, 166 U.S. 404 (1897). Fair market value usually is determined by comparable sales of similar vessels. Where comparable sales are not available, a court may determine the value from opinion testimony or from such factors as reproduction cost less depreciation, the condition of repair of the vessel, the uses to which the vessel could be put, its insured value, and its mortgage value. The general rule is that there can be no recovery for loss of use of a vessel which has been lost or destroyed. However, there is authority that such damages should be awarded if the plaintiff establishes his inability to obtain an immediate replacement and can demonstrate that the award of "loss of use" damages will not result in "double recovery," such as where prejudgment interest is not awarded. Punitive damages would seem to be available in an appropriate case. *See generally*, *Atlantic Sounding Co. v. Townsend*, 129 S.Ct. 2561 (2009) (recognizing availability of punitive damages in admiralty cases); *Exxon Shipping Co. v. Baker*, 128 S.Ct. 2605 (2008).

If a vessel is damaged, the owner is entitled to recover the cost of repairs, together with loss of use or profits, sometimes referred to as detention damages or demurrage damages. *See, e.g.*, Gilmore & Black, *supra*, p. 526. If repair necessitates replacement of parts, there is no deduction for depreciation if the parts, though old, were in good working order at the time of the collision. Since the owner has a duty to mitigate damages, he must effect the repairs in the manner likely to produce the least amount of loss of use. The "fleet" rule prohibits an owner from recovering detention damages when the damaged vessel is removed from service and is merely replaced by an idle substitute vessel from the owner's fleet.

The *Robins Drydock* rule (*see* Chapter XI, *supra*), proscribing recovery of economic harm without contemporaneous physical damage to the plaintiff's property, applies generally in collision cases. However, it may not bar such recovery where the damaging conduct was intentional. *See, e.g.*, *Nautilus Marine Inc. v. Niemela*, 170 F.3d 1195 (9th Cir. 1999).

Cargo damage claims in collision cases present a peculiar problem. The consignee of cargo shipped under a bill of lading may not recover from the carrying vessel the damage caused by negligence in the operation and management of the vessel. *See* Chapter IV, *supra.* If the consignee brings an action against a vessel involved in the collision other than the carrying vessel, COGSA and the Harter Act do not apply, and under American law the consignee may recover the full amount of his damages from the negligent non-carrying vessel; collision tortfeasors are jointly and severally liable. *Transorient Navigators Co., S.A. v. M/S Southwind*, 788 F.2d 288 (5th Cir. 1986). (The 1910 Brussels Collision Convention, to which the United States does not adhere, allows cargo to recover from the non-carrying vessel only to the extent of that vessel's fault.) The non-carrying vessel, having paid the damages as a joint tortfeasor with the carrying vessel, may then seek contribution from the carrying vessel; again, COGSA and the Harter Act do not bar such recovery. The result is that the carrying vessel pays a portion of the damages to its cargo caused by a risk that COGSA and Harter allocate to the cargo (the shipper or consignee). Carriers have sought to avoid this result by inserting into bills of lading clauses providing that the consignee will indemnify the carrier for any damages paid by the carrier to a non-carrying vessel which represents the claim of the consignee for a risk allocated to the consignee by COGSA and the Harter Act; however, the Supreme Court has declared these "both to blame" clauses invalid. *United States v. Atlantic Mutual Insurance Co.*, 343 U.S. 236 (1952).

C. IMPAIRMENT OF RIVERS AND HARBORS

1. The Wreck Act

33 U.S.C.A. § 409 provides that:

whenever a vessel ... is wrecked and sunk in a navigable channel, accidentally or otherwise, it shall be the duty of the owner of such sunken craft to immediately mark it and to maintain such marks until the sunken craft is removed or abandoned ... and ... to commence the immediate removal of the same, and prosecute such removal diligently, and failure to do so shall be considered as an abandonment of such craft, and subject the same to removal by the United States.

The statute imposes two affirmative duties upon the owner of a sunken vessel that constitutes an obstruction to navigation or navigable capacity—the duty to mark and the duty to remove. The duty to mark is non-delegable. Formerly, the non-negligent owner could abandon the vessel to the United States and thus avoid the cost of removal. However, 33 U.S.C.A. § 414(b) now imposes liability upon any owner for the cost of removal of the wreck. The requirement that the owner of a sunken vessel must mark and remove it apparently does not apply when he has made a full, good faith search for the vessel but cannot find it. *Allied Chemical Corp. v.*

Hess Tankship Co. of Delaware, 661 F.2d 1044 (5th Cir. 1981).

The owner of the sunken vessel also may be liable to third persons who are injured as a result of his failure to mark or to remove the vessel, even though the sinking occurred without any fault on the owner's part. The failure of the owner to mark or to remove the vessel becomes a "proximate cause" of any subsequent collision between the wreck and another vessel. The party who negligently caused the initial sinking is liable to the owner, or to the United States, for the removal costs. In *Southern Scrap Material Co., LLC v. ABC Ins. Co.*, 541 F.3d 584 (5th Cir. 2008), the court held that the government can state a personal liability claim under the Wreck Act for the recovery of its actual costs of removal without alleging that the vessel owner negligently caused the sinking. The lower courts are divided on the issue of whether the owner is liable to third persons for damages resulting from a subsequent collision with the wreck. *Compare Red Star Towing & Transp. Co. v. Woodburn*, 18 F.2d 77 (2d Cir. 1927), and *Nunley v. M/V Dauntless Colocotronis*, 727 F.2d 455 (5th Cir. 1984).

33 U.S.C.A. § 408 imposes liability without fault for injury, obstruction or impairment of the usefulness of a structure built by the United States for the improvement of navigable waters or for flood prevention. It is not clear whether liability is only *in rem* or includes an *in personam* remedy against the owner of the offending vessel. *Compare Hines,*

Inc. v. United States, 551 F.2d 717 (6th Cir. 1977), with *In Re Barnacle Marine Management, Inc.*, 233 F.3d 865 (5th Cir. 2000). 33 U.S.C.A. § 403, which prohibits the "creation of an obstruction . . . to the navigable capacity of any of the waters of the United States," also has been applied to vessels sunk in navigable waters.

P & I insurance policies insure against the cost of removal of wrecked vessels when such removal is "compulsory by law." In the leading case, the U.S. Fifth Circuit, sitting en banc, concluded that removal is "compulsory by law" even though there has been no judicial or administrative order requiring removal; it is sufficient that a reasonable owner, fully informed, would conclude that failure to remove would likely expose him to liability imposed by law sufficiently great in amount and probability of occurrence to justify the expense of removal. *Continental Oil Co. v. Bonanza Corp.*, 706 F.2d 1365 (5th Cir. 1983).

2. Marine Pollution

Imposition of civil liability upon a vessel operator for damages caused by water pollution—primarily through the discharge of oil—has attracted much legislative and judicial attention in recent years. The most important Congressional regulation is the Oil Pollution Act of 1990, 33 U.S.C.A. §§ 2701 et seq., which imposes liability upon the polluter for damages which are limited both in type and amount. The most significant type of damages recoverable is the cost of restoring natural resources damaged from the oil pollution. These damages are paid to a trustee representing the affected sovereign and are used for the restoration work. *See, e.g.*, 33 U.S.C.A. § 2706(f).

Under the Oil Pollution Act, the owner and the operator of the vessel or facility from which the pollution emanates and who is "responsible" for the discharge is strictly liable; the only defenses are that the discharge was caused solely by Act of God, act of war, or act or omission of a third party. 33 U.S.C.A. § 2703(a). A third party who is the "sole cause" of the pollution is subject to the same liability for damages. 33 U.S.C.A. § 2702(d)(1)(A).

Discharge of hazardous substances other than petroleum and related products is primarily regulated by the Comprehensive Environmental Response, Compensation and Liability Act (CERCLA), 42 U.S.C.A. §§ 9601–9675. CERCLA also limits the amount of liability (based upon the size or type of vessel or facility) and the types of damages, which include removal costs and natural resource damages. The limitation on the amount of liability does not apply if the cause of the discharge was violation of applicable regulations or "willful" misconduct within the "privity or knowledge" of the defendant. 42 U.S.C.A. § 9607(c)(2).

Oil and other pollution also are regulated by the Clean Water Act, 33 U.S.C.A. §§ 1251–1397, and by the Outer Continental Shelf Lands Act. *See* 43 U.S.C.A. § 1811 et seq.

Negligent or intentional discharge of pollutants into navigable waters constitutes a maritime tort under general admiralty principles. Damage to the water and to vessels on the water has the "locality" and "flavor" required for maritime tort jurisdiction; damage to shoreside property caused by a vessel "spill" arguably lacks "locality," but should fall within maritime jurisdiction through the provisions of the Admiralty Extension Act, 46 U.S.C.A. § 740. It thus would appear that maritime tort law may afford a remedy to private persons damaged through pollution of navigable water and may also supplement recovery by the United States where such additional recovery is not prohibited by the federal legislation, including the recovery of punitive damages. *Exxon Shipping Co. v. Baker* (allowing, but reducing, punitive damages in maritime oil spill case and holding that maritime punitive damages are not preempted by the Clean Water Act). The Oil Pollution and Clean Water Acts may preempt some but not all state remedies. *Compare Askew v. American Waterways Operators, Inc.*, 411 U.S. 325 (1973) (applying state law), with *United States v. Locke*, 529 U.S. 89 (2000) (holding that state regulations regarding general navigation watch procedures, crew English language skills and training, and maritime casualty reporting are preempted by the comprehensive federal regulatory scheme governing oil tankers (Ports and Waterways Safety Act and Oil Pollution Act)).

CHAPTER XIII

WORKER INJURY CLAIMS

A. INTRODUCTION

The remedies available to an employee against his or her employer and a vessel on which the employee is working are determined by the employee's "status," i.e., whether the employee is (1) a seaman, (2) a non-seaman maritime worker, or (3) a non-maritime worker.

Two of the seaman's major claims—negligence against the employer and unseaworthiness against the vessel as to which he or she is a seaman—are governed by tort principles. The other—the right to recover maintenance and cure—is akin to worker compensation but is governed not by statute but by judicially developed principles of maritime law.

The non-seaman maritime worker's recovery against the employer ordinarily is through the Longshore and Harbor Workers' Compensation Act (LHWCA), a traditional worker's compensation scheme. The non-seaman maritime worker's claim against the vessel upon which he or she is working is governed by tort principles.

The non-maritime worker's action against his or her employer is regulated by the applicable state worker's compensation scheme, except when the injury is caused by the employer's maritime tort.

Claims by seamen and maritime workers against third persons are governed either by maritime tort law or state law, depending upon whether maritime tort jurisdiction attaches. However, the seaman or maritime worker's claim against a third party often is affected by the maritime law discussed in this chapter, and decisions defining the rights of seamen and other maritime workers often may impact the rights of non-maritime workers. For example, decisions involving the proper standard of causation and the types of damages available to seamen in claims against their employers have been applied, rightly or wrongly, by the lower courts in determining the similar issues in claims by seamen against third parties and tort claims by non-maritime workers. Noteworthy decisions are discussed specifically in the following sections.

Non-maritime worker tort claims against third parties will be governed by maritime tort law or state law, or some combination of the two.

B. SEAMAN'S REMEDIES

1. Introduction

Prior to the Twentieth Century, employees in American industry fared poorly in their claims against their employers for work-related injuries. Before the advent of worker compensation, the employee who was injured in a workplace accident and who sought recovery against his employer had to establish the employer's fault. Even if the plaintiff worker could make a colorable claim of fault, he faced an "unholy trinity" of defenses: contributory negligence, assumption of risk, and the "fellow servant" rule. Under the doctrine of contributory negligence as a bar to recovery, even the slightest fault on the plaintiff's part meant no recovery. Additionally, a plaintiff employee often would be held to have assumed any risks of the employment and could not recover if he was injured as a result of one of the risks. Thirdly, under the "fellow servant" rule, the negligence of an employee was not imputed to the employer in an action by an injured co-employee; the fault of the fellow servant was one of the risks the employee was deemed to have assumed.

The seaman fared somewhat better than his or her land-based counterparts. In 1903 the Supreme Court observed:

[W]e think the law may be considered as settled upon the following propositions:

1. That the vessel and her owners are liable, in case a seaman falls sick, or is wounded, in the service of the ship, to the extent of his maintenance and cure, and to his wages, at least so long as the voyage is continued.

2. That the vessel and her owners are, both by English and American law, liable to an indemnity for injuries received by seamen in consequence of the unseaworthiness of the ship, or a failure to

supply and keep in order the proper appliances appurtenant to the ship....

3. That all the members of the crew, except perhaps the master, are, as between themselves, fellow servants, and hence seamen cannot recover for injuries sustained through the negligence of another member of the crew beyond the expense of their maintenance and cure.

4. That the seaman is not allowed to recover an indemnity for the negligence of the master, or any member of the crew, but is entitled to maintenance and cure, whether the injuries were received by negligence or accident.

The Osceola, 189 U.S. 158 (1903).

Thus, while the seaman did not have a negligence action against the employer based upon the fault of a co-employee, he or she had other valuable remedies. A seaman incurring injury or illness while in the service of the ship was entitled to his wages to the end of the voyage and to maintenance and cure, even though the employer was free from fault. Maintenance and cure provided the seaman with medical expenses until attainment of maximum cure, and an allowance for living expenses while undergoing treatment. Additionally, the operator of a vessel owed to the members of the crew a duty to furnish a safe place to work and live aboard the vessel. A breach of that duty gave rise to a claim for general damages under the doctrine of unseaworthiness.

Early in the twentieth century, state legislatures provided the employee with limited recovery against the employer for workplace injuries by adopting worker's compensation laws. Under those laws, if the employee suffers disabling injury in the course and scope of employment, the employer is liable, without regard to fault, for the payment of fixed benefits. The employer thus trades limited exposure to unlimited tort damages for a form of absolute liability for the payment of limited amounts.

Rather than adopt a worker's compensation program for seamen, Congress chose to remove the barriers to a seaman's recovery in a negligence action against his or her employer. With the right to recover maintenance and cure and general damages for unseaworthiness, the seaman did not need all of the no fault protection a worker compensation scheme would provide. However, Congress did not limit the seaman to his traditional maritime remedies, i.e., the right to recover maintenance and cure and for breach of the warranty of seaworthiness. Instead it gave the seaman a right to sue his employer in negligence. Its initial effort was unsuccessful. Apparently sensing that the "fellow servant" rule (point three in *The Osceola*, page 208, *supra*) was the barrier, Congress in 1915 passed an act which provided:

> in any suit to recover damages for any injury sustained on board vessel or in its service seamen having command shall not be held to be fellow-servants with those under their authority.

Section 20 of the Act to Promote the Welfare of American Seamen, 38 Stat. 1164 (1915). However, the act did not achieve the intended purpose, because the Supreme Court, in *Chelentis* (page 4, *supra*), held that it was not the "fellow servant" doctrine which barred the seaman's action against the employer for the negligence of a co-employee, but rather the maritime rule that a seaman could not recover against the vessel owner for the negligence of any member of the crew (point four in the excerpt from *The Osceola*, page 208, *supra*). Thus the abolition of the fellow servant rule merely deprived the employer of a defense but did not provide the employee with what he needed—a negligence action against his employer, a logically antecedent necessity for recovery.

Congress previously had adopted the Federal Employers' Liability Act (FELA), 45 U.S.C.A. § 51 et seq., which granted an interstate railroad worker a negligence claim against his employer. The statute essentially made a railroad employer liable, through *respondeat superior*, for the negligence of an employee causing injury to a co-employee. In addition, the FELA abolished assumption of risk and the fellow servant rules as defenses, and provided that contributory negligence reduced but did not bar recovery.

After the *Chelentis* setback, Congress in 1920, through the Jones Act, 46 U.S.C.A. § 688, extended the provisions of the FELA to negligence claims by seamen against their employers. The Jones Act makes the FELA applicable to seamen, which means that any decision interpreting the substantive reach of the FELA usually will apply in a Jones Act claim.

A seaman thus has three major remedies against the employer and the vessel as to which he is a seaman: maintenance and cure, a "warranty" of seaworthiness, and a negligence action through the Jones Act. Below, we explore seaman "status" and the seaman's major remedies.

2. Who Are Seamen?

The determination of what maritime workers are "seamen" has generated a body of law on its own. Generally speaking, a "seaman" is a "member of the crew of a vessel." A seaman is a worker on a vessel who is exposed to the perils of the sea as an incident of employment. The traditional seaman is one working on a vessel, sailing the high seas in maritime commerce. He may be certified as an "able seaman" by the federal inspecting authority. The crew of a merchant vessel must contain a certain percentage of "able seamen," who usually agree by contract to serve the ship for a specified voyage or period of time.

Title 46 U.S.C.A. section 10101(3) provides " 'seaman' means an individual (except scientific personnel, a sailing school instructor, or a sailing school student) engaged or employed in any capacity on board a vessel." In addition to this definition, Congress has excluded the master or member of the crew of any vessel from LHWCA coverage. The exclusive definition in the LHWCA results in mutually exclusive remedies for seamen and longshore-men. In the 1990s, after nearly forty years of si-lence, the United States Supreme Court articulated the modern test for seaman status: "an employ-ment-related connection to a vessel in navigation." This definition requires that the worker (1) contrib-ute to the mission or work of the vessel, and (2) have a connection to the vessel which is substantial in duration and nature.

It bears noting that not all those who have been classified as seamen fit this traditional definition of a seaman. *See Mahramas v. American Export Is-brandtsen Lines, Inc.*, 475 F.2d 165 (2d Cir. 1973) (a hairdresser on a cruise ship is a seaman). Further, seamen may work on a vessel on one of America's great water ways—like the Mississippi or the Great Lakes, or in some cases, on a structure engaged in the production of oil, gas, or other natural re-sources. Workers who sail the high seas are com-monly referred to as "bluewater" seaman and those who work on waters other than the high seas, especially those who work in the oil and gas produc-tion business, are commonly called "brownwater" seaman, although these descriptions are not legal terms.

The threshold question in determining seaman status is whether the vehicle or instrumentality to which the putative seaman is connected is a vessel. The majority of decided vessel status cases involve putative seaman's claims. *See Chapter II, supra.* Because seaman status requires an employment-related connection to a vessel, a worker may not attain seaman status by performing work on a fixed platform or on a vessel under construction. He or she must work on a vessel, although the injury giving rise to the claim need not occur on a vessel. A claimant cannot be a seaman if the vessel to which he is permanently assigned is neither operating on navigable waters nor preparing for navigation on such waters. *See Stanfield v. Shellmaker, Inc.*, 869 F.2d 521 (9th Cir. 1989) and *Reeves v. Mobile Dredging & Plumbing Co.*, 26 F.3d 1247 (3d Cir. 1994). One important issue in "brownwater" seaman status is whether a barge which is being used as a work platform is a vessel for seaman status purposes. *See, e.g., Stewart v. Dutra Construction Co.*, 543 U.S. 481 (2005) (work platform with dredge was a vessel). The status of a floating gambling casino as a vessel probably will depend upon the method of its construction, it dockside connections, and the likelihood of movement. *See, e.g., Pavone v. Mississippi Riverboat Amusement Corp.*, 52 F.3d 560 (5th Cir. 1995); *see also Howard v. Southern Illinois Riverboat Casino Cruises, Inc.*, 364 F.3d 854 (7th Cir. 2004).

The development of the modern test for seaman status began in 1959. As in many other areas of the law, new technologies and businesses forced the law to reexamine and adapt entrenched doctrine. In that year, in the celebrated case of *Offshore Co. v. Robison*, 266 F.2d 769 (5th Cir. 1959), the Fifth Circuit held that floating drilling structures are "vessels" and that the amphibious oil workers aboard them are entitled to the seaman's remedies against their employers and the operators of the "vessels" on which they are employed. *Robison* articulated a broad definition of a "seaman" as one who (1) has a more or less permanent connection with, or performs a substantial part of his work aboard, (2) a vessel, (3) in navigation and (4) who is aboard the vessel primarily in aid of navigation *or*, if the vessel is a "special mission" vessel, aids in the special mission of the vessel. *Robison* involved a new type of seaman; this was not Billy Budd, but an oil field worker. Some circuits did not follow *Robison*, however, and held that a worker could not attain seaman status unless he or she performed a transportation-related function on the vessel.

The Supreme Court provided the basis for the currently used definition of seaman status in *McDermott International, Inc. v. Wilander*, 498 U.S. 337 (1991). In *Wilander*, the Court held that "[t]he key to seaman status is employment-related connection to a vessel in navigation." Indicating approval of *Robison*, the Court wrote:

> There is no indication in the Jones Act, the LHWCA, or elsewhere, that Congress has excluded from Jones Act remedies those traditional seamen who owe allegiance to a vessel at sea, but who do not aid in navigation.... [T]he better rule is to define "master or member of a crew" under the LHWCA, and therefore "seaman" under the Jones Act, solely in terms of the employee's connection to a vessel in navigation. We are not called upon here to define this connection in all details, but we hold that a necessary element

of the connection is that a seaman perform the
work of a vessel. In this regard, we believe the
requirement that an employee's duties must
"contribut[e] to the function of the vessel or to
the accomplishment of its mission" captures well
an important requirement of seaman status. It is
not necessary that a seaman aid in navigation or
contribute to the transportation of the vessel, but
a seaman must be doing the ship's work.

Consequently, the putative seaman must be doing
the work of the ship. Under this criterion, a paint
foreman on a paint boat, a hairdresser or a bartend-
er on a cruise ship, or a waiter or entertainer on a
casino vessel are doing the work of the particular
ship without further analysis.

In *Chandris, Inc. v. Latsis*, 515 U.S. 347 (1995),
the Court held that the "employment-related connection" must be a connection to a vessel in navigation (or to an identifiable group of such vessels)
that is substantial in terms of both duration and its
nature. The Court in *Chandris* wrote that:

The duration of a worker's connection to a vessel
and the nature of the worker's activities, taken
together, determine whether a maritime employee is a seaman.... [S]eaman status is not merely
a temporal concept, but ... it necessarily includes
a temporal element.... Generally, the Fifth Circuit seems to have identified an appropriate rule
of thumb for the ordinary case: a worker who
spends less than about 30 percent of his time in
the service of a vessel ... should not qualify as a

seaman under the Jones Act.... [W]e see no reason to limit the seaman status inquiry ... exclusively to an examination of the overall course of a worker's service with a particular employer.... If a maritime employee receives a new work assignment in which his essential duties are changed, he is entitled to have the assessment of the substantiality of his vessel-related work made on the basis of his activities in his new position.

After *Wilander* and *Chandris*, the quantity and quality of the worker's duties aboard a vessel at the time of his injury govern his status as a seaman. Neither alone is determinative, as is illustrated by the *Chandris* court's rejection of the "voyage rule," which would provide seaman status to an employee of a ship injured at sea in the course of his employment. The Court observed that "land-based maritime workers do not become seaman because they happen to be working on board a vessel when they are injured, and seamen do not lose Jones Act protection when the course of their service to a vessel takes them ashore."

The general rule set forth in *Chandris* is that a worker must spend at least 30% of his time aboard a vessel in navigation. This determination should be made in light of the seaman's employment with the particular employer as a whole. If, however, the putative seaman is reassigned to new job responsibilities, his or her status should be determined in light of that reassignment. Thus if a worker, after serving for ten years in an office environment, is made a captain of a ship for the same employer and subsequently injured on his fifth day on board, the durational inquiry would apparently be answered in reference to the five days (post-reassignment) and not in reference to the employer's total ten-year, five-day employment with the same employer. At least one case has gone beyond the "reassignment" language in *Chandris* by requiring that, for a new work assignment to effect a status change, the seaman must establish that his status was permanently changed by the reassignment. *See Becker v. Tidewater, Inc.*, 335 F.3d 376 (5th Cir. 2003).

The standard for seaman status in *Chandris* is designed to separate those "who go down to the sea in ships" and are regularly exposed to the perils of the sea from those who are not. Under the *Chandris* test, however, it is not clear what a putative seaman would have to prove in order to show that his or her connection to the vessel is substantial in nature. Frequently, a worker will be employed to work regularly on more than one vessel. *Chandris* confirmed lower court jurisprudence holding that a worker may become a seaman if he has the requisite connexity with a "fleet of vessels." The lower courts required that the "fleet" be "an identifiable group of vessels acting together or under one control." *Barrett v. Chevron, U.S.A., Inc.*, 781 F.2d 1067 (5th Cir. 1986). The Supreme Court dealt with this issue and others in *Harbor Tug & Barge v. Papai*, 520 U.S. 548 (1997).

In *Papai*, a worker received short term work assignments through a union hiring hall; some of the assignments required him to go to sea. On the day in question he was assigned to an employer and was injured while doing maintenance on a docked vessel. The Court held that the worker was not a seaman. First it indicated that the fleet on which he worked was not subject to common ownership and control. *See also, St. Romain v. Industrial Fabrication and Repair Service, Inc.*, 203 F.3d 376 (5th Cir. 2000). The vessel owners' use of the same union hiring hall did not make it so. Secondly, the Court indicated that, in determining seaman status, it would not look at the employee's job history with all his employers but only with the employer in question. Finally, the Court held that the relevant employment period for the injury in question was the day on which the plaintiff was injured—i.e., the particular discrete employment involved—and not the previous times he worked for the defendant. *See also, Foulk v. Donjon Marine Co., Inc.*, 144 F.3d 252 (3d Cir. 1998) (jury question on whether diver injured on first day of ten-day assignment was a seaman). The *Papai* Court implied that the durational inquiry must be made in light of the nature inquiry—i.e., a court or jury must decide if the putative seaman spent 30% or more of his or her work time in employment that exposed him or her to the perils of the sea. *See O'Hara v. Weeks Marine Inc.*, 294 F.3d 55 (2d Cir. 2002) (no evidence worker derived his living from sea-based activities). Some courts have questioned whether the *Papai* requires that a putative seaman must show that he or she actually goes to sea, with one court holding not. *In re Endeavor Marine*, 234 F.3d 287 (5th Cir. 2000).

Before *Papai*, the question arose whether a worker whose job title is one listed in the LHWCA cannot be a seaman as a matter of law because the LHWCA explicitly excludes seamen from its coverage. In *Southwest Marine, Inc. v. Gizoni*, 502 U.S. 81 (1991), the Supreme Court held that a maritime worker whose occupation is one of those enumerated in the LHWCA nevertheless may be a seaman within the meaning of the Jones Act. The Court observed that "[a] maritime worker is limited to LHWCA remedies only if no genuine issue of fact exists as to whether the worker was a seaman under the Jones Act. . . . Because a ship repairman may spend all of his working hours aboard a vessel in furtherance of its mission—even one used exclusively in ship repair work—the worker may qualify as a Jones Act seaman." In refusing to draw a bright line rule between seaman status and LHWCA status, the Court found that substance rather than form should govern a worker's rights.

Seaman status ordinarily is a mixed question of law and fact for the jury. However, the Court's decisions of the 1990s, most notably *Chandris* and *Papai*, somewhat limit the number of cases that juries will decide. Under *Chandris,* the 30% threshold for the durational connection to a vessel seems to require that unless the worker satisfies the quantitative 30% threshold, summary judgment would be appropriate. *Papai*, by adopting a "discrete employment" rule and a "fleet doctrine" requiring common ownership and control, further limits the number of seaman status questions that will go to the jury. *But see Wisner v. Professional Divers of New Orleans,* 731 So.2d 200 (La. 1999) (fleet doctrine not limited to vessels under common ownership and control in case involving a diver). *Compare Roberts v. Cardinal Services, Inc.,* 266 F.3d 368 (5th Cir. 2001). When such a case does go to the jury, there is some abiding confusion whether the burden of proof of seaman status is the "more probable than not" test generally applied in civil litigation, or the "scintilla" test applied to the issues of causation in Jones Act cases. The better view is that the "more probable than not" test applies. Use of the "scintilla" test represents special protection which the law affords a seaman; a litigant should not be given that protection until there has been a determination that he is a seaman.

3. Maintenance and Cure

An employer must provide maintenance and cure to a seaman who suffers injury or illness while "in the service of" his or her ship. The remedy is similar to worker's compensation, but more closely resembles limited health and accident insurance. As with worker's compensation, liability for maintenance and cure is imposed upon the employer without regard to fault, but unlike most worker compensation schemes, benefits are limited to the seaman's medical expenses (cure) until he reaches maximum medical cure (for his condition), wages only to the end of the voyage, and a sum (not related to the wages the seaman was earning) for living expenses (maintenance) during the period of treatment and convalescence. *The Osceola*, page 208, *supra*.

Maintenance and cure is derived from ancient sea codes and was incorporated into American maritime common law in the nineteenth century. The maintenance and cure claim is independent of the claims based upon unseaworthiness or Jones Act negligence, but nearly all of the benefits payable under maintenance and cure overlap with categories of damages that may be recovered in those actions. The major role of maintenance and cure is to provide a seaman with medical treatment from his employer or the vessel on which he is a seaman when his illness or injury was not caused by unseaworthiness or employer negligence. As a practical matter, it also is useful as a means of providing the seaman with living expenses, by way of maintenance, while he is undergoing medical treatment and is awaiting the outcome of his action for general tort damages against his employer, the shipowner, or a third party tortfeasor.

The seaman's employer is liable for maintenance and cure. Ordinarily, the vessel owner is the seaman's employer. If the vessel owner is not the employer, a situation not uncommon in offshore mineral production, the vessel owner will not be personally liable for maintenance and cure, but there is respectable authority indicating that the vessel as to which he is a seaman will be liable *in rem* to the seaman for maintenance and cure. *Solet v. M/V Capt. H. V. Dufrene*, 303 F.Supp. 980 (E.D.La. 1969).

The obligation to pay maintenance and cure arises if the injury occurs, or the illness becomes manifest, while the seaman is "in the service of the ship." For seamen aboard oceangoing vessels, coverage is almost absolute; all injuries aboard the vessel are covered, and injuries off the vessel also are covered, even though the seaman is on shore leave and pursuing personal pleasures. The classic case, which probably has not escaped the attention of any admiralty student through the years, is *Koistinen v. American Export Lines, Inc.*, 83 N.Y.S.2d 297 (N.Y. 1948). There, the court held that a seaman, injured in a foreign port when he jumped from the window of a prostitute's room to avoid mayhem at the hands of her male associate, was entitled to maintenance during the recuperative period which followed. Several theories are advanced in support of this kind of result. One is that a "bluewater" seaman who has signed articles is bound, during the term of those articles, to report to the ship upon the master's order; hence he is "answerable to the call of duty" while on shore leave, and such leave is within the course and scope of his or her employment. Another is that the nature of the employment requires the seaman to pursue recreation in strange environments; thus injury sustained while on such pursuits is fairly chargeable as a cost of the employer's enterprise. Finally, a variation of the theory contends that since the employer would not be able to secure seamen for long voyages unless the employer provided them with the opportunity for recreation ashore while the vessel was in port, a seaman while ashore for rest and recreation actually is furthering the employer's interests.

Workers aboard offshore mineral production structures, and some workers who are engaged in providing services to those structures, may be seamen even though they do not go to sea in the traditional sense. These "brownwater" seamen, and those working aboard tugs and other port service vessels, frequently return to shore on a weekly or daily basis. If one is injured while at home, or while en route to or from the dock, is the injury compensable under maintenance and cure? The courts have not formulated a satisfactory answer, but most decisions analogize from cases providing maintenance and cure to "bluewater" seamen. Thus if at the time of injury the seaman, by the terms of his or her employment, is under an obligation to return to the vessel if called, he, like the "bluewater" seaman, is "answerable to the call of duty." If the seaman is not under an obligation to return if called, the proper inquiry may be whether the employer has a significant interest in the seaman's activities at the time of injury. One indication of such an interest is whether the employer provides transportation from an inland point to the dock. Other indicia are whether the vessel has living quarters, or is located at such a place that crew members could reasonably be expected to live elsewhere and "commute" to the vessel or to some other geographic point at which their employment commences.

The employer owes maintenance and cure if the seaman suffers an illness which manifests itself while the seaman is in the service of the ship. What if the illness manifested itself before the seaman entered the service of a ship, and manifests itself again during such service? This issue usually is resolved by determining whether the seaman "willfully concealed" the illness at the commencement of his or her service. If the employer requires a medical examination as a condition of employment, the seaman's only obligation may be to answer honestly those questions posed by the examining health care provider. If the employer does not require a medical examination, the seaman only may be required to voluntarily disclose any illness or condition that he reasonably could be expected to know the employer would consider in making an employment decision. Even where "concealment" is found, it will not defeat the employer's obligation to pay maintenance and cure unless it is the "cause" of the obligation; if the shipowner would have employed the seaman even though disclosure had been made, the concealment should not bar recovery. *Brown v. Parker Drilling Offshore Corporation*, 410 F.3d 166 (5th Cir. 2005); *Wactor v. Spartan Transportation Corp.*, 27 F.3d 347 (8th Cir. 1994); *McCorpen v. Central Gulf Steamship Corp.*, 396 F.2d 547 (5th Cir. 1968). The "McCorpen rule" that a seaman's willful concealment of a pre-existing condition defeats recovery for maintenance and cure does not apply to the

seaman's Jones Act claim; however, such concealment may be considered contributory negligence in
the Jones Act claim where the seaman conceals
material information about his pre-existing condition from his employer. *Johnson v. Cenac Towing
Inc.*, 544 F.3d 296 (5th Cir. 2008).

A seaman is not entitled to maintenance and cure
if the injury or illness occurred through his or her
own "willful misconduct." This term of art has
defied definition, but it is clear that it means something more than negligence. Two classic examples of
misconduct which will defeat the seaman's claim
are intoxication and venereal disease. There has
been some tendency to relax the intoxication defense, *see e.g.*, *Garay v. Carnival Cruise Line, Inc.*,
904 F.2d 1527 (11th Cir. 1990), but the courts have
not been so forgiving of drug use. Surprisingly, in
the light of changing community standards, the
venereal disease defense remains viable. Mere
"horseplay" usually will not be treated as "willful
misconduct"; fighting may be "willful misconduct,"
particularly if the injured seaman was the aggres-
sor.

When a seaman is injured in the service of the
ship, the employer must furnish medical treatment
until maximum cure is achieved but not thereafter.
Whitman v. Miles, 387 F.3d 68 (1st Cir. 2004). The
prevailing rule is that maximum cure does not
include palliative treatment, and thus maximum
cure is achieved, and the employer's obligation terminates, when improvement in the seaman's condition is no longer possible. However, in *Vella v. Ford*

Motor Co., 421 U.S. 1 (1975), the Supreme Court expressly reserved the question, which it found unnecessary to decide under the facts of the case before it. Even if maximum cure is attained when improvement is no longer possible, the obligation to provide medical treatment may re-arise if progress in medical science subsequently produces a new curative treatment. One court has held that even though a seaman's condition is permanent, he is entitled to maintenance and cure where long-term improvement might result from treatment. *In re RJF International Corp.*, 354 F.3d 104 (1st Cir. 2004).

From 1798 to 1981, the federal government provided free medical care for disabled seamen, first through special seamen's hospitals and later through Public Health Service hospitals. Because Congress has closed those hospitals, the employer now may designate the physicians and medical facilities that he or she will supply. Free medical care available to a seaman through government benefits such as Medicare or Medicaid may satisfy the obligation to furnish cure. *See Moran Towing & Trans. Co. v. Lombas*, 58 F.3d 24 (2d Cir. 1995).

If the employer offers the seaman medical treatment but the seaman obtains treatment from another source, the better view is that the seaman may recover the costs of such treatment unless the employer proves that the seaman's choice caused the employer to incur medical expenses in excess of those that he or she would have incurred from the source he or she offered. *Caulfield v. AC & D*

Marine, Inc., 633 F.2d 1129 (5th Cir. 1981). Logically, if the employer would have been liable for maintenance payments even if the seaman had accepted the proffered treatment, the seaman's wrongful refusal of treatment may result in forfeiture of the medical costs but not the maintenance payments. A seaman also may forfeit the right to maintenance and cure by failing to follow the medical treatment prescribed by his physician, unless the seaman's failure was reasonable. *Coulter v. Ingram Pipeline, Inc.*, 511 F.2d 735 (5th Cir. 1975).

Maintenance and cure imposes upon the employer the obligation to furnish adequate medical treatment aboard the vessel and after the seaman is discharged. In some cases, the vessel must transport the seaman to shoreside medical facilities, and pay his travel expenses from his home to the place of treatment.

The employer obligated to furnish medical treatment also must provide the seaman with maintenance, an additional sum for living expenses during treatment. Traditionally, the courts made small standard awards ($6–$8 per day) for maintenance, but recent decisions indicate a change in judicial attitude. Some courts have increased the fixed daily stipend to a more realistic sum ($15 per day or more), and some other courts now permit a seaman to offer evidence of his or her living expenses, from which the court makes an *ad hoc* award. The majority of courts now hold that a seaman is bound by the maintenance rate set in a collective bargaining agreement between the seaman's employer and union. *Baldassaro v. United States*, 64 F.3d 206 (5th Cir. 1995); *Ammar v. United States*, 342 F.3d 133 (2d Cir. 2003); *Stanton v. Buchanan Marine, L.P.*, 2009 WL 2447823 (S.D.N.Y. 2009). *But see, Daniels v. Standard Marine Transport Service, Inc.*, 680 N.Y.S.2d 41 (N.Y. 1998). Of course what that agreement provides requires interpretation of the relevant contract. *Marcic v. Reinauer Transp. Companies*, 397 F.3d 120 (2d Cir. 2005).

Maintenance is owed only if the seaman proves he or she has incurred living expenses while undergoing treatment; the seaman is not entitled to maintenance if hospitalized, or if expenses are furnished by a friend or relative at no cost to the seaman. Thus the seaman must establish some real loss or expense to recover maintenance, but the standard recovery is the daily allowance, a sum often unrelated to the actual expense incurred. However, some maintenance awards have been based on the amount necessary to maintain a family home. Such an award seems more compensatory in nature.

In one case, *Hall v. Noble Drilling (U.S.) Inc.*, 242 F.3d 582 (5th Cir. 2001), the U.S. Fifth Circuit attempted to comprehensively analyze and restate the law relating to maintenance. The court indicated that a seaman may not recover maintenance unless he presents evidence of actual expenses. If he does, the court must then estimate the seaman's actual costs of food and lodging and the reasonable cost of food and lodging for a single seaman in the locality of the plaintiff. In determining the reasonable costs the court may consider evidence of the seaman's actual costs, evidence of reasonable costs in the locality or region, union contracts stipulating a rate of maintenance or per diem payments for shoreside food or lodging while in the service of a vessel, and maintenance rates awarded by other courts for seamen in the same region. A seaman need not present evidence of the reasonable rate; a court may take judicial notice of the prevailing rate in the district. Thereafter, the court must compare the seaman's actual expenses to reasonable expenses; the seaman is entitled only to reasonable expenses for his or her locality. There is one exception to this rule that the court must consider: if the court concludes that the seaman's actual expenses were inadequate to provide him with reasonable food and lodging, the plaintiff is entitled to the amount the court determines is the reasonable cost of food and lodging. Setting forth these principles, the Fifth Circuit ruled that where a seaman paid the rent or mortgage of a home he shared with his family, the total amount of the rent or mortgage, and not a pro-rated amount, represented the seaman's actual expenses. Reaching these conclusions, the court opined that "[a]warding a standardized rate of maintenance is appropriate as long as the seaman provides evidence that his actual expenses meet or exceed the standard, reasonable amount." However, the court declined to adopt a circuit standard, "leav[ing] that task to the district courts...."

If a seaman is forced to seek employment because of the shipowner's willful refusal to pay maintenance, the amount the seaman earns may not be deducted from the maintenance payment. *Vaughan v. Atkinson*, 369 U.S. 527 (1962). There is authority for the proposition that a seaman does not forfeit his or her right to maintenance payments even though he or she voluntarily obtains another type of employment while undergoing cure. *Wood v. Diamond M Drilling Co.*, 691 F.2d 1165 (5th Cir. 1982). There is also authority that the receipt of Social Security benefits does not satisfy the shipowner's obligation to pay maintenance and cure because such benefits do not provide the "exact equivalent" of maintenance. *Delaware River & Bay Authority v. Kopacz*, 584 F.3d 622 (3d Cir. 2009).

If the employer's failure to provide prompt, adequate medical treatment causes the seaman's condition to worsen, the employer may be liable for compensatory damages, including an award for additional pain and suffering. If the employer's failure to provide maintenance and cure is "willful," "persistent," or "callous," the seaman also is entitled to an award of attorney's fees. *Vaughan v. Atkinson*, 369 U.S. 527 (1962). The *Vaughan* court did not decide whether the seaman also could recover punitive damages in excess of attorney's fees. Prior to *Miles v. Apex Marine Corp.*, 498 U.S. 19 (1990), the majority of the post-*Vaughan* decisions in the lower courts permitted awards of both attorney's fees and punitive damages when the employer failed to provide maintenance and cure and did not have a reasonable excuse. Following *Miles* the trend was to deny punitive damages for failure to pay maintenance and cure. *See, e.g., Glynn v. Roy Al Boat Mgt.*

Corp., 57 F.3d 1495 (9th Cir. 1995); *Guevara v. Maritime Overseas Corp.*, 59 F.3d 1496 (5th Cir. 1995). In *Atlantic Sounding Co., Inc. v. Townsend*, 129 S.Ct. 2561 (2009), the Supreme Court found that neither *Miles* nor the Jones Act eliminated the availability of punitive damages for the willful and wanton disregard of the maintenance and cure obligation, and thus such damages remained available as a matter of general maritime law.

An action for maintenance and cure may be brought *in personam* against the employer, either as an admiralty claim in federal or state court, or, if there is diversity jurisdiction, as a law claim in federal court. If the seaman joins his action for maintenance and cure with a Jones Act claim in which he asks for a jury trial, he also may obtain a jury trial on his maintenance and cure claim. *Fitzgerald v. U.S. Lines Co.*, 374 U.S. 16 (1963). If, as some cases hold, a maintenance and cure claim can be brought *in rem* against the vessel as to which the plaintiff enjoys seaman status, that action must be brought in federal court as an "admiralty claim."

When a seaman is entitled to maintenance and cure, the court awards a lump sum encompassing benefits due to the date of trial and for a brief period thereafter for which medical evidence establishes that cure will be required. If the seaman does not achieve maximum cure by the expiration of the period for which payments were awarded, he or she may pursue a claim for additional benefits. However, one appellate court has approved a judgment that ordered the shipowner to pay benefits until maximum cure was achieved, thus shifting to the employer the onus to return to court and establish that benefits are no longer due. *Lirette v. K & B Boat Rentals, Inc.*, 579 F.2d 968 (5th Cir. 1978).

Prior to 1980, the doctrine of laches governed whether a maintenance and cure claim was time-barred. In that year Congress adopted 46 U.S.C.A. § 763a, providing a three-year statute of limitations on suits ''for recovery of damages for personal injury . . . arising out of a maritime tort.'' Maintenance and cure payments are owed without regard to the employer's fault, and thus it is arguable that the ordinary claim for maintenance and cure might not come within the statute, but will continue to be governed by the laches test, i.e., unreasonable delay and prejudice to the defendant. *See, e.g., Reed v. American Steamship Co.*, 682 F.Supp. 333 (E.D.Mich. 1988).

The seaman may join his maintenance and cure claim with his Jones Act and unseaworthiness claims, but he is not required to do so. Where he does not join them, judgment in one of the suits may preclude litigation of all or part of the claims in the other. For example, if there is a determination in the maintenance and cure claim that the employee is a seaman, collateral estoppel could bar the employer from contesting seaman status in the Jones Act claim. If the Jones Act claim is successfully prosecuted to judgment, the recovery of benefits in that suit may preclude subsequent recovery of most, if not all, of the maintenance and cure benefits, since Jones Act damages include accrued and future medical expenses and past and future lost wages.

One often overlooked element of damages in Jones Act cases is "found," the sum which represents the living expenses furnished to the seaman by his employer as a condition of employment. Where the seaman is entitled to "found," he may recover it as an element of damages in his Jones Act claim. "Found" and maintenance are strikingly similar, and recovery of one should preclude subsequent recovery of the other. *See e.g.*, *McCarthy v. American Eastern Corp.*, 175 F.2d 727 (3d Cir. 1949).

If an injury occurs while the seaman is in the service of the ship, the employer is liable for maintenance and cure, even though the injury was caused by the fault of a third person. Where the tort that injures the employee is non-maritime, state law may govern the employer's rights to recover from the tortfeasor the maintenance and cure he has paid to his seaman. Where maritime law governs (as when the tort to the employee is maritime), the employer may be entitled to contribution or indemnity from the tortfeasor. If the employer's fault contributed to the seaman's injury, he may recover under the maritime rule of comparative contribution. *See* Chapter XVII, *infra*. If the employer is free from fault, the procedural context in which the seaman's claim is presented may dictate the employer's indemnity rights. If the seaman joins the maintenance and cure claim with the damage suit against the tortfeasor, judgment for all damages (including sums otherwise payable as maintenance and cure) must run first against the tortfeasor, with the employer being liable only in the event the tortfeasor is unable to satisfy the judgment. If the seaman proceeds first against the tortfeasor and is successful, the employer thereafter sued by the seaman is entitled to a credit for maintenance and cure expenses that the seaman has recovered from the tortfeasor. If the seaman first recovers maintenance and cure payments from the employer, who then seeks indemnity from the tortfeasor, some courts have denied indemnity, probably under the influence of the traditional common-law rule that a third person may not recover damages for economic harm resulting from negligent interference with his contract with the tort victim. Other courts, taking what is obviously the better view, have permitted recovery.

The seaman's illness may become manifest while he or she is in the service of a ship, but the illness may have developed over a longer period of time during which the seaman was employed elsewhere. The seaman's employer at the time the illness manifests itself may be entitled to recover, under the theory of unjust enrichment, part of the maintenance and cure payments from those employers of the seaman during the earlier periods in which the injury was developing.

4. Unseaworthiness

A vessel and its operator owe members of the vessel's crew the duty to furnish a seaworthy vessel, i.e., one which is reasonably fit for its intended use. The duty of seaworthiness is owed by the operator of the vessel. Usually the shipowner is both the operator of the vessel and the seaman's employer. However, the vessel operator need not be the employer of the seaman; the operator owes the duty of seaworthiness to members of the crew of the vessel who are employed directly by others. Where the vessel is under a demise or bareboat charter, the charterer becomes the operator (the owner *pro hac vice*) and assumes the obligation of placing and maintaining the vessel in a seaworthy condition. However, the owner who has leased the vessel under a demise charter may be liable *in personam* to a member of the crew for injury caused by an unseaworthy condition existing before the owner surrendered control to the charterer. One court has gone one step further, holding that the owner is liable *in personam* to seamen aboard the vessel for unseaworthy conditions arising after the owner has let the vessel to another under a demise charter. *Baker v. Raymond International, Inc.*, 656 F.2d 173 (5th Cir. 1981). *Compare Backhus v. Transit Cas. Co.*, 549 So.2d 283 (La. 1989), and the cases cited therein. While the majority rule is that the owner is not liable *in personam* for post-charter unseaworthiness, all courts hold that the vessel is liable *in rem* for both pre-and post-charter unseaworthiness. The difference may be critical, depending upon the value of the vessel at the relevant time.

The seaman's claim for damages caused by unseaworthiness has had a turbulent history in American maritime law. Prior to the adoption of the Jones Act, the seaman could recover general damages from his or her employer only if the latter failed to furnish the seaman with a safe place to work, i.e., a seaworthy vessel. It was not clear whether this duty was absolute or could be satisfied by the exercise of due diligence. After the passage of the Jones Act, the initial perception of the legal community was that a seaman was required to elect between his Jones Act and unseaworthiness claims; since the Jones Act encompasses negligence by fellow servants as well as employer negligence in failing to provide a safe place to work, the seaman usually chose the Jones Act remedy. During the next quarter century, three developments had a startling effect upon the doctrine of unseaworthiness. The Supreme Court held that the duty to furnish a seaworthy vessel was absolute and was not based upon the failure to exercise due care—i.e., it was a type of strict liability. The courts also determined that the seaman was not required to choose between unseaworthiness and the Jones Act remedy, but could urge both in a single action. Then, in *Seas Shipping Co. v. Sieracki*, 328 U.S. 85 (1946), and in *Pope & Talbot, Inc. v. Hawn*, 346 U.S. 406 (1953), the Supreme Court extended the duty of seaworthiness to persons who were not members of the crew, but who were aboard the vessel doing work traditionally performed by a member of the crew. These persons usually were longshoremen engaged in loading and unloading or persons engaged in ship repair. During the period from 1946 to 1972 the courts were deluged with suits by these "*Sieracki* seamen" against vessel owners. In the latter year, the Longshore and Harbor Workers' Compensation Act was amended to provide that persons covered by the Act may not maintain an unseaworthiness action against the vessel, but can recover (under section 905(b), *see* page 298, *infra*) only if the shipowner is negligent. This eliminated most, if not all, of the *Sieracki* suits. However, the volume of unseaworthiness claims during the "*Sieracki* era" impacted heavily on the doctrine as it now applies to both true seamen and any remaining *Sieracki* seamen.

The general, if not complete, demise of the *Sieracki* seaman has lessened the importance of unseaworthiness in seaman claims. Usually, a harmful condition aboard a vessel is caused or continued by the negligence of a crew member. Since the seaman can recover against his employer under the Jones Act for injuries caused by such a condition, the unseaworthiness remedy often is unnecessary. It remains important, however, in those cases in which (1) an unseaworthy condition arises without employer negligence, (2) the plaintiff must establish a lien against the vessel (recovery under the Jones Act does not give rise to a maritime lien), or (3) the seaman is not an employee of the vessel owner (the Jones Act applies only in a suit by a seaman against his employer).

Since the intended use of the vessel by the seaman is as a place to live and work, "seaworthiness," in the context of a seaman's claim, means that the vessel must be a reasonably fit place to both live and work. Because the duty is absolute, it sometimes is called a warranty. The obligation to provide a seaworthy vessel arises out of the seaman's relationship to the vessel, but it has much more a tort flavor than a contractual one.

The duty of seaworthiness owed to a member of the crew is greater than the seaworthiness duty owed to others, such as shippers and insurers. To the crew, the shipowner's duty to furnish a seaworthy vessel is absolute; it does not require shipowner fault, and extends to conditions arising after the voyage has begun (unless the owner has bareboat chartered the vessel to another, in which case the owner's *in personam* liability for unseaworthiness may be limited to pre-charter unseaworthy conditions). It also applies to conditions created by the acts of third persons without any knowledge or negligence on the part of the shipowner or his employees.

The shipowner, however, is not required to furnish an accident-free ship, but only one reasonably fit for its intended use. Some conditions may render a vessel unseaworthy under certain circumstances but not under others. Ice on a walkway in a frigid climate, while the vessel is underway, may not constitute unseaworthiness, but the same condition may make the vessel unseaworthy if the vessel is in a warmer climate or is in port. Water on deck during turbulent weather, or during cleaning operations, may not constitute unseaworthiness, but the result may be different if the weather was calm or the clean-up activities had ceased for an appreciable period of time. Determining when a work area for a hazardous occupation is not reasonably fit for its intended use is not easy, and the courts apparently have not yet formulated a workable test. One judge, called upon to draw the line, remarked:

[a] seaman is not absolutely entitled to a deck that is not slippery. He is absolutely entitled to a deck that is not unreasonably slippery. . . .

It seems only fair that men who make their livelihood on the water can be expected to cope with some of the hazardous conditions that must prevail even on a seaworthy vessel. Any stricter rule would require the intervention of traveling companions to guide and protect sailors in going about the vessel to perform their duties.

Colon v. Trinidad Corp., 188 F.Supp. 97 (S.D.N.Y. 1960). *See also, Henry v. Bally's Louisiana, Inc.*, 982 So.2d 860 (La. App. 4th Cir. 2008) (holding that a cashier on a casino boat who slipped and fell on a shore-side deck returning from lunch must accept the naturally occurring conditions that came with working on a vessel to avail herself of the benefits of a seaman).

Some courts hold that a vessel is unseaworthy when the risk of the relevant vessel condition outweighs its utility under the circumstances. Under this test the difference between unseaworthiness and negligence is that in unseaworthiness the seaman need not prove that the defendant knew or should have known of the unreasonably dangerous condition. This type of test for unseaworthiness resembles some tests for determining if a product is unreasonably dangerous in a products liability case.

A vessel also may be unseaworthy because it lacks certain equipment, such as thermal boots for seamen required to go ashore in arctic weather, *Webb v. Dresser Industries*, 536 F.2d 603 (5th Cir. 1976), or because it provides improper recreational facilities for its crew, such as where it is "operating . . . a floating dramshop" for the seamen. *Reyes v. Vantage S.S. Co., Inc.*, 558 F.2d 238 (5th Cir. 1977). A vessel may be unseaworthy because the owner provides improper equipment to do a job, including an improper cleaning solution. *Vargas v. McNamara*, 608 F.2d 15 (1st Cir. 1979). A vessel may be unseaworthy because the operator fails to provide proper tools or equipment, or because the tools are defective. Even the misuse of properly functioning equipment may render a vessel unseaworthy. *Taylor v. Teco Barge Line, Inc.*, 517 F.3d 372 (6th Cir. 2008).

The duty of seaworthiness extends to the vessel's appurtenances, even those not owned by the shipowner and brought aboard the vessel by third persons. The term "appurtenance" is one of art, and its definition is often a matter of policy. A gangplank is an appurtenance of a vessel. Equipment normally kept aboard a vessel may remain an appurtenance after it has been removed if it is still being used in the performance of a function for the vessel. The duty should not extend to equipment that normally is kept on shore and that is neither on, nor attached to, the vessel at the time of injury.

The duty of seaworthiness requires that the shipowner provide a competent crew. An incompetent seaman, as opposed to a merely negligent one, will make a vessel unseaworthy. *See, e.g., Szymanski v. Columbia Transp. Co.*, 154 F.3d 591 (6th Cir. 1998) (no recovery for job-related stress caused by an incompetent co-worker). One line of cases distinguishes between the normally boisterous or combative seaman and the "savage" seaman, who is "incompetent" and whose presence aboard the vessel makes it unseaworthy. One court has suggested that the distinction between the two is whether the seaman fights with a weapon or only with his fists. Another has held that an intoxicated seaman who is involved in a fight does not render a ship unseaworthy unless the seaman has a wicked disposition, a propensity to evil conduct, or a savage and vicious nature. *Hasty v. Trans Atlas Boats, Inc.*, 389 F.3d 510 (5th Cir. 2004). Courts have found a breach of the duty of seaworthiness where the ship's complement was too small for its operations, and where the complement was adequate but too few workers were assigned to perform a specific task.

The Supreme Court found unseaworthiness when a crew member used defective equipment although proper equipment was available, *Mahnich v. Southern Steamship Co.*, 321 U.S. 96 (1944), and when a seaman improperly used proper equipment. This latter development, in *Crumady v. The Joachim Hendrik Fisser*, 358 U.S. 423 (1959), led many to believe that the expanded concept of unseaworthiness would "swallow" employer negligence under the Jones Act, at least as to shipboard accidents; if "operational negligence," as in *Crumady,* constituted unseaworthiness, then there simply could be no employer negligence aboard the vessel which did not also constitute unseaworthiness.

In *Usner v. Luckenbach Overseas Corp.*, 400 U.S. 494 (1971), the Supreme Court, retreating from *Crumady,* held that unseaworthiness does not arise until the negligent act becomes a "condition," and that a single, isolated negligent act is not, in and of itself, such a condition. The line between mere "operational negligence" and the point at which the negligence rises to the level of a "condition" has not been clearly drawn. With the demise of the *Sieracki* seaman, the issue has declined in importance.

A vessel must be seaworthy only while it is in navigation. When members of the regular crew remain aboard while the vessel undergoes extensive repairs, the court may be required to determine whether the vessel remained in navigation or whether it became a "dead ship," thus relieving the operator of his duty to maintain a seaworthy vessel for the crew. The issue turns upon the control of the vessel during the repairs and the nature and extent of the repairs. Where the vessel is under the control of the repairman, and the repairs are major, the vessel should not owe the duty of seaworthiness. In determining whether the repairs are major, relevant factors include the cost of repairs compared with the value of the vessel, the period of time encompassed by the repairs, and whether the repairs invade the "watertight integrity" of the vessel. *See, e.g., Wixom v. Boland Marine and Manufacturing*, 614 F.2d 956 (5th Cir. 1980).

The contributory negligence of the seaman diminishes but does not defeat recovery for unseaworthiness; "pure" comparative negligence applies. Conduct that would constitute "implied assumption of risk," and thus overlap with contributory negligence, will not defeat but may diminish recovery.

Prior to 1980, an unseaworthiness claim was time barred only if laches applied, and thus it was an important remedy if the Jones Act claim was barred by its three-year statute of limitations. However, the adoption of Title 46 U.S.C.A. section 763a, providing a three-year statute of limitations for all claims for personal injury or death arising out of a maritime tort, probably eliminated that important difference between the remedies.

An unseaworthiness claim may be urged in the same manner as a claim for maintenance and cure. The jurisprudence requires joinder of the unseaworthiness and Jones Act claims; if there is no joinder, the omitted claim is waived. *Baltimore S.S. Co. v. Phillips*, 274 U.S. 316 (1927). This rule developed at a time when the shipowner who was liable for unseaworthiness and the employer who was liable for Jones Act negligence were usually the same person, and it may have been a simple application of the "might have been pleaded" *res judicata* rule. A different result may be reached if, as is now often the case, the shipowner and the seaman's employer are not the same person. When the unseaworthiness claim brought as an admiralty claim is joined in federal court with a Jones Act claim in which trial by jury is sought, the seaman is entitled to a jury trial of the unseaworthiness claim, under the *Fitzgerald* doctrine (*see* Chapter XIX).

The seaman successful in an unseaworthiness action recovers the usual tort damages, including awards for pain and suffering, disability, loss of earnings, and medical expenses. Most of the damages recoverable under the unseaworthiness and Jones Act remedies are the same. The fact that the two claims must be joined prevents "double recovery."

Two important types of damages have been available under the general maritime law (and thus in an unseaworthiness claim) but not under the Jones Act. Punitive damages are not recoverable under the FELA, and thus, *a fortiori*, are not recoverable under the Jones Act. However, it had been held that a seaman could recover punitive damages from a shipowner who was "grossly negligent" or "willful" in the violation of his duty to furnish a seaworthy vessel. *See, e.g., Complaint of Merry Shipping, Inc.*, 650 F.2d 622 (5th Cir. 1981). Damages for loss of consortium with an injured seaman are not recoverable under the Jones Act. However, it was held that the spouse of a worker injured by an unseaworthy condition of the vessel could recover damage for loss of consortium. *American Export Lines v. Alvez*, Chapter XI, *supra*. Then, in 1990, the Supreme Court, stressing the need for uniformity, ruled that although there is a general maritime cause of action for the wrongful death of a seaman, the damages recoverable in such an action do *not* include loss of society. *Miles v. Apex Marine Corporation*, page 165, *supra*.

Strictly construed, *Miles* merely banned recovery of non-pecuniary damages by a seaman's relatives in unseaworthiness claims, thus providing uniformity in seamen's remedies. However, in *Miles* the Court alluded to a Congressional intent to limit recovery in maritime claims to pecuniary damages, and to a need for uniformity. Some lower courts read *Miles* as barring recovery of almost all non-pecuniary damages in admiralty. *See, e.g., Guevara v. Maritime Overseas Corp.*, 59 F.3d 1496 (5th Cir. 1995); *Michel v. Total Transportation, Inc.*, 957 F.2d 186 (5th Cir. 1992); *Lollie v. Brown Marine Service, Inc.*, 995 F.2d 1565 (11th Cir. 1993); *Miller v. American President Lines, Ltd.*, 989 F.2d 1450 (6th Cir. 1993); *Horsley v. Mobil Oil Corp.*, 15 F.3d 200 (1st Cir. 1994). Others did not. *See, e.g., Wheelings v. Seatrade Groningen, B.V.*, 516 F. Supp. 2d 488 (E.D.Pa. 2007) (holding that punitive damages are available in a case involving the death of a longshore worker in territorial waters). The Supreme Court, in *Atlantic Sounding Co., Inc. v. Townsend*, page 165, *supra,* held that neither *Miles* nor the Jones Act eliminated the availability of punitive damages as a matter of general maritime law for the willful and wanton disregard of maintenance and cure obligations. The scope of *Miles* is still uncertain in the wake of *Townsend*, although it is now clear that non-pecuniary damages are viable in admiralty where they are available as a matter of general maritime law and not otherwise barred by Congress or prior Supreme Court precedent. After *Townsend*, *Miles* will probably not bar recovery of non-pecuniary damages brought by a seaman (or in the case of wrongful death, his survivors) against third parties under general maritime law. *See, e.g., Scarborough v. Clemco Industries*, 391 F.3d 660 (5th Cir. 2004). Even after *Townsend*, however, the uniformity principle alluded to in *Miles* should bar recovery of loss of consortium with a seaman who is injured by the unseaworthiness of his *employer's* vessel because the Jones Act does not allow such a claim. Moreover, one may persuasively argue that a seaman should not be able to recover punitive damages as a result of unseaworthiness from his *employer* because the Jones Act does not allow such damages.

There is some duplication between damages recoverable in unseaworthiness and the benefits payable under maintenance and cure. Consequently, recovery under one theory may bar recovery of the same benefits under the other. Similarly, a determination in a maintenance and cure action that a claimant is not a seaman should bar, through estoppel by judgment, litigation of the claimant's action for unseaworthiness. Recovery of interest on judgments for unseaworthiness, and removal of unseaworthiness claims from state to federal court, are discussed in the following section on the Jones Act.

5. Negligence: *The Jones Act*

The general maritime law did not provide a seaman with a cause of action against his employer for damages caused by the negligence of co-employees. *See, e.g., Chelentis v. Luckenbach Steamship Co.,* page 4, *supra.* Congress remedied this by adopting the Jones Act, which now provides:

A seaman injured in the course of employment or, if the seaman dies from the injury, the personal representative of the seaman may elect to bring a civil action at law, with the right of trial by jury, against the employer. Laws of the United States regulating recovery for personal injury to, or death of, a railway employee apply to an action under this section....

46 U.S.C.A. § 30104. The "laws ... regulating recovery for personal injury to, or death of, a railway employee" is the Federal Employers' Liability Act (FELA), 45 U.S.C.A. § 51 et seq., which provides, in relevant part:

Every common carrier ... shall be liable in damages to any person suffering injury while he is employed by such carrier ... resulting in whole or in part from the negligence of any of the officers, agents, or employees of such carrier ...

45 U.S.C.A. § 51. Thus the Jones Act provides a seaman a cause of action against his employer for the negligence of a co-employee. Because the Jones Act is remedial legislation, it is liberally construed to accomplish its beneficent purposes and thus is an

extremely effective method of recovery for work-related injuries.

The Jones Act applies only to a claim by a seaman against his or her employer; the seaman's claim against others is governed by general maritime tort law, if the tort is maritime, or by state law. However, a Jones Act employer need not own or operate the vessel on which his or her employee serves as a member of the crew. *Guidry v. South Louisiana Contractors*, 614 F.2d 447 (5th Cir. 1980). Thus where an employee of X injures another employee of X on a vessel which is owned by Y but as to which the injured employee is a seaman, X could be liable under the Jones Act through *respondeat superior*.

The borrowed servant or borrowed employee doctrine applies to the Jones Act so that a seaman may have a claim against an employer who is not the general (payroll) employer but who has borrowed the seaman, i.e., has exercised sufficient control over the seaman to be treated as the employer. It has been held that a seaman may have only one employer for Jones Act purposes, but the U.S. Fifth Circuit has reached the opposite conclusion. The rule in that circuit, where many of the cases arise, appears to be that the general employer who maintains some control over the seaman will be treated as the seaman's Jones Act employer without more, but the seaman also may prove that some other person had sufficient control over him or her, or sufficient connexity with his or her employment, to be treated as an additional employer for the purposes of the Act. *Guidry v. South Louisiana Contractors, Inc., supra.*

The Jones Act applies only if the employee is injured (or killed), *see* Chapter XIV, during the course of his employment. A seaman who is "in the service of the ship" for the purposes of maintenance and cure probably also will be "in the course of his or her employment" for Jones Act purposes, but the two concepts are not necessarily identical. A seaman who is assigned temporarily to shoreside employment is "in the course of his or her employment" with the employer for Jones Act purposes, but for maintenance and cure purposes may not be "in the service of the ship" as to which he or she is a seaman.

Negligence chargeable to the employer is the gravamen of a Jones Act claim. As at common law, Jones Act negligence is the failure to exercise reasonable care under the circumstances. *Gautreaux v. Scurlock Marine, Inc.*, 107 F.3d 331 (5th Cir. 1997). The employer may be personally negligent, as when he or she fails to furnish the seaman with a safe place to work. *See, e.g., Colburn v. Bunge Towing, Inc.*, 883 F.2d 372 (5th Cir. 1989). If the seaman's employer is the operator of the vessel and the seaman is working aboard the vessel, the duty to furnish a safe place to work may be subsumed into the employer-operator's absolute duty to furnish a seaworthy vessel, including the means of ingress and egress. If the seaman is working off the vessel, or the employer is not the operator of the vessel, the non-delegable duty to furnish a safe place to work imposed by the Jones Act becomes significant. In such situations, the employer's duty to furnish a safe place for his or her employee to work probably extends to those premises over which the employer has control, and to those dangerous conditions of which the employer is aware. *Verrett v. McDonough Marine Service*, 705 F.2d 1437 (5th Cir. 1983); *Martin v. Walk, Haydel & Associates, Inc.*, 742 F.2d 246 (5th Cir. 1984).

Recovery against the Jones Act employer also may be premised upon the violation of a safety statute. In *Kernan v. American Dredging Co.*, 355 U.S. 426 (1958), the Supreme Court ruled that violation of a statute by a Jones Act employer constitutes negligence *per se* if the violation contributes in fact to the injury, even though the statute was not designed to prevent that harm to that victim. Violation of an OSHA regulation may not be negligence *per se*. *Jones v. Spentonbush–Red Star Co.*, 155 F.3d 587 (2d Cir. 1998). Several courts have held that the *Pennsylvania* rule, see Chapter XII, *infra*, (which shifts the burden of proof to a vessel that has violated a navigational rule and been involved in a collision) may *not* apply in a Jones Act case. *Wills v. Amerada Hess Corp.*, 379 F.3d 32 (2d Cir. 2004); *Poulis–Minott v. Smith*, 388 F.3d 354 (1st Cir. 2004).

The most common Jones Act claim is one in which the employer is charged with the negligence of an employee that injures a co-employee. The Jones Act makes the employer liable for the negligence of any of its "officers, agents or employees," but the negligence must be within the course and scope of the offending employee's employment. This requirement may be satisfied if the act of the negligent employee was in furtherance of, or in an attempt to further, the employer's business.

A Jones Act defendant may seek to avoid liability by establishing that the tortfeasor is an independent contractor, or an employee of an independent contractor. The relevant inquiry in making such a determination under the Jones Act is the same as that at common law generally, i.e., did the defendant retain control over the manner in which the work was done by the tortfeasor? Even if the tortfeasor is an independent contractor, or the employee of an independent contractor, the Jones Act employer nevertheless may be liable for the negligence, either because (1) the tortfeasor became the employer's "borrowed servant," or (2) because the activity in which the tortfeasor was engaged was a "vital part" of the employer's operations. This "vital part" exception springs from the Supreme Court's ruling in *Hopson v. Texaco*, 383 U.S. 262 (1966) that a Jones Act employer may not delegate to a third person, and thus escape responsibility for, any act which is "a vital part of the ship's total operations." In *Hopson* the vessel owner engaged a taxi to carry seamen to a hospital to obtain medical services; seamen subsequently were injured in an accident caused by the negligence of the taxi driver. Because transporting the seamen to the medical facility met the "vital part" test, the fact that the taxi driver was an independent contractor did not relieve the vessel owner of liability for the taxi driver's negligence in the claim by the injured seamen. The *Hopson* doctrine frequently is overlooked or ignored by court and counsel or restricted in its application. *See, e.g., Craig v. Atlantic Richfield Co.*, 19 F.3d 472 (9th Cir. 1994).

The Jones Act employer owes a "duty to rescue" a seaman who has jumped or fallen overboard without antecedent employer negligence. If the seaman's presence in the water is discernable, the ship's officers must use every reasonable means to retrieve him. If the seaman apparently is overboard, but his presence or location in the water is not readily discernable from the vessel, the officers are required to search the area traversed by the ship so long as it is possible that the seaman remains alive in the water. The seaman's survivors are afforded a rebuttable presumption that any breach of the duty to rescue was a cause-in-fact of the seaman's death by drowning. *Reyes v. Vantage S.S. Co., Inc.*, 609 F.2d 140 (5th Cir. 1980).

The employer also may be negligent in failing to provide adequate medical care, although the same damages for such conduct may be recoverable through maintenance and cure or may overlap with the benefits recoverable under maintenance and cure.

Courts frequently stated that a Jones Act employer owes a high duty of care for the safety of its seamen. *See, e.g., Litherland v. Petrolane Offshore Constr. Serv., Inc.*, 546 F.2d 129 (5th Cir. 1977).

However, in *Gautreaux v. Scurlock Marine, Inc.*, 107 F.3d 331 (5th Cir. 1997), the appellate court reviewed the origin of the "high duty" rule and observed in dicta that the employer owes only the duty to exercise ordinary care under the circumstances. The court explained that the "high duty of care" rule that it and other courts apparently had embraced arose out of language in FELA cases concerning the burden of proof for causation, and not the duty owed to the employee. *Compare Williams v. Long Island Railroad Co.*, 196 F.3d 402 (2d Cir. 1999).

A seaman may recover for negligent infliction of emotional distress if the plaintiff was either in the "zone of danger" or suffered some "impact." *Gottshall*, page 175 *supra*. However, fear of developing a disease from exposure to a toxic substance is not compensable until the worker has manifested some symptom of the disease. *Metro–North Commuter Ry.*, page 176, *supra*, but if the worker has some disease, such as asbestosis caused by exposure, damages for fear of developing cancer may be recoverable. *Norfolk & Western Rwy. Co. v. Ayers*, 538 U.S. 135 (2003). *See also, West v. Midland Enterprises, Inc.*, 227 F.3d 613 (6th Cir. 2000) (emotional distress may be the basis for a maintenance and cure action even if not recoverable under the Jones Act). It is unclear if medical monitoring damages may be recovered under the Jones Act. *See Metro–North Commuter Rwy.*, page 176, *supra*; *In re Marine Asbestos Cases*, 265 F.3d 861 (9th Cir. 2001).

The FELA provision on causation (employer is responsible for injuries caused "in whole or in part" by its negligence) applies to Jones Act cases *Rogers v. Missouri Pacific Rwy. Co.*, 352 U.S. 521 (1957). Consequently the Jones Act plaintiff's burden of proof on causation is "featherweight," and thus liability will exist where the employer's negligence contributed "in the slightest" to the seaman's injury. *See Poulis–Minott v. Smith*, 388 F.3d 354 (1st Cir. 2004).

Consistently with general maritime tort law, a negligent Jones Act employer is subject to joint and several liability with other tortfeasors. *Simeon v. T. Smith & Son, Inc.*, 852 F.2d 1421 (5th Cir. 1988).

The successful plaintiff in a Jones Act claim may recover standard tort damages. The interplay of Jones Act damages and benefits under maintenance and cure is discussed in the section on unseaworthiness.

There is a three-year statute of limitations on Jones Act claims. 45 U.S.C.A. § 56; *see also* 46 U.S.C.A. § 30106. However, the employer may be estopped from asserting the defense if it has misled the seaman into withholding suit, by conduct such as active misrepresentation of the seaman's rights, or a promise to pay or settle the claim if the seaman foregoes legal action.

The seaman's contributory negligence reduces (through "pure" comparative negligence) but does not bar recovery in a Jones Act case. 45 U.S.C.A. § 53. The seaman's substandard conduct may not reduce his or her recovery if the injury was caused in part by the employer's violation of a statute enacted for the safety of employees. 45 U.S.C.A. § 53; *Roy Crook & Sons, Inc. v. Allen*, 778 F.2d 1037 (5th Cir.1985). An OSHA regulation may not be a safety statute for this purpose. *Jones v. Spentonbush–Red Star Co.*, 155 F.3d 587 (2d Cir. 1998). In a case brought under FELA, which applies to a seaman's Jones Act claim, *Norfolk Southern Rwy. Co. v. Sorrell*, 549 U.S. 158 (2007), the Supreme Court held that the same standard of causation applies when assessing the negligence of the employer and the contributory negligence of the employee. In deciding the question, the Court expressly declined to revisit prior case law addressing the "slight" standard of causation set forth in *Rogers*, page 254, *supra*.

Many courts had held that the seaman's duty to protect himself or herself was "slight." However, the precise holding of *Gautreaux*, page 249, *supra*, is that the employee owes a duty to exercise reasonable care for his safety under the circumstances, which include his reliance on his employer to provide a safe work environment and his own experience, training or education. A seaman may not be held contributorily negligent for carrying out an order that results in injury even if the seaman recognizes a possible danger and does not delay to consider a safer alternative. *Simeonoff v. Hiner*, 249 F.3d 883 (9th Cir. 2001).

Express assumption of the risk should not affect a seaman's recovery in a Jones Act case; 45 U.S.C.A.

§ 55 provides that "[a]ny contract ... the purpose or intent of which shall be to enable any common carrier to exempt itself from any liability created by this chapter, shall to that extent be void." *See, e.g., Miles v. American Seafoods Co.*, 197 F.3d 1032 (9th Cir. 1999) (employer may not by language in a settlement agreement insulate itself from liability for future injury to the same part of the employee's body caused by a subsequent event).

Where the assumption of risk is implied from the seaman's conduct, the answer is less clear. Section 54 provides that an employee covered by the provisions of the FELA "shall not be held to have assumed the risks of his employment," but section 53 provides that "the fact that the employee may have been guilty of contributory negligence shall not bar recovery, but the damages shall be diminished...." Where conduct that constitutes implied assumption of risk also constitutes contributory negligence, courts are faced that a dilemma: should they apply the statutory prohibition against assumption of risk and bar the jury from consideration of the seaman's conduct, or should they apply comparative negligence and allow the jury to reduce the damages because of such conduct? Some courts have taken the latter course. Others, however, have refused to diminish a seaman's recovery for his or her conduct that constitutes both assumption of risk and contributory negligence. Under this latter approach, the seaman's contributory negligence does not reduce recovery if his or her substandard conduct consists solely of assuming the risk, such as where the seaman realizes that the job is dangerous but does it anyway. However, if the seaman elects to do the job in an unsafe manner when a safe way is readily available, or if the seaman fails to protest the dangerous nature of the work when such protest may have avoided the danger, the seaman may be guilty of contributory negligence that is independent of assumption of the risk, and reduction for that conduct through comparative negligence may be permitted. The better rule probably is that implied assumption of the risk should reduce plaintiff's recovery.

An interesting defense to Jones Act (and unseaworthiness) claims is the "primary duty" rule illustrated by the case of *Walker v. Lykes Bros. S.S. Co.*, 193 F.2d 772 (2d Cir. 1952). In *Walker*, the ship's master was injured when struck by a drawer of a steel filing cabinet; the drawer's latch apparently had been defective when the master took command of the vessel five months earlier. The trial judge refused to direct a verdict for the shipowner but instructed the jury that if the shipowner was negligent, the master's recovery should be reduced by his contributory negligence. Reversing a jury verdict for the master, the Second Circuit observed that:

> We shall therefore accept the conventional rubric and think of contributory negligence as the breach of a duty to the wrongdoer. The important thing in situations like that at bar is to distinguish between such a duty, which the law imposes upon the injured person, regardless of any

conscious assumption of a duty towards the wrongdoer, *and a duty which the injured person has consciously assumed as a term of his employment.* By 'contributory negligence' which results in no more than reducing the amount of an employee's recovery, the [Jones] Act means the first; *the second is a bar to any recovery.* . . . In the case at bar, since the plaintiff was master of the ship, he fell within this doctrine, because it is well settled that the 'duty of the master in the case of damage to the ship is to do all that can be done towards bringing the adventure to a successful termination; to repair the ship, if there be a reasonable prospect of doing so at an expense not ruinous;' . . . . *Thus, if the plaintiff failed to repair the catches, although he was able to do so, his failure was not only 'contributory negligence' in the first sense, but also a breach of his duty to the defendant which barred his recovery absolutely.*

Walker, 193 F.2d 772, 773–774 (emphasis added) (footnotes omitted).

The "primary duty" rule has been rejected by some courts and limited by others. *See, e.g., Bernard v. Maersk Lines, Ltd.*, 22 F.3d 903 (9th Cir. 1994). It may be limited to those situations in which the seaman either created the condition or had actual knowledge of it before the accident. *See, e.g., Joia v. Jo–Ja Service Corp.*, 817 F.2d 908 (1st Cir. 1987), and *Villers Seafood Co. v. Vest*, 813 F.2d 339 (11th Cir. 1987). The doctrine continues to endure however. *See, e.g., Northern Queen, Inc. v. Kinnear*, 298 F.3d 1090 (9th Cir. 2002); *Wilson v. Maritime*

Overseas Corp., 150 F.3d 1 (1st Cir. 1998). However, most of the cases where the doctrine is applied involve masters, officers, chief mates, or similar management level employees of the vessel. *See, e.g., Park v. Stockstill Boat Rentals, Inc.*, 492 F.3d 600 (5th Cir. 2007). Application of the "primary duty" doctrine to less sophisticated seamen would undercut the maritime policy of protecting them from their foibles, a policy which is illustrated by the law's treatment of the seaman's contributory negligence and assumption of the risk.

A claim under the Jones Act may be brought as an admiralty claim in federal court or in state court, and, because the claim arises under an act of Congress, it also may be brought as a law claim in federal court. A Jones Act claim brought in state court may not be removed to federal court. 28 U.S.C.A. § 1445(a). An unseaworthiness claim may be removed to the law "side" if diversity jurisdiction is present. (*See* Chapter XIX). However, where the unseaworthiness and Jones Act claims arise out of the same injury and occurrence and are joined in state court, the unseaworthiness claim becomes nonremovable because it is not a "separate and independent" claim within the meaning of 28 U.S.C.A. § 1441(c). *Lirette v. N.L. Sperry Sun, Inc.*, 810 F.2d 533 (5th Cir. 1987). The same result has been reached when maintenance and cure and Jones Act claims arising out of the same injury and occurrence are joined in state court, but there is some dissent. *Compare Addison v. Gulf Coast Contracting Services, Inc.*, 744 F.2d 494 (5th Cir. 1984)

and Sawyer v. Federal Barge Lines, Inc., 510
F.Supp. 39 (S.D.Ill. 1981).

A seaman may prosecute a Jones Act claim in
federal court without prepayment of costs, pursuant
to a statute, 28 U.S.C.A. § 1916, which provides for
prosecution without advance payment of costs of
suits by seamen "for wages or salvage or the enforcement of laws enacted for their health or safety." A claim under the Jones Act is not secured by a
lien on the vessel, even though the employer is the
vessel's operator. *Plamals v. The Pinar Del Rio*, 277
U.S. 151 (1928). The result is unfortunate, but
appears too well settled for judicial change.

Jones Act and unseaworthiness claims frequently
are tried together and submitted to a jury for decision by special verdict, under which the jury must
give affirmative or negative answers to questions
such as: (1) was the defendant negligent, (2) was
that negligence the cause of plaintiff's injury, (3)
was the vessel unseaworthy, and (4) was that unseaworthiness the cause of the plaintiff's injury? A
jury may give conflicting answers to these questions, such as where the only basis for a finding of
employer negligence is the maintenance of a shipboard condition that existed for a substantial period
of time, and the jury concludes that the defendant,
who is both employer and vessel operator, was
negligent, but that the vessel was not unseaworthy.
In such a case, the court must attempt to reconcile
the verdict; if it cannot, it must grant a new trial.

Another problem arising out of a joint jury trial of unseaworthiness and Jones Act claims is the seaman's right to pre-judgment interest. Such interest is available almost as a matter of course in general maritime law claims (including unseaworthiness), whether the claims are tried to a judge or to a jury. *See* Chapter XI. When a Jones Act claim is tried to a judge, pre-judgment interest is discretionary; when it is tried to a jury, the claimant is not entitled to pre-judgment interest. The rationale for denial of pre-judgment interest in a jury trial probably is the assumption that in assessing damages the jury will consider the delay that elapsed between injury and trial. One solution sometimes utilized is that when Jones Act and unseaworthiness claims are tried together to a jury, pre-judgment interest may be awarded only on that part of the damages that is attributable solely to unseaworthiness. The practical effect of the rule is that in most cases a seaman must choose between a jury trial and pre-judgment interest.

6.   Choice of Law in Seamen's Claims

The employer's liability under the Jones Act, and the absolute duty imposed upon a vessel operator by American maritime law to furnish his seamen with a seaworthy vessel, are among the most liberal theories of recovery for maritime personal injuries. Thus frequently, a foreign seaman whose shipboard injury has some connection with the United States may institute his action in an American court and ask that American law be applied to the controversy. If the suit is brought in an American court exercising admiralty jurisdiction, and jurisdiction over the person of the defendant can be obtained, the issues become choice of law and forum non conveniens. If American law applies, the court ordinarily will retain jurisdiction, but if foreign law applies, the court may dismiss under forum non. This has led to a two-step analysis in which the court first determines the applicable law and then considers *forum non* in the light of that determination. *See, e.g., Neely v. Club Med Management Services, Inc.*, 63 F.3d 166 (3d Cir. 1995).

The Supreme Court has spoken several times to the issue of when the American maritime remedies apply to a seaman whose work-related injury has foreign connections. The cases are *Hellenic Lines Ltd. v. Rhoditis*, 398 U.S. 306 (1970), *Romero v. International Terminal Operating Co.*, 358 U.S. 354 (1959) and *Lauritzen v. Larsen*, 345 U.S. 571 (1953). The general rule gleaned from these cases probably is that if the seaman is an American citizen or resident, or in a "bluewater" seaman's case if the vessel is an American flag vessel or is owned by an American citizen or a shipowner whose "base of operations" is in the United States, American maritime law should apply and the court should take jurisdiction. If that rule existed, both Congress and the lower courts have eroded it. In 1982, Congress approved Public Law 97–389, now 46 U.S.C.A. § 30105(b), providing that

[A] civil action for maintenance and cure or for damages for personal injury or death may not be brought under a maritime law of the United States if—

(1) the individual suffering the injury or death was not a citizen or permanent resident alien of the United States at the time of the incident giving rise to the action;

(2) the incident occurred in the territorial waters or waters overlaying the continental shelf of a country other than the United States; and

(3) the individual suffering the injury or death was employed at the time of the incident by a person engaged in the exploration, development, or production of offshore mineral or energy resources, including drilling, mapping, surveying, diving, pipelaying, maintaining, repairing, constructing, or transporting supplies, equipment, or personnel, but not including transporting those resources by a vessel constructed or adapted primarily to carry oil in bulk in the cargo spaces.

This statutory limitation on the use of the American law does not apply if the person bringing the action establishes that no remedy is available to him under the laws of the nation asserting jurisdiction over the area where the incident occurred, or under the laws of the nation with which the victim maintains citizenship or residency. Title 46 U.S.C.A. section 30105(c). Literally, the statute seems to bar only claims based on American law and not to bar the prosecution of foreign law claims in American courts, even though that result may seem somewhat illogical.

The Congressional act makes obvious inroads on the *Rhoditis–Romero–Lauritzen* doctrine, such as where the vessel is an American flag vessel and its owner is American, but the injured seaman is a foreign national. Further erosion of the doctrine has come from lower court decisions which reflect a general shift from the more rigid *Rhoditis–Romero–Lauritzen* formula to the more flexible general choice-of-law approach, i.e., a consideration of the interests and policies of the sovereigns involved. *See, e.g., Chiazor v. Transworld Drilling Co., Ltd.*, 648 F.2d 1015 (5th Cir. 1981); *Koke v. Phillips Petroleum Co.*, 730 F.2d 211 (5th Cir. 1984); *Neely v. Club Med Management Services, Inc.*, page 262, *supra*.

When foreign law applies, dismissal is not automatic; the court must apply forum non conveniens principles to determine whether jurisdiction should be maintained and foreign law applied. The key case is *Piper Aircraft Co. v. Reyno*, 454 U.S. 235 (1981), an aircraft case in which the Supreme Court held that dismissal of an action because of forum non conveniens was not automatically barred solely because the law of the alternative forum was less favorable to the plaintiff than the law of the American forum which he had selected. That same rule probably applies in a maritime claim; indeed, the decision of the Supreme Court in *Canada Malting Co. v. Paterson S.S., Ltd.*, 285 U.S. 413 (1932), supports that view. However, litigation delay may render an alternative forum so "clearly unsatisfactory" as to be inadequate, thus precluding forum non conveniens. *Bhatnagar v. Surrendra Overseas Ltd.*, 52 F.3d 1220 (3d Cir. 1995).

Where dismissal through forum non conveniens is proper, the court may condition dismissal upon concessions by the defendant that will assure that the plaintiff has the opportunity to litigate effectively in the foreign forum. These concessions may be that defendant (1) will not object to the jurisdiction of the foreign forum, (2) will waive in the foreign forum any statute of limitation defense maturing after the commencement of the action in the American court, (3) will make available in the foreign forum all relevant witnesses and evidence within his control, and (4) will satisfy any final judgment rendered in the foreign forum.

The United States Supreme Court has ruled that in cases filed in state court under the Jones Act and the "saving to suitors" clause, federal law does not pre-empt application of the state law's doctrine of forum non conveniens. *American Dredging Co. v. Miller*, 510 U.S. 443 (1994). Thus a foreign claimant often may assure litigation in an American forum by initially selecting the right state court. If the claimant first goes to a federal forum and is dismissed on forum non, may he then relitigate the forum non issue in a state court? The answer is not clear. *Compare Chick Kam Choo v. Exxon Corp.*, 486 U.S. 140 (1988), and *American Dredging Co. v. Miller, supra.*

One increasingly common issue in foreign seaman's claims is whether foreign choice of law/choice of forum clauses are enforceable. One circuit has held that forum selection clauses are presumptively enforceable, absent a strong showing that they are unfair or unreasonable. *Marinechance Shipping, Ltd. v. Sebastian*, 143 F.3d 216 (5th Cir. 1998).

C. MARITIME WORKERS

1. Introduction

The employee's difficulty in recovering against the employer for work-related injuries before the start of the twentieth century is well known. As society perceived a need to impose the cost of a work-related injury upon the industry that generated it, lawmakers responded by adopting worker's compensation statutes. For maritime employees who qualified as seamen, Congress made a different choice. Through the Jones Act, it incorporated the FELA into maritime law and thus provided the seaman with a negligence action against his employer in which neither the "fellow servant" rule, contributory negligence, nor assumption of risk barred recovery.

However, many persons engaged in maritime-related employment are not seamen. Among them are the longshoremen, shipbuilders, shiprepairers, and others whose work on or near navigable waters facilitates the transportation of goods and passengers over water. Congress initially assumed that these employees would be covered by state worker's compensation laws and made no provision for their claims against their employers. That assumption proved false. In 1917, in the celebrated case of *Southern Pacific Co. v. Jensen*, 244 U.S. 205 (1917), the U.S. Supreme Court ruled that if a longshoreman's injury or death occurred on navigable waters, state worker's compensation law could not apply. The decision left maritime workers, other than seamen, without an adequate remedy against their employers for work-related injuries occurring on water. Because such workers usually lacked a sufficient relationship with a vessel, they could not qualify as seamen and pursue a remedy under the Jones Act. If injured on land, they could recover state worker's compensation benefits. If injured on water, however, their claims against their employers were subject to the traditional common-law barriers to recovery, such as contributory negligence and the fellow servant rule.

Congress' first reaction was to extend state worker's compensation laws to maritime workers injured on navigable waters. A 1917 act amended what is now 28 U.S.C.A. § 1333 to reserve to claimants "the rights and remedies under the workmen's compensation law of any state;" however, this was struck down by the Supreme Court as an unconstitutional delegation of the federal legislative power, a novel and seldom used basis for decision. *Knickerbocker Ice Co. v. Stewart*, 253 U.S. 149 (1920). Subsequently, Congress made another attempt to apply state worker's compensation laws to the non-seaman injured on water, but that act also was declared unconstitutional. *State of Washington v. W. C Dawson & Co.*, 264 U.S. 219 (1924).

Other decisions by the Supreme Court did afford some relief to the maritime worker. In *Grant Smith–Porter Ship Co. v. Rohde*, 257 U.S. 469 (1922), the Court held that some injuries to maritime workers on navigable waters, although "maritime," were sufficiently "local" in nature to permit application of state worker's compensation laws. Then in 1926, in *International Stevedoring Co. v. Haverty*, 272 U.S. 50 (1926), the Court held that a maritime worker aboard a vessel and engaged in work normally done by a member of the crew could be treated as a seaman for Jones Act purposes.

In the following year, Congress finally responded directly to the problem by adopting the Longshoremen's (now Longshore) and Harbor Worker's Compensation Act (LHWCA, 33 U.S.C.A. § 901 et seq.), a comprehensive worker's compensation scheme for maritime workers who do not qualify as seamen. The Act, patterned after the New York compensation statute, provides benefits for disability caused by a work-related injury, without regard to employer fault. The system is administered through the Department of Labor, with subsequent review by the federal courts of appeal.

The determination of which work-related injuries are covered by the Act has required much judicial effort. In adopting the LHWCA, Congress sought to provide compensation for worker injuries which, because of *Jensen,* were not covered by either the Jones Act or state worker's compensation. Accordingly, the only requirements for coverage should have been that (1) claimant was not a seaman, and (2) he or she sustained a work-related injury on navigable waters. The original LHWCA, however, provided coverage for worker injuries "occurring upon the navigable waters of the United States ... *if recovery ... through workmen's compensation proceedings may not validly be provided by State law."* 33 U.S.C.A. § 903.... (emphasis supplied). The effect of that language was to make the "maritime but local" exception developed in *Grant Smith–Porter Ship Co.* and other decisions a jurisdictional limitation upon application of the LHWCA; if an injury occurring on navigable waters was "maritime but local," "recovery ... through workmen's compensation proceedings" could "be provided by state law," and thus the employee could not recover under the LHWCA. As a result, many non-seaman workers injured on navigable waters ran the risk of pursuing the wrong remedy, only to learn about their error at the conclusion of lengthy and expensive litigation and at a time when a statute of limitations barred their pursuit of the proper remedy.

The problem was somewhat alleviated by the development of the "twilight zone." The Supreme Court, in *Davis v. Department of Labor and Industries of Washington*, 317 U.S. 249 (1942), ruled that if the injury occurred on navigable waters but arguably fell within the "maritime but local" exception, the claimant's choice of federal or state remedy should be upheld. As could be expected, that "exception to the exception" generated its own share of judicial fodder. Two decades later, the Supreme Court, in *Calbeck v. Travelers Insurance Co.*, 370 U.S. 114 (1962), remedied the situation by holding that the language of the 1927 Act limiting coverage to injuries in which recovery could not be provided by state law did not prevent LHWCA coverage of all work-related injuries occurring on navigable waters.

The *Calbeck* decision moved the coverage of the LHWCA firmly to the water's edge, but the Court refused to move it further inland. In *Nacirema Operating Co. v. Johnson*, 396 U.S. 212 (1969), the Court rejected an attempt to extend LHWCA coverage to dockside injuries. Since some state compensation statutes afforded compensation benefits which were substantially less than those provided by the LHWCA, the *Jensen* hiatus continued in degree, if not in kind.

By 1972, the parties most affected by the LHWCA were in the mood for a revision of the Act. The shipowner wanted relief from the *Sieracki* doctrine, which made him liable without fault for injuries to maritime workers caused by his ship's unseaworthy conditions, which often were created by the maritime workers. The maritime employer, who was bearing much of the brunt of the *Sieracki* doctrine through the judicially imposed implied warranty of workmanlike performance, *see* Chapter XVII, wanted immunity from indemnity claims arising out of injuries to his employees. The maritime employee who was losing the *Sieracki* claim wanted increased benefits and the extension of coverage to work-related injuries occurring on piers, docks, and other inland harbor areas. In 1972 Congress accommodated all three interests—shipowner, maritime employer, and maritime employee—with a comprehensive revision of the LHWCA.

Twelve years later, Congress made another major revision of the LHWCA. The 1984 amendments withdrew LHWCA coverage from many harbor and dock workers, altered the rights of employer and employee in claims against third-party tortfeasors, and made a number of procedural changes in the administration of the LHWCA. It also changed the name to the Longshore and Harbor Workers' Compensation Act. 33 U.S.C.A. § 901 (1984). On the following pages, we discuss the LHWCA in light of the 1972 and 1984 amendments and the judicial interpretations of the original act and the amendments.

It should also be noted that in 2009 additional amendments to the LHWCA were proposed to improve the compensation system, but as of the publication of this edition of the *Nutshell* they had not passed.

2. Longshore and Harbor Workers' Compensation Act: Coverage and Benefits

a. *Introduction*

Coverage under the LHWCA has been the subject of much legislative and judicial attention. Initially, an employee was covered by the LHWCA if injured on actual navigable waters and if the employer was a covered employer. An employer was covered if one of its employees (the claimant employee or some other employee) was engaged in maritime employment. After the 1972 amendments, an "employee" of an "employer" is covered if the injury occurs on "the navigable waters of the United States." "Employer" is defined as one "any of whose employees are employed in maritime employment, in whole or in part upon the navigable waters of the United States," as defined in section 903. 33 U.S.C.A. § 902(4). An "employee" is defined as "any person engaged in maritime employment, including any longshoreman or other person engaged in longshoring operations, and any harborworker including a ship repairman, shipbuilder, and shipbreaker." 33 U.S.C.A. § 902(3). However, the 1984 amendments exclude from this "status" aspect of coverage certain workers who otherwise qualify as "engaged in maritime employment" under the 1972 amendments. "Navigable waters of the United States" includes "any adjoining pier, wharf, dry dock, terminal, building way, marine railway, or other adjoining area customarily used by an employer in loading, unloading, repairing, or building a vessel." 33 U.S.C.A. § 903(a). However, the 1984 amendments deny "status" to workers at certain shipbuilding facilities that might otherwise meet the "navigable waters" definition in the 1972 amendments.

Despite the confusion produced by the amendments, the basic pattern for coverage provided by the 1972 amendments remains unchanged. The essentials for coverage by the LHWCA are (1) a covered employer, and (2) an injured employee who meets both the "status" requirement of section 902(3) and the "situs" requirement of section 903.

b. *Covered Employer*

An employer probably is covered by the LHWCA if his injured employee is a covered employee. To qualify as an "employee," the claimant must be engaged in maritime employment. Thus if the claimant is covered, his employer is one "any of whose employees are employed in maritime employment," and thus is an "employer" under section 902(4). Attempts to limit an "employer" within the coverage of the Act to one who has at least one employee actually working on navigable waters have failed. One appellate court has observed that the "employer" status requirement in the Act has been rendered "largely tautological" by the 1972 amendments, and that when there is a determination that the claimant is a "maritime employee" under section 902(3), it "necessarily follows that ... his employer ... is a statutory 'employer' within in the meaning of the Act." *Hullinghorst Industries, Inc. v. Carroll*, 650 F.2d 750 (5th Cir. 1981). There is some dicta arguably to the contrary, however. In *Director v. Perini North River Associates*, 459 U.S. 297 (1983), the Court observed that

> when a worker is injured on the actual navigable waters in the course of his employment on those waters, he satisfies the status requirement ... and is covered under the LHWCA, *providing of course, that he is the employee of a statutory 'employer,'* and is not excluded by any other provision of the Act.

(emphasis added). However, *Perini* involved the issue of whether the 1972 amendments denied coverage to those who were covered before 1972, and perhaps the troublesome language quoted above should be read in that context, i.e, the Court was dealing with a pre–1972 coverage question in the guise of interpreting the post–1972 LHWCA.

Alternatively, one could persuasively argue that an employer cannot be expected to maintain insurance coverage for LHWCA benefits unless it can foresee the need for it. If the employer knows or should have anticipated that the injured employee would be covered by the LHWCA, the employer will have had a fair opportunity to obtain insurance protection. However, if the employer should not have anticipated that the injured employee will be covered by the Act, it should not be expected to obtain LHWCA coverage unless it has some other employee who is subject to the Act. In *Director v. Perini North River Associates*, the Supreme Court may have anticipated this kind of situation in which it may be patently unfair to impose LHWCA liability upon an employer.

c. The Covered Employee: Status

If the employer qualifies as an "employer" under the LHWCA, the employee is entitled to benefits if he or she is an "employee" within the meaning of the Act. To qualify as a covered employee, the worker must have both "status"—the nature of his work must be maritime—and "situs"—his injury must occur within a designated geographical area. *Northeast Marine Terminal Co. v. Caputo*, 432 U.S. 249 (1977).

A person has "status" if he or she is "engaged in maritime employment." 33 U.S.C.A. § 902(3). Several types of employment—longshoreman, longshoring, harbor worker, shipbuilder, ship repairer, and shipbreaker—are covered because they are specifically enumerated in section 902(3). Is this statutory listing exclusive, or only illustrative? There are conflicting indications from the Supreme Court. In *Northeast Marine Terminal Co., Inc. v. Caputo, supra,* the Court stated that the listings were illustrative. A later case, *Herb's Welding, Inc. v. Gray*, 470 U.S. 414 (1985), suggested that "status" extends only to those who are engaged in the loading, unloading, construction or repair of ships. Some lower courts, motivated by *Caputo*, have fashioned a general definition of "maritime employment" and have identified some employments, other than those specifically named in Section 902(3), which fall within that broad, general definition of "status." *See, e.g., Sidwell v. Virginia Intern. Terminals, Inc.*, 372 F.3d 238 (4th Cir. 2004); *Cunningham v. Di-*

rector, Office of Workers' Compensation Programs, 377 F.3d 98 (1st Cir. 2004).

Three other Supreme Court pronouncements bear directly on the determination of "status." In *P.C. Pfeiffer Co. v. Ford*, 444 U.S. 69 (1979), the Court rejected the argument that a person is "engaged in maritime employment" only if he is working, or may be assigned to work, over actual navigable waters, i.e., not including the adjoining shoreside areas which were added to the statutory definition of "navigable waters" by the 1972 amendments. In *Chesapeake and Ohio Railway Co. v. Schwalb*, 493 U.S. 40 (1989), the Court ruled that an employee injured while maintaining or repairing equipment essential to the loading or unloading process is "engaged in maritime employment" for the purposes of LHWCA coverage. However, in neither case did the Court specify that a worker is not engaged in maritime employment unless he is participating in the loading or unloading process.

In the third case, *Director v. Perini North River Associates, supra*, the Court ruled that if a worker is injured while performing his job upon "actual navigable waters," he is "engaged in maritime employment" and within the coverage of the Act. The Court's logic was that (1) these workers would have been covered by the LHWCA before the 1972 amendments; (2) the Court was "unable to find any Congressional intent to withdraw coverage of the [Act] from those workers injured on navigable waters in the course of their employment, and who would have been covered by the Act before 1972";

(3) *a fortiori,* these workers remain covered. The Court emphasized that it was not abandoning the "status" requirement for workers injured on "actual navigable waters." Thus mere injury on water may not suffice, such as where the worker is only "transiently or fortuitously" upon navigable waters at the time of injury. *Director v. Perini North River Associates, supra.* One prestigious court has held that a worker who is injured on navigable waters is only "transiently or fortuitously" on the water and not thereby a maritime employee unless he performs a "not insubstantial" amount of his work on navigable waters. *Bienvenu v. Texaco, Inc.,* 164 F.3d 901 (5th Cir. 1999).

One other piece in the LHWCA "status" puzzle is the 1984 amendments, which provide that certain workers whose employment otherwise might give them "status" are not covered by the LHWCA if they are covered by state worker's compensation. The excluded workers are those employed:

(1) exclusively to perform office, clerical, secretarial, security or data processing work;

(2) by a club, camp, recreational operation [*see Boomtown Belle Casino v. Bazor,* 313 F.3d 300 (5th Cir. 2002) (floating casino's chief engineer)], restaurant, museum or retail outlet;

(3) by a marina and not engaged in construction, replacement or expansion of the marina;

(4) by suppliers, transporters or vendors, [*See Daul v. Petroleum Communications, Inc.,* 196 F.3d 611 (5th Cir. 1999)] if such individuals are

temporarily on a covered situs and are not engaged in work normally done by the covered employer;

(5) as aquaculture workers [*See Alcala v. Director*, 141 F.3d 942 (9th Cir. 1998)];

(6) to build or repair recreational vessels under 65 feet in length.

33 U.S.C.A. § 902(3)(A)–(F).

Another 1984 amendment to 33 U.S.C.A. § 903 excludes from LHWCA coverage workers who are employed at a facility certified by the Secretary of Labor as exclusively engaged in building or repairing small vessels (defined as commercial barges under 900 lightship displacement tons, commercial tugboats, crewboats, fishing vessels and other work vessels under 1,600 gross tons), unless (1) the injury occurs on navigable waters or on an adjoining pier, wharf, dock, or facility over land for launching, hauling, listing or drydocking vessels; or (2) the facility receives federal maritime subsidies; or (3) the employee is not entitled to state worker's compensation coverage. 33 U.S.C.A. § 903(d).

The unclear state of the present law may be summarized in this manner:

1. A worker has "status" if he is injured while performing his job on actual navigable waters, i.e., if he meets the *Director v. Perini North River Associates* test, *unless* he is excluded by the 1984 amendments to sections 902(3) and 903 of the LHWCA. Arguably, the worker must spend more

than an insubstantial amount of time working on the water.

2.   A worker who does not meet the *Director v. Perini North River Associates* test (a) has status if "engaged in maritime employment," which includes, but is not limited to, loading; unloading; building and repairing vessels, i.e., if the worker falls within the broad test supported by the Court's decision in *Caputo* and is not excluded by the 1984 amendments to sections 902(3) and 903, *or* (b) has "status" *only* if he is engaged in an integral part of the loading, unloading, building or repairing of vessels, and is not excluded by the 1984 amendments to sections 902(3) and 903.

Other significant issues remain. One issue is whether "maritime employment" encompasses occupations other than those enumerated in Section 902(3), i.e., loading, unloading, building and repairing vessels. If it does, what is the test for such employment? Is it the general "maritime flavor" test, i.e., the employment bears a realistically significant relationship to traditional maritime activities?

Another important issue is the identification of the activities that constitute "essential elements" of the loading, unloading, repairing or building of vessels. The loading and unloading of containers, and the repair of equipment used in the loading, unloading, building and repair process, should qualify. *See, e.g.*, *Chesapeake and Ohio Railway Co. v. Schwalb*, *supra*.

The employee need not be engaged in maritime employment at the time of injury if he or she spends "at least some of [his or her] time in indisputably longshoring operations." *Northeast Marine Terminal Co. v. Caputo*, 432 U.S. 249 (1977). How much is "some"? It may be as little as a "substantial portion" of his time, but that "substantial time" may be as little as two and one-half percent of total work time. *Boudloche v. Howard Trucking Co., Inc.*, 632 F.2d 1346 (5th Cir.1980); *In re CSX Transportation, Inc.*, 151 F.3d 164 (4th Cir. 1998) (employee had "status" where 15% of time spent unloading maritime freight, even though he was unloading nonmaritime freight at the time of his injury). But is a worker covered if he is in fact engaged in maritime employment at the time of the injury, although he does not spend "some" (a substantial portion) of his time in that employment?

d.   *The Covered Employee: Situs*

A worker who has "status" is covered if his injury occurs on a covered "situs." The 1972 amendment to 33 U.S.C.A. § 903 extends coverage to "employees" injured on navigable waters and "any adjoining pier, wharf ... and other adjoining area customarily used by an employer in loading, unloading, repairing or building a vessel." This language does not require that the "other adjoining area" also adjoin navigable waters. In *Caputo* the Court indicated that there is sufficient connexity although the "other adjoining area" does not adjoin navigable waters but adjoins a pier or wharf that adjoins navigable waters. Thus a claim has "situs" if it occurs (1) upon navigable waters; (2) upon an adjoining pier, wharf or similar structure, *Fleischmann v. Director*, 137 F.3d 131 (2d Cir.1998) (bulkhead is covered site), or (3) in an area that adjoins a pier, wharf or similar structure, and is customarily used by an employer in loading, unloading, repairing or building a vessel. The "customary usage" required for this third type of situs must be by a maritime employer, but not necessarily by the claimant's employer. *See, e.g., Cunningham v. Director*, 377 F.3d 98 (1st Cir. 2004); *Texports Stevedore Co. v. Winchester*, 569 F.2d 428 (5th Cir. 1978). *Compare Thibodeaux v. Grasso Production Management Inc.*, 370 F.3d 486 (5th Cir. 2004) (fixed oil production platform built on pilings over marsh and water, but inaccessible from land, is not a covered situs). In *Coastal Production Services, Inc. v. Hudson*, 555 F.3d 426 (5th Cir. 2009), the court held that a platform to which was attached a sunken oil barge from which vessels were loaded with fuel was a covered situs because it was integral to the operation of the loading barge.

May the "other adjoining area" be separated from the pier, wharf, or structure which it adjoins, or from navigable waters, by other areas which are not customarily used for loading, unloading, building or repairing vessels? Some courts have insisted upon contiguity. Others hold that "situs" exists if the "other adjoining area," although separated from navigable waters or adjoining piers and wharves by facilities used for nonmaritime purposes, is located as close to the water's edge as is practical under all of the circumstances. *Compare Brady–Hamilton Stevedore Co. v. Herron*, 568 F.2d 137 (9th Cir. 1978) and *Jonathan Corp. v. Brickhouse*, 142 F.3d 217 (4th Cir. 1998). *See also*, *Sidwell v. Express Container Services, Inc.*, 71 F.3d 1134 (4th Cir. 1995); *Sisson v. Davis & Sons, Inc.*, 131 F.3d 555 (5th Cir. 1998). Proponents of the requirement of contiguity can glean some support from dicta in *Director v. Perini North River Associates*, *supra*. There, the majority opinion observed that one of the purposes of the 1972 amendments to the LHWCA was to "extend coverage of the Act to include certain *contiguous* land areas" (emphasis supplied). "Contiguity" between the "area adjoining navigable waters" and the area "adjoining the area adjoining navigable waters" may be important only if it is necessary to provide an employer with "fair notice" that his employee is working within a "situs" covered by LHWCA. However, there has been little, if any, judicial recognition of this. Recent cases arguably stress contiguity and proximity.

The traditional wisdom was that "situs" was limited to American territorial waters and that a worker injured outside those waters was not covered by the LHWCA, unless he came under the provision of the Outer Continental Shelf Lands Act extending LHWCA coverage to mineral production workers on the Shelf. *See* "The Covered Employee: The Outer Continental Shelf Lands Act," *infra*. Section 903 of the LHWCA provides coverage only for injury "occurring upon the navigable waters of the United States," and section 902(9) appears to limit the term "United States" to the states and their territorial waters. However, courts have permitted recovery under the LHWCA to shipbuilders and to shiprepairers injured beyond three miles. *See Kollias v. D & G Marine Maintenance*, 29 F.3d 67 (2d Cir. 1994); *Reynolds v. Ingalls Shipbuilding Division*, 788 F.2d 264 (5th Cir. 1986); *Cove Tankers Corp. v. United Ship Repair, Inc.*, 683 F.2d 38 (2d Cir. 1982). This extension of jurisdiction arguably is supported by the presidential proclamation extending territorial waters to 24 miles, since the LHWCA by its terms extends to injuries incurred on the territorial waters of the United States. 33 U.S.C.A. §§ 902(9), 903(a).

e. The Covered Employee: The Outer Continental Shelf Lands Act

A large group of employees falls within the coverage of the LHWCA without regard to the "status" and "situs" requirements of sections 902(3) and 903. The Outer Continental Shelf Lands Act (OCS-LA) makes the LHWCA applicable to injury to an employee occurring as a result of operations conducted on the Shelf for the purpose of exploring for, developing, removing or transporting by pipeline the natural resources of the Shelf, unless the employee is a seaman or public employee. 43 U.S.C.A. § 1333(b). The effect of this provision, and the judicial gloss placed upon the term "seaman," is that (1) oil production workers aboard floating drilling structures on the Shelf or within territorial

waters usually qualify as "seamen" and are entitled
to seamen's benefits, since they aid in the "special
mission" of the "vessel"; (2) oil production workers
aboard fixed platforms on the Shelf are entitled to
the benefits provided by the LHWCA unless they
qualify as "seamen" through connection with some
vessel; and (3) oil production workers on fixed platforms within a state's territorial waters are covered
by state worker's compensation, unless they qualify
as seamen or they meet the "status" and "situs"
requirements of sections 902(3) and 903 of the
LHWCA. The Supreme Court has ruled that production of minerals from a fixed platform is not
"maritime employment" within the meaning of Title 33 U.S.C.A. Section 902(3). *Herb's Welding, Inc.
v. Gray*, 470 U.S. 414 (1985). This precludes oil
production workers on fixed platforms within territorial waters from LHWCA coverage unless (1) they
are engaged (either at the time of injury, or, under
Caputo, "some" of the time) in a covered activity
(such as loading or unloading a vessel) at a covered
situs (such as an area of the platform adjoining
navigable waters) and customarily used for loading
or unloading vessels, *but see*, *Munguia v. Chevron
USA, Inc.*, 999 F.2d 808 (5th Cir. 1993), or (2) they
are injured "as a result of" operations conducted on
the Shelf for production of minerals.

When does an injury within territorial waters
occur "as a result of" operations on the Shelf? The
Supreme Court expressly reserved the question in
Herb's Welding, *supra*. The U.S. Fifth Circuit applies a "but for" and situs test; a worker is covered

by the LHWCA through the OCSLA only if the injury would not have occurred "but for" operations on the outer continental shelf (OCS), *and* the injury occurs either on a platform on the OCS or in waters above the OCS. *Pickett v. Petroleum Helicopters, Inc.*, 266 F.3d 366 (5th Cir. 2001); *Mills v. Director, OWCP*, 877 F.2d 356 (5th Cir. 1989). The Fifth Circuit clarified its location requirement in *Demette v. Falcon Drilling Co.*, 280 F.3d 492 (5th Cir. 2002) to include not only platforms but moveable rigs whose "legs" are attached to the seabed. In *Becker v. Tidewater, Inc.*, 335 F.3d 376 (5th Cir. 2003), the court said that a jack up rig can be an LHWCA situs. The Third Circuit does not require "situs," i.e., the injury need not occur on the OCS; it only requires the "but for" connection. *Curtis v. Schlumberger Offshore Service*, 849 F.2d 805 (3d Cir. 1988).

f. Other Coverage Issues

Ordinarily the claimant's payroll employer is his LHWCA employer. However, there are two situations in which some other person may also be treated as the claimant's employer for the purposes of the Act. Section 904(a) imposes liability upon a contractor for the payment of LHWCA benefits to the employees of a subcontractor who has failed to secure payment of benefits. This contingent liability apparently does not provide the contractor with immunity from tort suits by his subcontractor's employee unless the contractor is required to pay LHWCA benefits to that employee. The Supreme

Court reached a different conclusion in *Washington Metropolitan Area Transit Authority v. Johnson*, 467 U.S. 925 (1984), but that result was quickly overturned by 1984 amendments to sections 904 and 905(a) of the LHWCA.

An employer may be liable for LHWCA benefits to the employee of another (and immune from tort suit by that employee) through application of the "borrowed servant" doctrine. In determining when an employee has been "borrowed," the extent to which the "borrowing" employer exercises control over the employee is relevant but not dispositive. The courts also look to other factors such as the existence of an agreement between the original and borrowing employer, the length of time during which the arrangement continued, which employer had the right to discharge and the obligation to pay the employee, which employer was responsible for working conditions, and whether the employment was of such duration that the employee reasonably could have evaluated and acquiesced in the risks of the work situation. The latter two factors have been deemed the most pertinent by the U.S. Fifth Circuit, which gets most of these cases. *Gaudet v. Exxon Corp.*, 562 F.2d 351 (5th Cir. 1977). *See also*, *Peter v. Hess Oil Virgin Islands Corp.*, 903 F.2d 935 (3d Cir.1990).

An employer subject to the Act must secure compensation, either by obtaining insurance or by qualifying as a self insurer. 33 U.S.C.A. § 932. If he does not, the employee has the option of seeking compensation benefits or pursuing a claim in tort against the employer. If the employee seeks recovery in tort, the employer may not interpose the "fellow servant," assumption of risk or contributory negligence defenses. 33 U.S.C.A. § 905(a).

As with other worker's compensation statutes, the injury or illness causing disability to an employee covered by the LHWCA must arise out of and occur in the course and scope of his employment. 33 U.S.C.A. § 902(2). The "arising out of" and "course and scope" requirements rarely were significant in pre–1972 cases, because coverage extended only to injuries occurring on navigable waters, and nearly all of such injuries were clearly work-related. With the extension of coverage to shoreside injuries, the "arising out of" and "course and scope" requirements have become more important in the disposition of LHWCA claims. These two requirements for coverage are given the same interpretation under the LHWCA as under most worker's compensation statutes. The Supreme Court has written that:

Arising 'out of' and in the course of' employment are separate elements; the former refers to injury causation; the latter refers to the time, place, and circumstances of the injury. Not only must the injury have been caused by the employment, it also must have arisen during the employment.

United States Industries/Federal Sheet Metal, Inc. v. Director, Office of Workers' Compensation Programs, 455 U.S. 608 (1982). Indeed, injuries suffered by an off-duty employee during foreseeable horseplay in a bar on an atoll in the Pacific were compensable where they resulted from reasonable and foreseeable recreational activities in an isolated locale—employment created a "zone of special danger." *Kalama Services, Inc. v. Director*, 354 F.3d 1085 (9th Cir. 2004).

g. *Benefits*

Benefits under the LHWCA include disability benefits and medical rehabilitation services. An employee who is totally disabled is entitled to two-thirds of the average weekly wages he earned prior to his injury for the period of the total disability, which may be permanent. 33 U.S.C.A. § 908(a) & (b). An employee who is permanently but only partially disabled is entitled to two-thirds of his average weekly wages for a fixed period of weeks, depending upon the type of injury or the portion of the body to which the disability attaches. 33 U.S.C.A. § 908(c)(1)–(20). If an employee is permanently and partially disabled but his injury and disability is not one of those listed in Section 908(c)(1)–(20), he is entitled to two-thirds of the difference between his average weekly wages before the injury and his "wage earning capacity" thereafter. 33 U.S.C.A. § 908(c)(21). For the purposes of calculating these benefits, the employee's average weekly wage is subject to minimum and maximum limits based upon a percentage of the average national weekly wage. 33 U.S.C.A. § 906(b). Wages may include per diem for food and lodging expenses that are made regardless of whether food and lodging costs were incurred. *Custom Ship Interiors v.*

Roberts, 300 F.3d 510 (4th Cir. 2002). Additionally, in *B&D Contracting v. Pearley*, 548 F.3d 338 (5th Cir. 2009) the court held that where per diem payments were calculated based on the number of hours worked, were paid in the same paycheck as the employee's normal wages, were not related to actual costs of meals, lodging or travel, were paid to all employees regardless of where they lived and constituted almost one half of worker's gross pay, the per diem was wages, not fringe benefits.

Disability justifying an award of benefits under the LHWCA is defined as "incapacity ... to earn the wages which the employee was receiving at the time of injury in the same or any other employment." 33 U.S.C.A. § 902(10). A claimant makes out a prima facie case of total disability when he proves that he is unable to perform the duties of his previous job because of a work-related injury; the burden then shifts to the employer to show that there are jobs that the claimant is capable of performing and which are reasonably available to him or her. *See, e.g., Louisiana Ins. Guar. Ass'n v. Abbott*, 40 F.3d 122 (5th Cir. 1994). The courts are divided over the precision with which the employer must establish job availability. *Compare Lentz v. Cottman Co.*, 852 F.2d 129 (4th Cir. 1988) and *P & M Crane Co. v. Hayes*, 930 F.2d 424 (5th Cir.1991). If the employer meets his burden, the employee is not entitled to benefits unless he or she can show the diligent attempt but inability to secure employment. *See Norfolk Shipbuilding & Drydock Corp. v. Hord*, 193 F.3d 797 (4th Cir. 1999).

The employee is entitled to medical services for injury or illness arising out of and in the course and scope of his or her employment. 33 U.S.C.A. § 907(a). The employee may select a physician (other than one who has been "disapproved" by the Office of Worker Compensation) and may be required to submit to examination by another physician. 33 U.S.C.A. § 907. The employee may have the right to select between alternative treatments. *Amos v. Director*, 153 F.3d 1051 (9th Cir. 1998).

The LHWCA provides wrongful death benefits to designated survivors and also provides for survival of benefits if a claimant dies from a cause other than the work-related injury that caused disability under the Act. The rights of beneficiaries of a deceased worker covered by the LHWCA are discussed in Chapter XIV, *infra*.

Benefits are payable if disability results from accidental injury or from an occupational disease which "arises naturally out of such employment." This term of art usually is interpreted as requiring that the disease result from working conditions which are peculiar to the claimant's employment with the LHWCA employer.

An employer is encouraged to employ or continue the employment of a partially disabled employee through the "Second Injury" fund. If the partially disabled employee's "manifest" pre-employment disability exposes the employer to greater LHWCA liability than that which would have resulted from the work-related injury alone, the employer's liability is limited to compensation for 104 weeks, and the employee's subsequent benefits are paid from the "Second Injury" fund. *See* 33 U.S.C.A. § 908(f); *Director v. Vessel Repair, Inc.*, 168 F.3d 190 (5th Cir. 1999).

When the disability arises from an "occupational injury" incurred while working for different employers, the last employer who exposes the claimant to the injury-causing condition may be responsible for all of the benefits. *Metropolitan Stevedore Co. v. Crescent Wharf and Warehouse Co.*, 339 F.3d 1102 (9th Cir. 2003); *Avondale Industries v. Director, OWCP*, 977 F.2d 186 (5th Cir. 1992).

h. Processing the LHWCA Claim

LHWCA claims initially are processed administratively within the Department of Labor. An employee must give notice of his claim within thirty days of its occurrence, 33 U.S.C.A. § 912(a), and must file a formal claim within a year. 33 U.S.C.A. § 913(a). Failure to give notice will not bar recovery if the employer knew about the injury or otherwise was not prejudiced by the failure, or if the deputy commissioner excuses the failure. 33 U.S.C.A. § 912(d). Sections 912(a) and 913, and case law provide that the delays for giving notice and for filing a claim begin to run when the employee reasonably should have known of the existence of the illness and of its work-related genesis. The difficulty has been alleviated somewhat by a 1984 amendment which extends the delays for giving notice and filing claims arising out of certain occupational diseases. 33 U.S.C.A. §§ 912(a), 913(b).

The employer also must give notice of a disabling injury or illness of which he has knowledge, 33 U.S.C.A. § 930(a); his failure to do so will toll the running of the statute of limitations. 33 U.S.C.A. § 930(a). In cases involving non-traumatic injuries or illnesses, the employer may not have knowledge that the employee's disabling condition is work-related. However, the circumstances of the injury or illness may be such that the employer "should have known" that it was work-related, or at least should have inquired further, and he may be charged with the knowledge he would have gained from such inquiry. *See, e.g, Strachan Shipping Co. v. Davis*, 571 F.2d 968 (5th Cir. 1978).

The employer must either "controvert" the claim or commence voluntary payment within fourteen days after the occurrence of the accident. 33 U.S.C.A. § 914(b). When the employer controverts, the employee is relieved of the burden of giving notice, and the statute of limitations on the filing of the claim is tolled. 33 U.S.C.A. § 913(a). If the employer controverts or, after commencing payments, contends that no further payment is due, the claim is first processed through a conciliation procedure in which the deputy commissioner seeks to provoke an amicable resolution. *See, e.g.*, 20 C.F.R. 702.301. Settlement is subject to approval by the deputy commissioner (or the administrative law judge who is hearing the matter), but a settlement must be approved "unless it is found to be inadequate or procured by duress." 33 U.S.C.A. § 908(i)(1). If settlement or other amicable resolution is not effected, the claim is heard by an administrative law judge (ALJ). In proving his claim, the employee is aided by certain presumptions. 33 U.S.C.A. § 920 provides that "[i]n any proceeding for the enforcement of a claim for compensation ... it shall be presumed, in the absence of substantial evidence to the contrary ... [t]hat the claim comes within the provisions of [the LHWCA]." The reach of that presumption is uncertain. However, the Supreme Court has ruled that the "true doubt" rule— when the evidence is evenly balanced, the benefit claimant wins—does not apply in LHWCA claims. *Director v. Greenwich Collieries*, 512 U.S. 267 (1994). When the presumption of coverage does apply, the employer must produce substantial evidence that the injury was not work related. *Ortco Contractors, Inc. v. Charpentier*, 332 F.3d 283 (5th Cir. 2003). The apparent majority rule is that the presumption shifts the burden of producing evidence but not the burden of persuasion. *American Grain Trimmers v. OWCP*, 181 F.3d 810 (7th Cir. 1999). Neither common law nor statutory rules of evidence nor "technical or formal rules of procedure" are binding in the processing of LHWCA claims through the Office of Worker Compensation Programs. 33 U.S.C.A. § 921.

An aggrieved party may appeal the ALJ's decision to the Benefits Review Board, an administrative appellate tribunal, with further appeal to the United States Court of Appeals for the circuit in which the case initially arose. On appeal, the Benefits Review Board must uphold the findings of fact made by the ALJ if the findings are supported by "substantial evidence," which may consist only of the credible testimony of the claimant. The appellate court's review of the Benefits Review Board decision is limited to questions of law and to a determination of whether the Board adhered to the scope of its review of the findings of fact by the ALJ. An LHWCA award may be enforced by an action in federal district court. 33 U.S.C.A. §§ 918(a), 921(d).

An employer who fails to pay benefits timely is subject to penalties, 33 U.S.C.A. § 914(e), (f). For the purpose of imposing penalties, the relevant date is the filing of the order and not its being sent to the parties. *Carillo v. Louisiana Insurance Guaranty Assoc.,* 559 F.3d 377 (5th Cir. 2009). Any attorney's fee paid by the claimant must be fixed by the OWCP. *See, e.g.,* 33 U.S.C.A. § 928(e). However, if the employer unsuccessfully contests liability for compensation benefits, he must pay a reasonable fee to the claimant's attorney. 33 U.S.C.A. § 928(a).

If there is a ruling that the employee is not entitled to benefits under the Act, the decision may be modified only within one year. 33 U.S.C.A. § 922. If an award is made, however, and circumstances thereafter establish that the claimant has sustained disability to a greater or lesser degree, the award may be modified years later to reflect the change. Section 922 also permits modification of an award where the employee's wage-earning capacity increases because of the acquisition of new skills, although there has been no change in the employee's physical condition. *Metropolitan Stevedore Co. v. Rambo*, 515 U.S. 291 (1995).

3. The Sieracki Seaman and the 905(b) Action

a. Introduction

Prior to the 1972 amendments to the LHWCA, a maritime worker aboard a vessel doing the work of a member of the crew was owed the same duty of seaworthiness by the vessel and its operator that was owed to a member of the crew of the vessel. Such a worker was called a *"Sieracki* seaman," named after the case in which the Supreme Court extended him that protection. *Seas Shipping Co. v. Sieracki, supra*. The vessel owner obtained significant, arguably even complete, relief from the *"Sieracki"* doctrine in 1972 when Congress adopted section 905(b), providing that:

> In the event of injury to a person covered under this chapter caused by the negligence of a vessel, then such person may bring an action against such vessel as a third party

[but]

> [t]he liability of the vessel under this subsection shall not be based upon the warranty of seaworthiness or a breach thereof at the time the injury occurred.

The 1972 amendment to section 905(b) abolishes the unseaworthiness claim for a worker covered by the LHWCA (including those covered by the LHWCA through the Outer Continental Shelf Lands Act) and replaces it with a negligence action against the vessel and its owner. However, it may be erroneous to assume, as some have done, that the *Sieracki* seaman has totally disappeared. The express language of the 1972 amendment to section 905(b) merely abolishes the unseaworthiness remedy for persons who are covered by the LHWCA. In most cases, non-seamen aboard a vessel doing the work of members of the crew are covered by the LHWCA; however, there are a number of workers who fit the *Sieracki* mold but who are not covered by the LHWCA. Here are some examples:

1. An American citizen or resident (or, in some instances, a foreigner) who is employed as a maritime worker in international or foreign waters by an American-based corporation. Since the LHWCA may not extend beyond American territorial waters and the Outer Continental Shelf, such a worker may meet the *Sieracki* guidelines without being covered by the Act. (If a worker is a foreigner employed by one engaged in the production of offshore energy resources in foreign territorial waters, he may be barred by 46 U.S.C.A. § 30105(b), *infra*, from maintaining an action under "any ... maritime law of the United States ... for damages"; this presumably would deprive him of a *Sieracki* action.)

2. A seaman on one vessel who is temporarily working aboard another vessel.

3. Federal and state employees, who are expressly excluded from LHWCA coverage. 33 U.S.C.A. § 903.

4. Workers who are neither seamen nor LHWCA employees but who are injured working on a vessel. *See, e.g., Green v. Vermilion Corp.,* 144 F.3d 332 (5th Cir. 1998). These workers may be covered by state worker compensation but because they are injured on navigable waters, state worker compensation may not be their exclusive remedy, and thus they may pursue claims against their employers under *Sieracki* or tort law. *See* Chapter XV, *infra*.

Arguably, Congress *has* completely abolished the *Sieracki* doctrine. *See Normile v. Maritime Co. of Philippines*, 643 F.2d 1380 (9th Cir. 1981), and the cases cited therein. Some support for this position may be found in dicta in *Edmonds v. Compagnie Generale Transatlantique*, 443 U.S. 256 (1979). One panel of the U.S. Fifth Circuit recognized a federal employee as a *Sieracki* seaman after the 1972 amendments, *Aparicio v. Swan Lake*, 643 F.2d 1109 (5th Cir. 1981), but another panel of the same court denied *Sieracki* status to a seaman injured while working temporarily aboard another vessel. *Bridges v. Penrod Drilling Co.*, 740 F.2d 361 (5th Cir. 1984). More recently, in *Green v. Vermilion Corp.*, 144 F.3d 332 (5th Cir. 1998), the court concluded that the *Sieracki* remedy survives for a worker at a camp who was not a seaman and who was not covered by the LHWCA but who was injured on navigable waters.

Prior to the development of the *Sieracki* doctrine, a maritime worker covered by the LHWCA could maintain a negligence action against the vessel on which he was employed. The expansion of the LHWCA landward and the adoption of section 905(b) in 1972 have presented the question of whether section 905(b) merely restores this pre-*Sieracki* negligence action, or whether it creates a new remedy. If it creates a new remedy, that remedy would "arise under" a federal act and could be brought in federal court on the law "side," with trial by jury. If section 905(b) merely continues the pre-*Sieracki* negligence action, then, arguably, it can only be brought in federal court if the underlying tort is maritime or there is diversity jurisdiction, with trial by jury only if there is diversity jurisdiction. Since Congress instructed the courts to fashion a new body of negligence law in implementing the section 905(b) action, a logical conclusion is that the maritime worker's negligence action against the vessel "arises under" the Act and not under pre-existing maritime common law. The Supreme Court has remarked, quite ambivalently, that the

> [longshoreman's] right to recover from the shipowner for negligence was *preserved* in § 905(b), *which provided a statutory negligence action* against the ship.

Scindia Steam Navigation Co., Ltd. v. Santos, 451 U.S. 156 (1981) (emphasis added).

The prevailing rule in the U.S. Fifth Circuit, which handles many of these cases, is that a section 905(b) action may not be maintained unless the underlying tort is maritime and that the section 905(b) action does not "arise under" a federal statute for the purposes of "federal question" jurisdiction. *Richendollar v. Diamond M Drilling Co.*, 819 F.2d 124 (5th Cir. 1987); *Margin v. Sea–Land Services, Inc.*, 812 F.2d 973 (5th Cir. 1987).

The legislative history of section 905(b) reflects that Congress intended to impose upon the vessel owner the same duties that general tort law imposes upon a landowner. The courts, responding to the Congressional command, have fashioned a body of law drawn from common law principles. They also have complied with the legislative directive in section 905(b) that the liability of a vessel "shall not be based upon the warranty of seaworthiness" by rejecting the application of tort principles, which would impose upon the vessel owner strict or absolute liability for conditions on the vessel, and have held that a section 905(b) claim preempts claims under state tort law. However, section 905(b) does not preempt state law on a claim to which it does not apply. Thus in *McLaurin v. Noble Drilling (U.S.) Inc.*, 529 F.3d 285 (5th Cir. 2008), a worker was employed by a shipyard and was injured while working as a scaffold carpenter supporting construction work on the defendant's vessel, working about 200 feet from the vessel in fabricating "pontoon extensions." He was injured when the shell of one of the extensions crushed his hand and arm.

The court held that the worker's claim in tort against the vessel owner was not barred. Although he could not recover from the vessel owner as a vessel owner because he could not state a cognizable claim for vessel negligence under section 905(b), he could proceed under state law.

Because a special body of law applies in a section 905(b) action, it is necessary to distinguish the maritime worker's section 905(b) action against the "vessel" from his or her other third party claims, which are governed either by general maritime principles or by state tort law. The section 905(b) rules apply only when the maritime worker is injured "by the negligence of a vessel." A "vessel" is defined in 33 U.S.C.A. § 902(21) as "any vessel upon which or in connection with which" the maritime worker suffers injury "arising out of or in the course of his employment, and said vessel's owner, owner pro hac vice, agent, operator, charterer or bare boat charterer, master, officer, or crew member." Thus the essential requirements for a section 905(b) action are (1) a worker covered by the LHWCA (2) who suffers injury on or in connection with a vessel (3) through "vessel negligence."

Where the vessel owner is not the maritime worker's employer, the section 905(b) claim is a more or less standard third party maritime tort claim. However, there is one situation in which the existence of a section 905(b) claim is crucial to any tort recovery by the maritime worker. An LHWCA employer ordinarily is immune from tort suit by his employee; however, the immunity does not apply to section

905(b) actions by certain employees. Thus section 905(b) may provide the employee with a negligence action against his own employer in the employer's "vessel" capacity. In such a case, however, the liability of the employer-vessel defendant is limited. A maritime worker engaged in longshoring may maintain a section 905(b) action against his employer who is a vessel defendant, but that action is not permitted if the injury was caused by the negligence of persons engaged in providing stevedoring services to the vessel. If the employee is engaged in shipbuilding, repairing or breaking services, he may not maintain an action against his employer-vessel owner under section 905(b). An LHWCA employee engaged in some other activity (such as maintenance) apparently may maintain a section 905(b) action against an employer-vessel defendant in the same manner as he could a non-employer. *See, e.g., New v. Associated Painting Services, Inc.,* 863 F.2d 1205 (5th Cir. 1989).

When an LHWCA employee brings a section 905(b) action against his employer, the court must distinguish between "vessel negligence," for which the defendant is liable, and "shipyard or employer negligence," for which he is not. The line between the two has been described as elusive, at best. *See Morehead v. Atkinson–Kiewit, J/V,* 97 F.3d 603 (1st Cir. 1996) (refusing to impute knowledge gained by defendant as maritime employer to defendant in its vessel capacity). However, "unlike employers, vessel owners are not mentioned in Sec. 933, so a maritime worker may attempt to recover against a vessel owner for vessel negligence under 905(b), against a vessel owner as a third party tortfeasor under Sec. 933, or even against a vessel owner as a borrowing employer," under Sec. 904. It is not a vessel owner's status as a vessel owner that dictates which LHWCA provision a maritime worker may use; it is the type of negligence that the worker alleges and the duty that is owed by the vessel owner that is controlling.

b. *Vessel Negligence*

By far the greatest exposure for the vessel owner, and the source of most of the post–1972 litigation, is the duty which it owes to the maritime worker to guard against dangerous conditions on those parts of the vessel where the maritime worker reasonably can be expected to go in the performance of his or her duties. In *Scindia Steam Navigation Company, Ltd. v. De Los Santos*, 451 U.S. 156 (1981), the Supreme Court made a comprehensive statement of the vessel owner's duty. Although its decision is couched in terms of the duty owed by a vessel owner to a longshoreman aboard the vessel, the same general duty has been applied to other maritime workers aboard a vessel. In *Scindia*, the Court articulated three vessel duties under section 905(b): (1) the "turnover duty"; (2) the "active operations" duty; and (3) the duty to intervene. The Court in *Scindia* first defined the vessel's "turnover duty," observing that:

> [T]he vessel owes to the stevedore and his long-
> shoremen employees the duty of exercising due

care "under the circumstances." This duty extends at least to exercising ordinary care under the circumstances to have the ship and its equipment in such condition that an expert and experienced stevedore will be able by the exercise of reasonable care to carry on its cargo operations with reasonable safety to persons and property, *and to warning the stevedore of any hazards on the ship* or with *respect to its equipment* that are known to the vessel or should be known to it in the exercise of reasonable care, that would likely be encountered by the stevedore in the course of his cargo operations and *that are not known by the stevedore and would not be obvious to or anticipated by him if reasonably competent in the performance of his work....* [T]he shipowner thus has a duty with respect to the condition of the ship's gear, equipment, tools and work space to be used in the stevedoring operations; *and if he fails at least to warn* the *stevedore of hidden danger* which would have been known to him in the exercise of reasonable care, he has breached his duty and is liable if his negligence causes injury to a longshoreman. (emphasis added).

Subsequently, the Court in *Howlett v. Birkdale Shipping Co., S.A.*, 512 U.S. 92 (1994), pointed out that the "turnover duty" to warn the longshoreman of latent defects in the cargo stow and cargo area is a "narrow one" which attaches only to latent hazards (those which are not known to the stevedore and that would be neither obvious to nor anticipated by a skilled stevedore in the competent performance of its work). Furthermore, the duty encompasses only those hazards that are known or should be known to the vessel in the exercise of reasonable care, *see, Deyerle v. United States*, 149 F.3d 314 (4th Cir. 1998), and the allegedly dangerous condition must exist at the time of the vessel's turnover. *Laulusa v. Foss Maritime Co.*, 173 F.3d 860 (9th Cir. 1999). In *Hill v. Reederei*, 435 F.3d 404 (3rd Cir. 2006) the court said: "[w]hen a ship is turned over to the stevedore with an open and obvious hazard which injures a longshoreman, the ship will be liable, first, if avoiding the hazard would be impractical for the longshoreman, or second, if the ship should have known that the longshoreman would confront the hazard.... Our common maritime law finds duties where longshoremen regularly confront hazards and the ship should be reasonably aware of that practice.... If the longshoreman's only alternatives are to leave the job or face trouble for delaying the work—then the ship owner had a duty to warn of or mitigate the hazard ... even if it was open and obvious." In *Kirksey v. Tonghai Maritime*, 535 F.3d 388 (5th Cir. 2008), the court said that the open and obvious exception to the vessel owner's turnover duty extends to a defect in the cargo stow where there is no evidence that the shipowner negligently created a dangerous condition in the stow.

Under the "active operations" duty (conditions arising after the maritime employer commences his activities), the vessel owner owes a continuing duty to exercise reasonable care to make the vessel safe if

(1) it actively participates in the operations; (2) it maintains control over the area; or (3) such a duty is imposed upon the vessel owner by contract, positive law (such as federal regulations) or custom. Otherwise, the vessel owner does not owe a duty to discover defective conditions in the area controlled by the maritime employer that arise after the employer has commenced his activities; it is not required to supervise the maritime employer.

Turning to the "more difficult and recurring issue," the *Scindia* court discussed the vessel owner's duty when he learns that an apparently dangerous condition exists or has developed in the cargo operation that may cause injury to the maritime employee, and the condition is known to the stevedore. What makes this issue particularly difficult is that it requires a vessel owner to "second guess" the safety methods of an "expert" whom he has engaged to perform a dangerous work. The *Scindia* court was divided over the proper handling of this issue. The majority reasoned that inasmuch as the maritime employer possesses expertise in the area of its activities, and is charged by law with providing for the safety of its employees, the vessel owner ordinarily may rely upon the maritime employer's judgment that the condition does not present an unreasonable risk of harm to the workers. However, the majority reasoned, the vessel owner may owe a "duty to intervene" if the maritime employer's judgment is

  so obviously improvident that [the vessel owner], if it knew of the defect and that [the maritime employer] was continuing to use it, should have realized [that] the [condition] presented an unreasonable risk of harm to the longshoremen.

The majority observed that, in reaching this decision, the vessel owner should consider not only the maritime employer's duty to provide its employees with a safe place to work, but also whether statutes, regulations or custom place a continuing duty on the vessel to remedy defective conditions arising during the course of the operations. Three justices, concurring, would have held that if the vessel owner has actual knowledge of an unsafe condition and a reasonable belief that the maritime employer will not remedy it, he has the duty to halt the operation, eliminate the unsafe condition, or make the maritime employer eliminate it.

If there is vessel negligence, the maritime worker's contributory negligence will not bar his recovery, but will reduce it through the application of "pure" comparative negligence. Assumption of risk is not a defense; it may even preclude reduction of the maritime worker's recovery for contributory negligence when the two defenses overlap, such as when the maritime worker's only negligence is that he realized his work was dangerous but nevertheless did it.

Stale section 905(b) claims formerly were barred by the doctrine of laches; however, the three-year general maritime personal injury statute of limitations, 46 U.S.C.A. § 30106, should apply to all section 905(b) claims arising after its effective date.

4. The Maritime Employer's Rights Against Third Persons

The maritime employer may attempt to recover the LHWCA benefits it has paid from the third party whose tort caused the compensable injury to the employee. If the underlying tort is maritime, admiralty law should apply. But what law applies if the underlying tort is non-maritime, such as where the LHWCA worker is injured on the dock or on a fixed platform? One can argue that since federal law imposes the compensation obligation upon the maritime employer, that law should govern his right to recoupment from third persons. The counter-argument is that because the employer's claim is based upon subrogation, he may exercise only those rights that his employee has. Thus if the employee's tort claim is non-maritime, the subrogation claim also should be governed by the applicable state law. The cases have not provided a clear answer.

Where maritime law applies to the maritime employer's rights against a third person, the maritime employer has two avenues of approach. One is subrogation. Although the LHWCA is silent on the employer's subrogation rights, maritime law generally recognizes subrogation, and the courts have granted the remedy to the LHWCA employer. *See, e.g., Peters v. North River Insurance Co. of Morristown, N.J.*, 764 F.2d 306 (5th Cir. 1985). The maritime employer also has an independent claim against the third party for the damages the employer has sustained—its LHWCA liability to its employee—because of the tortfeasor's injury to the employee. *See, e.g., Federal Marine Terminals, Inc. v. Burnside Shipping Co., Ltd.*, 394 U.S. 404 (1969).

The employer who has paid LHWCA benefits may enforce its subrogation rights by intervening in the worker's action against the third party. When this occurs, the employee may attempt to impose upon the employer some of the burden of the employee's attorney's fees, especially if the amount recovered in excess of the employer's subrogation claim will not fairly compensate the employee and his or her attorney for their efforts in obtaining recovery against the third party. The Supreme Court has ruled that the maritime employer is entitled to reimbursement of the full amount of compensation payments made under the LHWCA, without reduction for any proportionate share of the employee's expense in obtaining recovery from the third party tortfeasor. *Bloomer v. Liberty Mutual Insurance Co.*, 445 U.S. 74 (1980). However, that result may have been changed by a 1984 amendment to 33 U.S.C.A. § 933(f) providing that "if the person entitled to compensation institutes proceedings [against the third party tortfeasor] ... the employer shall be required to pay as compensation ... a sum equal to the excess of the amount ... payable on account of such injury or death [under the LHWCA] over the net amount recovered against such third person. Such net amount shall be equal to the actual amount recovered less the expenses reasonably incurred ... (including reasonable attorneys' fees)." *See also, Ochoa v. Employers National Insurance Co.*, 754 F.2d 1196 (5th Cir. 1985).

If the maritime worker's injury is caused by the concurring negligence of his employer and a third party, the third party as a joint tortfeasor is liable to the worker for the full amount of the worker's damages. However, as explained below, the third party's ability to recover part of those damages from the tortfeasor-employer usually is barred by the provisions of 33 U.S.C.A. § 905. Some courts initially sought to avoid this seemingly unjust result by giving the third party an "equitable credit" against his liability to the maritime worker in an amount equal to what would be the employer's share of the damages if he were not immune from contribution to the third party. The Supreme Court has rejected this "equitable credit" doctrine, holding that the negligent third party must pay the full amount of the damages attributable to the conduct of both the tortfeasor and the employer. *Edmonds v. Compagnie Generale Transatlantique*, 443 U.S. 256 (1979).

What if the LHWCA worker's tort claim is based upon state law and the applicable state law allocates fault to the immune employer and holds the tortfeasor liable only for the tortfeasor's share of the fault? One court has ruled that state law should be applied. *Fontenot v. Dual Drilling*, 179 F.3d 969 (5th Cir. 1999).

5. Third Party Claims Against the Maritime Employer

A third party who pays tort damages to a maritime employee may attempt to recoup all or part of those damages from the employee's negligent employer. The third party's rights depend in part upon whether it is a "vessel defendant" as that term is used in sections 905(b) and 902(21).

If the third party is a "vessel defendant," recovery against the maritime employer apparently is barred. Contribution is not available because the rule of *Halcyon Lines v. Haenn Ship Ceiling & Refitting Corp.*, 342 U.S. 282 (1952) prohibits recovery of contribution in admiralty from a party who is immune from direct tort recovery by the victim (*see* Chapter XVII). One exception is where the employer is liable to the worker in tort under section 905(b). In that case, the employer is not immune from the employee's tort action and is also not immune from a contribution action.

Nor is indemnity ordinarily available. The language of section 905(b)—"the employer shall not be liable to the vessel for ... damages [owed to a maritime worker] directly or indirectly and any agreements or warranties to the contrary shall be void"—bars contractual indemnity in most cases. (The exception is section 905(c), adopted in 1984, which permits agreements by which the maritime employer of a worker entitled to receive LHWCA benefits by virtue of the Outer Continental Shelf Lands Act, 43 U.S.C.A. § 1333, and the vessel reciprocally agree to indemnify each other against claims arising out of injury to their employees.) Tort indemnity also is not available. Since the vessel owner's liability must be predicated upon negligence, the theory of tort indemnity which permits recovery from the tortfeasor by a person who is only vicariously liable is inapplicable. The other theory of tort indemnification—recovery by a "passive" or "slight" tortfeasor against a joint tortfeasor whose negligence was "active" or "gross"—should not have survived the arrival of comparative contribution in maritime law. *See* Chapter XVII, *infra.* Even if it has survived, this type of tort indemnification may be barred by the language of section 905(b) providing that the employer shall not be liable to the vessel, "directly or indirectly," for damages recoverable against the vessel by a maritime worker. In addition, section 905(a), applicable to both vessel and non-vessel negligence, provides that

> [t]he liability of an employer [for compensation benefits] shall be exclusive and in place of all other liability of such employer to the employee ... and anyone otherwise entitled to recover damages from such employer ... on account of such injury or death....

Since tort indemnification arguably arises "on account of" injury to the employee, that language may bar application of any tort indemnification principle against a maritime employer.

If the third party tortfeasor is not a "vessel defendant," he may be able to obtain contractual indemnification from the maritime employer since the provisions of section 905(b) barring such indemnity do not apply, and section 905(a) may be inapplicable because the obligation to indemnify may arise "on account of" the contract of indemnification and not "on account of" the injury to the employee. Recovery of indemnification through tort principles would depend upon the applicability and continued viability of those principles, as discussed above, and upon the reach of the exclusivity provision of section 905(a), quoted above.

A vessel owner may require the maritime employer with whom he contracts to obtain insurance protecting the maritime employer against tort claims by the maritime employer's employees and naming the vessel owner as a coinsured. This has the same practical effect as requiring the employer to indemnify the vessel against section 905(b) claims by employees. However, some courts have held that such an agreement does not violate the mandate of section 905(b) that "the employer shall not be liable to the vessel for such damages directly or indirectly and any agreements ... to the contrary shall be void." *Voisin v. O.D.E.C.O. Drilling Co.*, 744 F.2d 1174 (5th Cir.1984)*; Price v. Zim Israel Navigation Co., Ltd.*, 616 F.2d 422 (9th Cir. 1980).

6. Prosecution and Settlement of Third–Party Claims by the Maritime Employer and Maritime Employee

General tort principles govern the maritime worker's tort action against a third party. If the tort is maritime, admiralty law governs; otherwise, state law applies. However, federal law rigidly regulates the employer's rights into the employee's third-party tort claims.

The employee may settle his third party claim without the employer's approval. That settlement may defeat the employer's subrogation rights. *See e.g., Peters v. North River Insurance Co. of Morristown, N.J., supra.* However, any settlement without the prior written approval of the employer discharges the employer from liability for future compensation. 33 U.S.C.A. § 933(g). The discharge occurs even though at the time the employee settles with the third party the employer is neither paying nor subject to an order to pay compensation to the employee under the LHWCA. *Estate of Cowart v. Nicklos Drilling Co.*, 505 U.S. 469 (1992). The employee also owes a "duty to notify" the employer of any settlement obtained from or judgment rendered against a third person; failure to notify also can result in a termination of LHWCA benefits. *See* 33 U.S.C.A. § 933(g).

If the maritime worker does not institute the third-party action within a designated time period, the claim is automatically assigned to the employer. 33 U.S.C.A. § 933(b) provides that

[a]cceptance of compensation under an award in a compensation order filed by the deputy commissioner or Board shall operate as an assignment to the employer of all rights of the person entitled to compensation to recover damages against such third person unless [the maritime worker] shall commence an action against such third person within six months after such award.

If the assignment occurs, the employer may recover from the third party all of the tort damages to which the employee would have been entitled. The employer then retains the expenses it incurred in effecting recovery (including attorney's fees), its subrogation claim, and the present value of future compensation it owes to the worker; the worker is entitled to the remainder.

Section 933(b) defines an award for such purpose as "a formal order issued by the deputy commissioner, an administrative law judge, or [the Benefits Review] Board."

Another difficulty with the assignment provision under the 1972 Act was that when the assignment occurred, it was deemed absolute. Thus the employee effectively was deprived of his tort remedy if the employer elected not to proceed with the third-party tort claim (which was likely if the employer's LHWCA carrier and the tortfeasor's liability insurer were the same, or if the employer was economically dependent upon the tortfeasor). In *Rodriguez v. Compass Shipping Co., Ltd.*, 451 U.S. 596 (1981), the Supreme Court rejected the argument that the assignment did not take place if there was a "potential conflict of interest" between the employer and the employee over the third-party claim. However, a 1984 amendment to section 933(b) eliminates the problem by providing that if the employer fails to commence the action against the tortfeasor within 90 days after the assignment occurs, the claim automatically is reassigned to the employee.

D. STATE WORKER'S COMPENSATION

If an employee does not qualify as a seaman or as a maritime worker, his claims against his employer for a work-related injury ordinarily will be regulated by the worker's compensation laws of the state with the most significant connection with the employment relationship. The employer may be immune from tort liability to the injured employee, where state law provides for such immunity and the underlying wrongful conduct of the employer would otherwise be governed by state law. *Compare Garvin v. Alumax of South Carolina, Inc.*, 787 F.2d 910 (4th Cir. 1986) and *Gates v. Shell Oil Co.*, 812 F.2d 1509 (5th Cir. 1987). Where the underlying wrongful conduct is governed by maritime law, i.e., there is maritime tort jurisdiction, the result is different. The worker perhaps may qualify as a *"Sieracki"* seaman, if such a seaman still exists (*see* Chapter XIII, *supra*). Even if the worker does not have a claim under *Sieracki*, he may sue his employer in maritime tort, and the employer immunity provided by the state worker's compensation law does not bar the action. *Green v. Vermilion Corp., supra*; *Purnell v. Norned Shipping B.V.*, 801 F.2d 152 (3d Cir. 1986); *Thibodaux v. Atlantic Richfield Co.*, 580 F.2d 841 (5th Cir. 1978).

E. PUBLIC EMPLOYEES

The exclusive remedy of seamen and maritime workers employed by the United States is the Federal Employees' Compensation Act (FECA), 5 U.S.C.A. § 8101 et seq., which has the general attributes of a worker's compensation act. Despite FECA, there are instances in which a seaman can recover damages against the United States. *See* Chapter XVI, *infra.*

State and local public employees who qualify as seamen are entitled to coverage under the traditional seaman's remedies; however, they are excluded from coverage under the LHWCA by express provisions of that act, 33 U.S.C.A. § 903(b), and of the Outer Continental Shelf Lands Act. 43 U.S.C.A. § 1333(b)(1).

F. THE OVERLAP OF COMPENSATION REMEDIES

Often it is difficult to determine whether an employee's claim is compensable through the seaman's remedies, the Longshore and Harbor Workers' Compensation Act, or state worker's compensation. In such borderline cases, both worker and employer face certain risks. There is the danger that the worker's proper remedy may become time-barred while he or she is pursuing what ultimately is determined to be an improper remedy. The employer faces the risk that its exoneration from liability, or its payment of a claim under one remedy, may not bar a subsequent claim against it by the worker under another remedy. The area is one through which the employer and employee must navigate with care.

If a worker whose status as a seaman is doubtful elects to pursue seamen's remedies, there is no danger that his LHWCA claim will be time-barred if it ultimately is determined that he is a non-seaman maritime worker. The LHWCA provides, 33 U.S.C.A. § 913(d), that

> [w]here recovery is denied ... in a suit brought at law or in admiralty to recover damages in respect of injury ... on the ground that such person was an employee and that the defendant was an employer within the meaning of this chapter ... the limitation of time prescribed in [the LHWCA] shall begin to run only from the date of termination of such suit.

If the claimant pursues seamen's remedies and it ultimately is determined that the claim is governed by state worker's compensation, the question of whether the suit for seamen's remedies tolls the statute of limitations on the state remedy depends upon the applicable state law. Where state law does not provide tolling, a claimant should file a "protective suit" in state court to toll the state statute while prosecuting a seaman's claims.

Will the pursuit of a state worker's compensation remedy toll the one-year limitation on filing of a claim under the LHWCA? If the state worker's compensation claim is processed through an administrative agency, it may not qualify under 33 U.S.C.A. § 913(d) as "a suit brought at law," and where the state claim for compensation benefits is administered through the courts, the issue becomes whether it is "a suit brought ... to recover damages" within the meaning of that section. While the matter is not free from doubt, courts have held that the state worker's compensation claim, whether processed through an administrative agency or through the courts, will toll the LHWCA statute. *Ingalls Shipbuilding Division, Litton Systems, Inc. v. Hollinhead*, 571 F.2d 272 (5th Cir. 1978)*; Wilson v. Donovan*, 218 F.Supp. 944 (E.D.La. 1963). However, an untimely filed state worker's compensation proceeding will not toll the LHWCA limitations period. *Hill v. Director*, 195 F.3d 790 (5th Cir. 1999).

There is no general federal statute or jurisprudential rule that tolls the running of a statute of limitations such as 46 U.S.C.A. § 30106 by pursuit of a related claim in another forum. Thus the cautious attorney may file a protective suit to prevent the accrual of the statute of limitations on his seaman's claim pending the outcome of a LHWCA claim or state worker's compensation claim. *See, e.g., Wilson v. Zapata Off–Shore Co.*, 939 F.2d 260 (5th Cir. 1991). Whether an LHWCA claim or a seaman's suit for tort damages or maintenance and cure will toll the statute of limitations on a state worker's compensation remedy depends upon the applicable state law.

Another problem arising in "borderline" status cases is whether pursuit of one remedy will bar subsequent recovery under another. As to unseaworthiness and Jones Act claims against the same defendant, the answer is clear: they must be brought together or the omitted one is waived. *McAllister v. Magnolia Petroleum Co.*, 357 U.S. 221 (1958)*; Baltimore Steamship Co. v. Phillips*, 274 U.S. 316 (1927). The rule may be different if the shipowner is not the Jones Act employer.

The maintenance and cure claim need not be joined with either the Jones Act or the unseaworthiness claim; however, disposition of one of the claims for seamen's benefits (Jones Act/unseaworthiness or maintenance and cure) may bar or reduce recovery under the other. For example, if a seaman first recovers maintenance and cure, he cannot recover the same damages (such as lost wages or medical expenses) in his claim for tort damages under the Jones Act and unseaworthiness. Similarly, a claimant unsuccessful in his first suit may be estopped by judgment (collateral estoppel) from pursuing a second suit, such as when there is a ruling adverse to the claimant on the issue of seaman status, or, perhaps, if there is a holding that the claimant was not in the course and scope of his employment (in the service of the ship) at the time of injury.

Mere acceptance of LHWCA benefits does not bar a worker's subsequent pursuit of seamen's remedies. However, if an adjudication is made in the LHWCA proceeding that the worker is covered by the Act, he or she may be barred from subsequently pursuing seamen's remedies. *See, e.g., Fontenot v. AWI, Inc.*, 923 F.2d 1127 (5th Cir. 1991)*; McDermott International, Inc. v. Wilander*, 498 U.S. 337 (1991). *Compare Papai v. Harbor Tug and Barge Co.*, 67 F.3d 203 (9th Cir. 1995). Acceptance of state worker's compensation benefits without an award or judgment will not bar a later suit for seamen's benefits. *Reyes v. Delta Dallas Alpha Corp.*, 199 F.3d 626 (2d Cir. 1999).

The LHWCA is a compensation statute, similar to most state worker's compensation statutes. Mere acceptance of benefits under a state compensation statute should not preclude subsequent assertion of a LHWCA remedy, and vice versa. Problems arise, however, when a claimant obtains an award under one of the remedies and then seeks benefits under the other. If the remedies are mutually exclusive, i.e., there is no "twilight zone" in which an injury is compensable under both statutes, an adjudication that the worker is entitled to benefits under one remedy should estop him from establishing coverage under the other. *See, e.g.*, La. R.S. 23:1035.2 (no state worker's compensation payable to any employee covered by the FELA, the LHWCA, or the Jones Act.) However, generally there is a "twilight zone" in which both remedies apply. After the 1972 amendments, a worker's claim may be compensable under both the LHWCA and the applicable state worker's compensation statute, at least if the injury occurs on land, including docks and piers. *Sun Ship, Inc. v. Pennsylvania*, 447 U.S. 715 (1980). There is no definitive jurisprudence yet on whether the "twilight zone" also extends to territorial waters or to the Outer Continental Shelf where the LHWCA is made applicable through the provisions of the Outer Continental Shelf Lands Act, 43 U.S.C.A. § 1333(b).

When the case falls in this "twilight" area, a worker who recovers under one compensation system nevertheless may be barred from recovering under another system by application of the doctrine of full faith and credit. The LHWCA and some state worker's compensation statutes contain language to the effect that acceptance of benefits under the statute constitutes the employee's exclusive remedy against the employer. That language precludes a tort claim (except, perhaps, for an intentional tort) by the employee against the employer, but it is not clear whether it also bars the employee's recovery against the employer under the compensation system of another sovereign. If benefits are awarded under a compensation statute the "exclusivity" language of which was intended to preclude subsequent recovery under another compensation system, subsequently permitting such recovery may constitute a denial of "full faith and credit" to the first sovereign's statutes. The extent to which "full faith and credit" prevents such subsequent recovery remains uncertain after three Supreme Court decisions on the subject. *Thomas v. Washington Gas Light Co.*, 448 U.S. 261 (1980); *Industrial Commission of Wisconsin v. McCartin*, 330 U.S. 622 (1947); *Magnolia Petroleum Co. v. Hunt*, 320 U.S. 430 (1943). For an attempted accommodation of the conflicting opinions in *McCartin* and *Hunt* with the opinion in *Thomas*, see *Landry v. Carlson Mooring Service*, 643 F.2d 1080 (5th Cir.1981). If recovery is permitted under the LHWCA after the employee has recovered under a state compensation scheme, the employer is entitled to a credit for sums paid under the state remedy. 33 U.S.C.A. § 903(a). However, that credit may not include all of the sums paid, such as that portion of the first award that was paid to the claimant's attorney as a fee. *See, e.g.*, *Landry v. Carlson Mooring Service*, *supra*.

Even when full faith and credit does not prevent subsequent recovery under another compensation system, an adjudication under one system may bar recovery under another. An adverse adjudication of a fact in one proceeding may estop the claimant from proving that fact in the subsequent claim and effectively bar recovery. For example, a determination in a state worker's compensation proceeding that the injury did not arise in the course of the claimant's employment may bar recovery under the LHWCA claim, if the standard for proof of "course of employment" is the same for both statutes.

CHAPTER XIV

WRONGFUL DEATH

In the second half of the nineteenth century, the Supreme Court adopted for maritime law what had once been the prevailing American common law rule that there was no recovery in tort if the victim died. *The Harrisburg*, 119 U.S. 199 (1886). By the time of the decision, many jurisdictions already had abandoned the harsh common law rule. Thus the Court's judgment in *The Harrisburg* was supported neither by logic, precedent nor policy; nevertheless, the rule of *The Harrisburg* became settled maritime law.

State legislatures responded by adopting general wrongful death and survival actions, but Congress did not. However, in the Federal Employer's Liability Act of 1908 (FELA), Congress provided wrongful death and survival actions for railway workers, and when it adopted the Jones Act in 1920, it extended those FELA remedies to survivors of seamen. The Supreme Court, although not compelled to do so by the statutory language, restricted recovery in wrongful death actions under the FELA to "pecuniary" losses, *Michigan Central Railroad Co. v. Vreeland*, 227 U.S. 59 (1913), and that limitation was judicially applied to claims under the Jones Act. In the same year in which it adopted the Jones Act,

Congress also passed the Death on the High Seas Act (DOHSA), initially providing that

> Whenever the death of a person shall be caused by wrongful act ... occurring on the high seas beyond a marine league ... the personal representative of the decedent may maintain a suit for damages in the district courts of the United States, in admiralty, for the exclusive benefit of the decedent's wife, husband, parent, child, or dependent relative against the vessel, person, or corporation which would have been liable if death had not ensued.

46 U.S.C.A. § 761(a). It was recodified in 2006 as 46 U.S.C.A. § 30302. DOHSA applies where the wrongful act has an impact upon the victim, although the wrongful act is committed upon land or the death occurs on land. DOHSA does not expressly provide for a survival action and limits recovery to "pecuniary loss." 46 U.S.C.A. § 762(a) now 46 U.S.C. § 30303.

Legislative and executive action has impacted the general pattern provided in the initial DOHSA. The extension of U.S. territorial waters to 24 miles by Presidential Proclamation, Pres. Proc. No. 7219, 64 Fed. Reg. 48701 (Aug. 2, 1999), may have extended the seaward boundary of DOHSA. *See In re Air Crash Off Long Island, N.Y.*, 209 F.3d 200 (2d Cir. 2000) (term "high seas" in DOHSA means waters beyond territorial waters of U.S.; thus DOHSA does not apply to crash in U.S. territorial waters eight miles from coast). Thereafter the Wendell H. Ford

Aviation Investment and Reform Act for the 21st Century, Pub. L. No. 106–181, 114 Stat. 61 (2000), now 46 U.S.C. Sec. 30307, amended DOHSA to provide that in commercial aviation accidents: (1) DOHSA does not apply within 12 miles from shore, and (2) nonpecuniary damages, but not punitive damages, are recoverable for wrongful death beyond 12 miles. The failure of the amendments to observe the 24 mile line arguably means that the Presidential Proclamation extended the U.S. territorial sea for international law purposes only, and thus did not alter DOHSA's application beyond one "marine league" (three nautical miles) from shore. The legislation also raises questions about why nonpecuniary damages should be expressly available for deaths resulting from commercial aviation accidents but *not* vessel accidents.

The initial Congressional response in 1920 to the *Harrisburg* left large gaps in recovery for maritime torts resulting in death. If the act producing death occurred on the high seas, recovery of pecuniary damages was available, but there could be no recovery through DOHSA for nonpecuniary damages, such as loss of society. DOHSA did not provide a survival action; thus in all cases arising on the high seas other than those falling within the Jones Act, survival damages could be recovered only if maritime law could "borrow" the survival statute of a state with significant interest in the controversy. The jurisprudence did not set forth clearly when this could be done.

Where the maritime tort causing death occurred on territorial or inland waters, then, except in cases falling under the Jones Act, there was no federal statute permitting wrongful death recovery; there were no survival action statutes; and there was no maritime common law remedy. Recovery for wrongful death in such cases sometimes could be obtained by "borrowing" the applicable state wrongful death statute, but when that occurred the admiralty claimant took the state law with all of its restrictions, including its statute of limitations and, in many instances, the rule that contributory negligence barred recovery. *The Tungus v. Skovgaard*, 358 U.S. 588 (1959). Even "borrowing," where permissible, did not aid the beneficiaries of a seaman killed within territorial waters. In *Gillespie v. United States Steel Corp.*, 379 U.S. 148 (1964), the Supreme Court held that the Jones Act was the exclusive remedy of the seaman and his beneficiaries against his employer; hence the beneficiaries could not "borrow" the state wrongful death statute where the seaman's death was caused by some wrongful act other than negligence, such as unseaworthiness.

This legislative and judicial action and inaction produced a number of anomalies. One was that if an unseaworthy condition caused a seaman's death through injury on the high seas, his beneficiaries could recover under DOHSA, but if his death resulted from injury caused by an unseaworthy condition within territorial waters, there was no recovery. A second anomaly was that the beneficiaries of a

Sieracki seaman (*see* Chapter XIII, *supra*) killed in an accident occurring beyond three miles from shore could recover from the shipowner under DOHSA, but if the accident took place within territorial waters, recovery depended upon whether the applicable state statute encompassed an action for unseaworthiness. The third, and most intolerable anomaly, was that if a seaman and a *Sieracki* seaman were killed by an unseaworthy condition while working side by side in an American port, the *Sieracki* seaman's beneficiaries might recover, depending upon local law, but the seaman's beneficiaries could not.

These anomalies and the continued lack of congressional response led the Supreme Court in 1970 to abrogate the rule barring recovery for wrongful death in admiralty. In a superb opinion authored by Justice John Marshall Harlan, the Court ruled that the beneficiaries of a *Sieracki* seaman killed within territorial waters could recover wrongful death benefits under the maritime common law, regardless of whether a statute of the state in which the accident occurred permitted such recovery. *Moragne v. States Marine Lines, Inc.*, 398 U.S. 375 (1970). Initially there was some dispute over whether the *Moragne* remedy was limited to a longshoreman's unseaworthiness claims, but that view has not prevailed; *Moragne* provides a remedy whenever the defendant's conduct constitutes a maritime tort, including both negligence and unseaworthiness. *Miles v. Apex Marine Corp.*, 498 U.S. 19 (1990); *Norfolk Shipbuilding & Drydock Corp. v. Garris*,

532 U.S. 811 (2001). This is, of course, consistent with the remedial nature of a wrongful death claim.

Moragne raised a number of significant questions: (1) Did the remedy that it established extend beyond territorial waters? (2) If it did, would it supplant or be subservient to the Death on the High Seas Act? (3) Could the new remedy supplement the death provisions of the Jones Act? (4) Did *Moragne* include recovery for nonpecuniary losses? and (5) Did it include survival benefits as well as wrongful death damages?

Subsequent decisions by the Court have provided answers to some of those questions but have raised other questions. In *Sea–Land Services, Inc. v. Gaudet*, 414 U.S. 573 (1974), the Court ruled that the general maritime law wrongful death remedy includes nonpecuniary damages for loss of society but not for grief. In the wake of *Gaudet*, some courts authorized recovery of nonpecuniary damages in admiralty wrongful death cases but only where the plaintiff beneficiary also was financially dependent upon the decedent. Additionally, cases arose in which the victim was killed beyond three miles from shore and the beneficiaries sought recovery for loss of society. These cases presented two other post-*Moragne* issues: whether the general maritime wrongful death remedy applied beyond territorial waters and, if so, whether the benefits it provided could be used to supplement recovery under the Death on the High Seas Act. When one of these cases, *Mobil Oil Corporation v. Higginbotham*, 436 U.S. 618 (1978), reached the Supreme Court, it apparently concluded that the *Moragne* remedy is applicable beyond three miles from shore *but* held that in such cases, the survivors could not recover under *Moragne* the nonpecuniary damages—loss of society—that were not available under the Death on the High Seas Act. The Court observed:

> The Death on the High Seas Act . . . announces Congress' considered judgment on such issues as the beneficiaries, the limitations period, contributory negligence, survival, and damages. . . . The Act does not address every issue of wrongful death law . . . but when it does speak directly to a question, the courts are not free to "supplement" Congress' answer so thoroughly that the Act becomes meaningless.

See also, Zicherman v. Korean Air Lines Co., 516 U.S. 217 (1996).

Later, the Supreme Court ruled that state law may not supplement recovery to provide nonpecuniary damages in cases where the Death on the High Seas Act applies, despite the language of Section 7 of DOHSA (now Title 46 U.S.C. Sec. 30308) that "[t]he provisions of any State Statute giving . . . rights of action or remedies for death shall not be affected by this chapter." *Offshore Logistics, Inc. v. Tallentire*, 477 U.S. 207 (1986).

Still later, in *Miles v. Apex Marine Corporation*, 498 U.S. 19 (1990), the Supreme Court held that a seaman's beneficiaries could not recover for nonpecuniary loss, such as loss of society, under the general maritime law. The Court's logic was simple:

Congress in the Jones Act withheld recovery of nonpecuniary damages in seamen's death claims, and the courts were not free to "sanction more expansive remedies in a judicially-created cause of action in which liability is without fault than Congress has allowed in cases of death resulting from negligence." Although the language of *Miles* does not require an expansive reading, some courts have held that the decision precludes recovery of nonpecuniary damages in any maritime wrongful death action, including seaman death claims against third parties (non-employers and non-vessel owners) and non-seaman death claims. *Scarborough v. Clemco Industries*, 391 F.3d 660 (5th Cir. 2004); *Tucker v. Fearn*, 333 F.3d 1216 (11th Cir. 2003); *In the Matter of American River Transportation Company*, 490 F.3d 351 (5th Cir. 2007). Some even extended the *Miles* holding to bar recovery for other types of nonpecuniary damages such as punitive damages and recovery for negligent infliction of emotional distress.

Subsequently, the Supreme Court once again considered the issue of wrongful death recovery in admiralty cases. The issue was whether state law could be used to supplement the benefits available under the common law wrongful death remedy in a case where the decedent was not a seaman or longshore worker, and the death occurred in territorial waters. In *Yamaha Motor Corp. v. Calhoun*, 514 U.S. 1126 (1995), the Court ruled that in maritime wrongful death cases in which (1) no federal statute specifies the appropriate relief and the decedent was not a seafarer (seaman, longshore worker or person otherwise engaged in a maritime trade); (2) there was no Congressionally enacted comprehensive tort recovery regime; and (3) the death occurred in territorial waters, state remedies may remain applicable and not displaced by *Moragne*. The Court specifically reserved the question of whether state law could be applied to standards governing liability, as distinguished from rules on remedies. On remand, the appellate court applied maritime law in determining the standard for tort liability but state wrongful death law for the types of damages recoverable. *See also*, *In Re Amtrak "Sunset Limited" Train Crash*, 121 F.3d 1421 (11th Cir. 1997) (Yamaha does not embody unspoken rule that state interest must always trump competing admiralty principles, when the two collide in state territorial waters). The passage in 2000 of the Wendell H. Ford Aviation Investment and Reform Act for the 21st Century, *supra*, raises further issues because it allows recovery of nonpecuniary damages in wrongful death cases arising out of commercial aviation disasters on the high seas.

Under *Moragne* and under the Death on the High Seas Act, the beneficiaries of a victim may maintain an action for wrongful death although before death the victim recovered damages for the subsequently fatal injuries. *Sea–Land Services, Inc. v. Gaudet*, page 328, *supra*. The opposite result has been reached where the wrongful death claim is based upon the FELA, through which Jones Act wrongful death claims are maintained. *Mellon v. Goodyear*, 277 U.S. 335 (1928).

Another unresolved issue is the availability of a general maritime common law survival remedy. *Moragne* involved a wrongful death claim, and the Supreme Court thereafter expressly reserved the question of whether the *Moragne* remedy would include survival damages. *Miles v. Apex Marine Corporation,* page 165, *supra.* The lower courts generally hold that maritime common law provides a survival action. *See, e.g., Evich v. Morris*, 819 F.2d 256 (9th Cir. 1987). If there is such an action, however, it does not include recovery for the deceased seaman's loss of projected post-death earnings, *Miles v. Apex Marine Corporation*, page 165 *supra*, or pre-death pain and suffering on the high seas, *Dooley v. Korean Airlines Co., Ltd.*, 524 U.S. 116 (1998).

If there is a general maritime survival action, is it preempted beyond territorial waters by the Death on the High Seas Act? The only ''survival'' provision in DOHSA, section 765, provides that

if a person die[s] ... as a result of [a] wrongful act ... during the pendency ... of a suit to recover damages for personal injuries in respect of such act ... the personal representative ... may be substituted as a party and the suit may proceed as a suit under this chapter for recovery of the compensation provided in section 762 [wrongful death benefits].

This is not a survival statute, properly speaking, but is a type of non-abatement statute, since it converts a pre-existing suit for personal injury by the victim into a wrongful death action by his beneficiaries. However, the Supreme Court in *Higginbotham*, page 328, *supra*, wrote that section 765 announced Congress' "considered judgment" on "survival" actions on the high seas. Section 765 was recodified in its general form by 46 U.S.C.A. § 30305.

There is no statutory abrogation of the early common law rule that a cause of action in tort abates upon the death of the tortfeasor; however, it is not likely that the rule has survived. *See, e.g., McKeithen v. M/T Frosta*, 435 F.Supp. 584 (E.D.La. 1977).

A partial summary of recovery of wrongful death and survival damages in maritime law after *Moragne*, *Gaudet*, *Higginbotham*, *Miles* and *Yamaha* reads like this:

1. If a seaman is killed by employer negligence within or beyond three miles from shore, his beneficiaries may recover under the Jones Act. Both wrongful death and survival remedies are available, but wrongful death recovery is limited to pecuniary damages from the employer (and maybe even from third persons).

2. If a seaman is killed beyond three miles by an unseaworthy condition, his beneficiaries may recover wrongful death benefits under DOHSA. However, recovery is limited to pecuniary damages. DOH-

SA applies if the wrongful act occurs on the high seas (or has an effect on the high seas), even if death occurs later on land or on territorial waters. Whether a survival action is available depends upon whether (a) there is a maritime survival action which is not preempted by section 765, now Title 46 U.S.C. Sec. 30305, of DOHSA (creation or recognition of a general maritime law survival action would seem to make the most sense), or (b) recovery can be obtained through "borrowing" the survival action of an adjacent state. *See, e.g., Offshore Logistics, Inc. v. Tallentire,* page 329, *supra.* However, damages for pre-death pain and suffering are not available.

3. If a seaman is killed within three miles of the shore by an unseaworthy condition, his beneficiaries may recover wrongful death benefits under *Moragne*; however, they may not recover nonpecuniary damages under *Miles.* The beneficiaries also may be entitled to recover survival damages, either (a) under a maritime survival action, if one exists, or (b) by application of a state survival statute.

4. In other death actions beyond three miles from shore (including, probably, actions under Title 33 U.S.C.A. section 905(b), *see* Chapter XIII), wrongful death recovery may be obtained through DOHSA. However, only pecuniary damages are recoverable. A survival action is possible, depending upon the existence of a common law remedy or the preemption of such a remedy (or of a state remedy) by DOHSA. DOHSA may apply although the wrongful death occurs on land, if the death was caused by

negligent conduct having an impact upon the victim on the high seas. *See, e.g., Motts v. M/V Green Wave,* 210 F.3d 565 (5th Cir. 2000).

5.   If a seaman dies as a result of a maritime tort committed by a third party tortfeasor within territorial waters, wrongful death benefits should be available through *Moragne*. However, *Miles* may prevent the beneficiaries from recovering nonpecuniary damages. The beneficiaries' entitlement to survival damages depends upon the existence of a maritime common law remedy or the borrowing of a state survival statute.

6.   In all other maritime death actions within three miles of the shore, the beneficiaries may recover under *Moragne*. Damages will include nonpecuniary damages, unless *Miles* ultimately is interpreted to bar recovery of nonpecuniary damages in any maritime wrongful death setting. Even if *Miles* precludes recovery of nonpecuniary damages, that remedy may be available to some claimants through state law. *See Yamaha Motor Corp. v. Calhoun,* page 330, *supra.* Availability of a survival action depends upon the existence of a maritime common law survival remedy or the borrowing of a state survival statute.

Many Americans are employed by American-based employers to perform maritime work within the territorial waters of another nation. When one of these workers is killed, recovery by his representative or beneficiaries may turn, in part, upon whether the territorial waters are the "high seas" where DOHSA applies, or whether the general maritime common law, i.e., *Moragne* and *Gaudet*, applies. Most lower courts hold that DOHSA applies to death actions within the territorial waters of foreign sovereigns.

In the wrongful death action, the Jones Act beneficiaries take "by class." The presence of a wife or child precludes recovery by the beneficiaries in the next lower class—the parents—and the presence of an eligible parent precludes recovery by any member of the next class, other dependent relatives. Under DOHSA, all of these beneficiaries are eligible to recover and share in the award, even though some would be in a higher "class" than others under the Jones Act approach. In applying *Moragne*, the lower courts have utilized the DOHSA approach and permit all of the beneficiaries to recover. One unresolved question is whether the more remote *Moragne* beneficiaries, such as parents or siblings, must have been financially dependent upon the victim at death. The Jones Act and DOHSA demand that these relatives be "dependent," a logical requirement inasmuch as those acts permit recovery of pecuniary benefits only. If *Moragne* permits recovery of nonpecuniary benefits, such as loss of society, the requirement of beneficiary dependency would be a matter of policy, not logic. The weight of authority is that parents and siblings cannot recover under *Moragne* unless they were dependent on the victim. *See Sutton v. Earles*, 26 F.3d 903 (9th Cir. 1994), and the cases cited therein.

Under all three wrongful death actions—Jones Act, DOHSA and *Moragne*—the personal representative is the proper party plaintiff and controls the litigation, unless there is a conflict of interest between the representative and the beneficiaries. *See Calton v. Zapata Lexington*, 811 F.2d 919 (5th Cir. 1987), and the authorities cited therein. State law furnishes the rule for determining whether a claimant has the requisite legal relationship with the victim to qualify as a beneficiary in the wrongful death action. *Tidewater Marine Towing, Inc. v. Curran–Houston, Inc.*, 785 F.2d 1317 (5th Cir. 1986).

Formerly, the three maritime theories for wrongful death recovery were time-barred by different standards. The Jones Act was subject to a three-year statute of limitations, DOHSA had a two-year statute of limitations, and the common law remedy was governed by laches. The maritime tort personal injury and death statute of limitations, 46 U.S.C.A. § 763a, makes both DOHSA and the common law death actions subject to the same three-year limitation period as Jones Act claims.

A Jones Act death claim may be brought in federal court at law or in admiralty or in state court. A death action premised upon *Moragne* may be brought in admiralty or in state court or, if there is diversity jurisdiction, on the law side of federal court. DOHSA, 46 U.S.C.A. § 761, now Title 46 U.S.C. Sec. 30302, authorizes the personal representative of the decedent to bring an action "in a civil action, in admiralty." This language has led some courts to conclude that jurisdiction over a DOHSA claim is exclusively in the federal court sitting in admiralty, and the claimant is not entitled to trial by jury unless the claim is properly joined with some other claim (such as a Jones Act claim) triable to a jury. Later decisions, including strong dicta by the Supreme Court in *Offshore Logistics, Inc. v. Tallentire*, page 329, *supra*, indicate that jurisdiction over a DOHSA claim is concurrent between the admiralty court and state court.

The Longshore and Harbor Workers' Compensation Act (LHWCA) provides death benefits to designated beneficiaries if the work-related injury causes death, or if an employee who is permanently disabled in a compensable accident dies thereafter from other causes. 33 U.S.C.A. § 909. It also provides for survival of a claim for permanent partial disability where the employee dies from causes other than the work-related injury. 33 U.S.C.A. § 908(d)(1). The extension of survival benefits when the death is not related to the compensable injury was effected in the 1972 amendments to the LHWCA. Courts have held that these survival benefits are payable even though the compensable injury occurred prior to the effective date of the amendment. *See, e.g., Puig v. Standard Dredging Corp.*, 599 F.2d 467 (1st Cir. 1979), and the cases cited therein. Benefits payable to disabled workers under the LHWCA are subject to a maximum "ceiling" of 200% of the national average weekly wage of production or nonsupervisory workers on private, nonagricultural payrolls. Construing the 1972 amendments, the United States Supreme Court held that the "ceiling" did not apply to death benefits payable under the Act. *Director, Office of Workers' Compensation Programs v. Rasmussen*, 440 U.S. 29 (1979). However, a 1984 amendment imposes the 200% "ceiling" on death benefits. 33 U.S.C.A. § 909(e).

CHAPTER XV

PLATFORM INJURIES

A. HISTORY AND BACKGROUND

Exploration for minerals beneath navigable waters is conducted from movable drilling structures or from stationary platforms constructed over water and permanently attached to the subsoil and seabed. Maritime law treats the movable structures as vessels, and thus within admiralty jurisdiction, even when the structures are temporarily attached to the seabed. The stationary or "fixed" platforms, however, are treated as land, *see Rodrigue v. Aetna Cas. & Surety Co.*, 395 U.S. 352 (1969). The large number of accidents occurring on these stationary platforms has led to the development of a unique body of law which is intertwined with maritime personal injury law.

A little history aids a proper understanding of platform law. When exploration for minerals under the beds of navigable waters became feasible about the middle of the twentieth century, the United States, first by presidential proclamation and later by international convention, obtained ownership and dominion over the natural resources in the seabed and subsoil of the Continental Shelf, which in some areas extends as much as two hundred miles seaward from the American coastline. The United States Supreme Court thereafter held that all of the Shelf and its resources, from the coastline seaward, belonged to the federal sovereign. *United States v. California*, 332 U.S. 19 (1947). Subsequently, Congress ceded to each coastal state the lands beneath that state's territorial waters, i.e., those waters lying within the projection seaward of the state's boundaries for designated distances. 43 U.S.C.A. §§ 1301, 1311. Those statutes have been interpreted as extending the dominion of the states of Texas and Florida seaward a distance of three marine leagues (about nine nautical miles) and the boundaries of Louisiana, Mississippi and Alabama seaward a distance of three geographical miles. *See United States v. Louisiana, Texas, Mississippi, Alabama and Florida*, 363 U.S. 1 (1960); *United States v. Florida*, 420 U.S. 531 (1975). For the remainder of the Outer Continental Shelf, Congress provided:

> To the extent that they are applicable and not inconsistent with this subchapter or with other Federal laws and regulations . . . now in effect or hereafter adopted the civil and criminal laws of each adjacent State . . . are declared to be the law of the United States for that portion of the . . . outer Continental Shelf . . . which would be within the area of the state if its boundaries were extended seaward to the outer margin of the outer Continental Shelf. . . . 43 U.S.C.A. § 1333(a)(2)(A).

Thus if there is no applicable federal law: (1) state law applies on the Outer Continental Shelf (OCS) as "surrogate" federal law, and (2) state law applies of its own force within the state's territorial waters. The difference may be more than semantic. When federal law preempts state law under the Supremacy Clause (such as within a state's territorial waters), subsequently developing federal common law presumably takes precedence over state law. The result may not be the same if federal common law develops after Congress adopted state law in the Outer Shelf Lands Act (OSLA), since arguably the effect in such case would be to give federal common law priority over a federal statute. The Supreme Court alluded to but did not squarely face this intriguing question in *Gulf Offshore Co. v. Mobil Oil Corp.*, 453 U.S. 473 (1981).

In *Demette v. Falcon Drilling Co.*, 280 F.3d 492 (5th Cir. 2002), the court held that the OCSLA applies to: (1) the subsoil and seabed of the OCS; (2) any artificial island, installation, or other device if (a) it is permanently or temporarily attached to the seabed of the OCS, and (b) it has been erected on the seabed of the OCS, and (c) its presence on the OCS is to explore for, develop, or produce resources from the OCS; and (3) any artificial island, installation or other device if (a) it is permanently or temporarily attached to the seabed of the OCS, and (b) it is not a ship or vessel, and (c) its presence on the OCS to transport resources from the OCS. As noted in Chapter 2, *supra, Demette* may mean that a jack-up rig ceases to be a vessel when jacked up on the Outer Continental Shelf. Alternatively, one might read *Demette* for the proposition that a jack-up rig while jacked up on the Outer Continental Shelf can be a vessel for some purposes (i.e., seaman status) but a non-vessel for others such as the Outer Continental Shelf lands Act and the LHWCA.

B. TORT CLAIMS

If a platform is located on the Outer Continental Shelf, state tort law applies as "surrogate" federal law, unless there is applicable federal law. If the platform is within territorial waters, state tort law applies unless it is preempted by applicable federal law. Thus torts occurring on platforms ordinarily will be governed by state law unless there is some applicable federal law. One such law is the Admiralty Extension Act (AEA), 46 U.S.C.A. § 740 which applies only if the tort was "caused by a vessel on navigable waters" and has "maritime flavor." However, the AEA frequently will not apply to the platform injury because the accident is not due to a defect in an appurtenance of the vessel but is caused by personnel performing service for the vessel. *Dahlen v. Gulf Crews, Inc.*, 281 F.3d 487 (5th Cir. 2002). Similarly, a wrongful death occurring in connection with a platform may fall under the Death on the High Seas Act, if the wrongful act occurs on the high seas and, perhaps, has "maritime flavor." (*See* Chapter XIV, *supra*). Otherwise, torts occurring on a platform ordinarily do not fall within maritime tort jurisdiction since the maritime common law treats the platform as an "extension of the land" (and thus lacking in "locality") and deems exploration for oil and gas from fixed platforms as lacking in "maritime flavor." *Rodrigue v. Aetna Cas. & Surety Co.*, 395 U.S. 352 (1969); *Herb's Welding, Inc. v. Gray*, 470 U.S. 414 (1985). The same result may attain when an injury occurs on the water near a platform because of negligence in the platform drilling process; there is "locality," but "flavor" may be lacking. *See, e.g.*, *In re Dearborn Marine Service, Inc.*, 499 F.2d 263 (5th Cir. 1974). Accordingly, state law usually governs the resolution of tort claims that arise from activities on fixed platforms. When state law governs, the litigants take that law in its entirety, including a state statute of limitations which may be shorter than the federal maritime statute, 46 U.S.C.A. § 763a, or that provides a time bar different from that which would result through application of the maritime doctrine of laches. *Chevron Oil Co. v. Huson*, 404 U.S. 97 (1971). In short, platform injury claims are a trap for the unwary law student, lawyer, or judge.

State tort law may not apply to all non-maritime torts that occur on fixed platforms. There are numerous federal regulations governing safety on platforms, and many accidents occurring on the platforms are caused at least in part by violation of those regulations. Prior to 1978, the federal courts refused to imply a federal cause of action for damages from a violation of such regulations. In that year, however, the OCSLA was amended to provide:

It shall be the duty of any holder of a lease or permit ... to—

(1) maintain all places of employment within the lease area ... in compliance with occupational safety and health standards and ... free from recognized hazards to employees ... [and]

(2) maintain all operations ... in compliance with regulations intended to protect persons ... on the Outer Continental Shelf ... 43 U.S.C.A. § 1348(b)

and

Any resident of the United States who is injured in any manner through the failure of any operator to comply with any rule, regulation, order, or permit issued pursuant to this subchapter may bring an action for damages [including reasonable attorney and expert witness fees] only in the judicial district having jurisdiction under paragraph (1) of this subsection. 43 U.S.C.A. § 1349(b)(2).

Arguably, these provisions establish a federal statutory action for damages caused by unsafe conditions or the violation of federal safety regulations on platforms located on the Shelf; however, this view has yet to find judicial support. *See, e.g., Wentz v. Kerr–McGee Corp.*, 784 F.2d 699 (5th Cir. 1986). Even if the amendments did not create a new federal cause of action, a stronger argument now can be made that a federal cause of action should be implied from violation of the duties imposed upon lease holders by the provisions of the OCSLA and by regulations adopted pursuant to the Act. Applying the test provided by the Supreme Court in *Cort v. Ash*, 422 U.S. 66 (1975) to the original version of the OCSLA, the Fifth Circuit concluded that a federal damage action for maritime workers could not be implied. *Olsen v. Shell Oil Co.*, 561 F.2d 1178 (5th Cir. 1977). However, the 1977 amendments added the provisions cited above and other sections that reflect a strong Congressional purpose of promoting the safety of workers on the Shelf, an important ingredient in the *Cort* test for implying the existence of a federal cause of action. As noted, lawyers and courts have not yet adopted your authors' contentions on this issue and in *Dupre v. Chevron U.S.A., Inc.*, 109 F.3d 230 (5th Cir. 1997), the court held that federal regulations adopted pursuant to the OCSLA did not provide the basis for an implied federal right of action nor did they create an independent duty under state law.

Federal and state courts have concurrent jurisdiction over claims arising on the Outer Continental Shelf. *Gulf Offshore Co. v. Mobil Oil Corp.*, 453 U.S. 473 (1981). Venue is proper "in the judicial district in which any defendant resides or may be found, or in the judicial district of the State nearest the place the cause of action arose." 43 U.S.C.A. § 1349(b)(1).

Drilling operations on an offshore platform usually are conducted by contractors and specialized subcontractors. This presents nice legal questions such as the duty that the platform owner or operator owes to the contractor's employees. The owner or operator may not owe a duty to persons on the platform unless it has "operational control" over the contractor's work or expressly or impliedly approves the contractor's unsafe work practice. *Fruge v. Parker Drilling Co.*, 337 F.3d 558 (5th Cir. 2003).

Another interesting issue is whether the contractor's immunity from workplace negligence through worker compensation extends to the platform owner or operator. A most frequently litigated issue in platform injury cases is indemnification. The contracts for drilling operations on an offshore platform commonly contain indemnity agreements. Maritime law upholds the validity of an indemnity agreement in which the indemnitor agrees to indemnify against indemnitee negligence, but some of the oil producing states, such as Texas and Louisiana, have adopted statutes which invalidate indemnitee-negligence provisions in mineral exploration contracts. Thus determination of the validity of the indemnity provision in a platform operations contract may turn upon whether the contract is maritime. *See, e.g., Smith v. Penrod Drilling Corp.*, 960 F.2d 456 (5th Cir. 1992). Some indemnitee-negligence agreements for operations on the Outer Continental Shelf are validated by 33 U.S.C.A. § 905(c), which expressly authorizes "reciprocal" indemnity agreements between a vessel owner and the maritime employer of a worker who is covered by the LHWCA through the OCSLA.

In *Grand Isle Shipyard, Inc. v. Seacor Marine, LLC*, 543 F.3d 256 (5th Cir. 2008), the court held that under the holding in *Demette, supra,* the OCS-LA did not apply to an indemnity claim arising out of an injury to a worker being transported by vessel on the high seas where the vessel was in close proximity to a platform at the time of the accident but neither the worker nor the vessel was in physical contact with the platform when the accident occurred. There, the court also held that where the majority of work to be performed under a contract was to be performed on OCSLA situses, the OCSLA applied along with any state anti-indemnity laws.

The general rule is that the state law designated by the OCSLA applies, even though that state's choice of law rules would dictate the application of the law of a sister state.

OCSLA claims filed in state court may be removed to federal court.

C. WORKER'S COMPENSATION CLAIMS

Workers on movable drilling structures on navigable waters may qualify as seamen under the prevailing test for seaman status. *See* Chapter XIII. If a worker qualifies as a seaman, his claim against his employer is not affected by the fact that his injury occurs on a fixed platform. A seaman's recovery under the Jones Act and for maintenance and cure is not limited to accidents occurring on water, and in some situations, a seaman may recover damages from the vessel for injuries occurring on land but caused by an unseaworthy condition of the vessel.

If the exploration for minerals is conducted from a fixed platform as opposed to a movable rig that qualifies as a vessel, a worker ordinarily will not attain seaman status. A seaman must have the requisite connexity with a vessel, and in maritime law a fixed platform is land, not a vessel. Some workers on fixed platforms may qualify as seamen because of their relationship to a vessel used in support of the platform's drilling activities. However, those craft ordinarily serve merely as "floating hotels" for the workers, and only cooks and others who perform much of their duties aboard the support vessel will qualify as seamen. A non-seaman on a "jack up" rig jacked up on the OCS may be covered by the LHWCA if the rig is treated as a "device ... temporarily attached to the seabed." *Demette, supra.*

Claims against employers by non-seamen working on fixed platforms will be governed by the LHWCA or by state worker's compensation, depending upon the geographical area in which the injury occurs. The OCSLA provides:

With respect to disability or death of an employee resulting from an injury occurring as the result of operations conducted on the outer Continental Shelf for the purpose of exploring for, developing, removing or transporting by pipeline the natural resources, or involving rights to the natural resources, of the subsoil and seabed of the outer Continental Shelf, compensation shall be payable under the provisions of the Longshoremen's and Harbor Workers' Compensation Act. For the purposes of the extension of the provisions of the [LHWCA] under this section—(1) the term "employee" does not include a master or member of a crew of any vessel, or an officer or employee of the United States or of any State. . . . 43 U.S.C.A. § 1333(b).

The Act clearly covers the compensation claims of privately-employed non-seamen injured while working on platforms on the Outer Continental Shelf. It also may extend the benefits of the LHWCA to some workers injured in accidents while engaged in mineral production within territorial and inland waters and on land; section 1333(b) does not expressly require that the injury occur on the Outer Continental Shelf, but only that the injury "occur . . . as a result of operations conducted" on the Shelf. There is a split of authority on whether LHWCA coverage applies under section 1333(b) only if the worker suffers injury on the Shelf. *Compare Mills v. Director, Office of Workers' Compensation Programs*, 877 F.2d 356 (5th Cir. 1989), and *Curtis v. Schlumberger Offshore Service, Inc.*, 849 F.2d 805 (3d Cir. 1988).

May a worker injured on a platform on the Outer Continental Shelf claim benefits under a state worker's compensation statute? Many of the state statutes extend coverage to workers injured outside the state, if the contract of employment is made within the state. One state supreme court has held that the adoption by the OCSLA of the LHWCA does not preclude application of state worker's compensation laws to injuries occurring on platforms on the Shelf. *Thompson v. Teledyne Movible Offshore, Inc.*, 419 So.2d 822 (La. 1982). However, federal court decisions have cast doubt upon the validity of that holding. *See, e.g., LeSassier v. Chevron, USA Inc.*, 776 F.2d 506 (5th Cir. 1985); *Gates v. Shell Oil Co.*, 812 F.2d 1509 (5th Cir. 1987).

The claim of a worker against his employer for injury on a fixed platform within territorial or inland waters usually is governed by the applicable state worker's compensation law, since (1) the worker usually does not qualify as a seaman, (2) he is not within the coverage of the LHWCA through the OCSLA, and (3) he usually lacks "status" as a maritime worker under the LHWCA, *Herb's Welding Inc. v. Gray*, 470 U.S. 414 (1985), or is not injured on a covered situs, *Thibodeaux v. Grasso Prod. Mgmt., Inc.*, 370 F.3d 486 (5th Cir. 2004). *Herb's Welding*, however, may not preclude LHWCA coverage for a mineral exploration platform worker who spends some of his time in "indisputable longshoring operations," such as loading and unloading vessels supplying the platform.

Foreign workers on fixed platforms off the shores of foreign sovereigns generally will be precluded from coverage under the Jones Act or the LHWCA, either by statutory exclusion, (*see* 46 U.S.C. § 30105(b) and Chapter XIII, *supra*) or because they do not otherwise meet the requirements for such coverage. American workers on fixed platforms in foreign waters may qualify as seamen but probably do not meet the "situs" requirement (injury on navigable waters of the United States) of the LHWCA. Their remedy often is through the worker compensation scheme of an American state with close ties to the worker or his employment contract.

CHAPTER XVI

SOVEREIGN IMMUNITY

Prior to 1916, the doctrine of sovereign immunity barred suits against the United States on maritime claims. In that year, in the Shipping Act, Congress made a limited waiver of immunity; however, the waiver permitted the arrest *in rem* of vessels under federal control, and for that reason proved unsatisfactory. In 1919 Congress adopted the Suits in Admiralty Act (SIAA), now codified at Title 46 U.S.C. section 30901 et seq., which authorized suits *in personam* against the United States for damages caused by a "merchant vessel" owned by the United States, but prohibited arrest or seizure of the vessel. If a claim did not fit within the Suits in Admiralty Act, such as where the vessel was a warship, the claimant was required to seek special legislation authorizing an action against the sovereign. In 1925, Congress adopted the Public Vessels Act (PVA), now Title 46 U.S.C. section 31101 et seq., which permits actions *in personam* against the United States for torts committed by "public vessels," including warships.

This disjointed approach to the waiver of sovereign immunity resulted in one hiatus: a ship under federal control which was neither a "merchant vessel" nor a "public vessel" did not come within the waiver of immunity in either statute. To eliminate this loophole, Congress in 1960 amended the Suits in Admiralty Act to extend the waiver of immunity to all cases "where if such vessel were privately owned or operated ... or if a private person or property were involved, a proceeding in admiralty could be maintained." 46 U.S.C. § 30903. This raised another issue: since the 1960 amendment placed all vessels under federal control within the language of the SIAA, did that act supersede the Public Vessels Act? The issue is not one of great significance, since the acts contain many similar provisions (including prohibitions against *in rem* proceedings, provisions permitting the sovereign to limit liability, and authorizations for arbitration or compromise of claims) and only a few differences (the SIAA provides more liberal venue rules, permits prejudgment interest and does not require "reciprocity" in suits brought by foreign nationals). The Supreme Court answered the question in the negative in *United States v. United Continental Tuna Corp.*, 425 U.S. 164 (1976). Thus if a tort is committed by a vessel belonging to the United States but not engaged in trade or commerce (such as a warship, customs patrol boat, Coast Guard search and rescue boat, or Army Corps of Engineers utility boat), the waiver of sovereign immunity is governed by the Public Vessels Act, to the extent its provisions differ from the Suits in Admiralty Act.

A more important and as yet unresolved issue is whether the Suits in Admiralty Act applies to maritime but non-vessel negligent acts of the federal sovereign. In 1946, Congress made a general waiver of tort immunity through the Federal Tort Claims Act (FTCA), now 28 U.S.C.A. § 2671 et seq. From 1946 until the 1960 amendment to the Suits in Admiralty Act, maritime tort claims against the United States that were not caused by a vessel, either "merchant" or "public," were brought under the FTCA. The 1960 amendment to the Suits in Admiralty Act, however, can be read as encompassing all maritime tort claims against the federal sovereign, including non-vessel torts which between 1946 and 1960 were brought under the FTCA. The lower courts generally hold that the SIAA and PVA now preempt the FTCA in all maritime torts claims against the federal sovereign. *McCormick v. United States*, 680 F.2d 345 (5th Cir. 1982); *Kelly v. United States*, 531 F.2d 1144 (2d Cir. 1976). *Compare Jones & Laughlin Steel, Inc. v. Mon River Towing, Inc.*, 772 F.2d 62 (3d Cir. 1985). The issue is significant, since there are important differences between the Suits in Admiralty Act and the FTCA, such as the pre-suit procedures, the courts in which they may be brought, the standards for liability and the statutes of limitations. One important exception to the United States' liability under the FTCA is the "discretionary function exception." Under this exception, the United States is not liable for errors in the performance of, or for the failure to perform, a discretionary function or duty. *See* 28 U.S.C. § 2680; *United States v. Empresa de Viacao Aerea Rio Grandense (Varig Airlines)*, 467 U.S. 797 (1984). Neither the SIAA nor the PVA explicitly provide such an exception to sovereign liability, although the courts have read it into the SIAA. *See, e.g.*, *McMellon v. United States*, 387 F.3d 329 (4th Cir. 2004). The discretionary function exception has been held to apply to a federal agency's decisions in marking, rather than removing, a sunken barge, *Liner v. Dravo Basic Materials Co.*, 162 F.Supp.2d 499 (E.D. La. 2001), and in a federal agency's decisions in designing and marking an improved harbor channel, in providing notice to mariners of the changes, and its decisions with respect to the maintenance of aids to navigation. *Compagnie Maritime Marfret v. San Juan Bay Pilots Corp.*, 532 F.Supp.2d 369 (D.Puerto Rico 2008).

When the waiver of immunity applies, the federal government is liable in the same manner as a private party, except that an *in rem* action may not be maintained. The SIAA has a two-year time limitation for filing of suit; the majority view is that it is a peremptive period or statute of repose, and not a statute of limitations; thus it is not subject to tolling or waiver. 46 U.S.C. § 30905. *But see McCormick v. United States*, 680 F.2d 345 (5th Cir. 1982). Under the FTCA, filing an administrative claim (which is required) tolls the statute of limitations. In contrast, the submission of an administrative claim is not a prerequisite to bringing suit under the SIAA, and therefore, the SIAA does not provide for the tolling of the two-year period upon the filing of a claim with an administrative body. Thus if a plaintiff with a maritime tort claim against the government mistakenly files an administrative claim but does not file a suit within two years, the claim will be time barred. *See, e.g.*, *Williams v. United States*, 711 F.2d 893 (9th Cir. 1983); *Taghadomi v. United States*, 401 F.3d 1080 (9th Cir. 2005). Recently, a court has held that the two-year statute may be subject to equitable tolling. *Hedges v. United States*, 404 F.3d 744 (3d Cir. 2005). Another trap for the unwary may arise from the operation of the Admiralty Extension Act, 46 U.S.C. § 740(b), which provides that in AEA suits against the United States, a plaintiff must present a written claim, and then wait six months before filing suit. The presentation of the written claim does not toll the two-year statute of limitations. Thus, in a case where the claim is made to the agency owning or operating the injury-causing vessel *less than* six months before the expiration of the two-year statute of limitations, the claim will be time barred. *Anderson v. United States*, 317 F.3d 1235 (11th Cir. 2003).

Federal employees sustaining injuries in a maritime setting usually are relegated to proceedings against their employer under the Federal Employees Compensation Act, 5 U.S.C.A. § 8101 et seq.; 33 U.S.C.A. § 903(B). However, a seaman employed by a private party who is under contract with the United States for the operation of one of its vessels may recover damages against the United States. In such a case, the exclusivity provision of the Suits in Admiralty Act, incorporated by reference in the

Public Vessels Act, allows the seaman to recover damages under the Jones Act and general maritime law. *See, e.g.*, *Arthur v. Maersk, Inc.*, 434 F.3d 196 (3d Cir. 2006); *Gavagan v. United States*, 955 F.2d 1016 (5th Cir. 1992).

The immunity of foreign states from maritime (and non-maritime) claims in American courts is governed by the Foreign Sovereign Immunities Act, adopted in 1976. The act provides sovereign immunity for claims arising out of noncommercial activities but does not provide immunity for claims based upon commercial activities carried on in, or having a direct effect in, the United States, or to acts performed in this country in connection with commercial activity elsewhere. 28 U.S.C.A. § 1604 et seq. The Act permits foreclosure upon a maritime lien *in personam* but does not permit an *in rem* proceeding against a vessel under the control of a foreign sovereign. 28 U.S.C.A. § 1605. A claimant may not obtain trial by jury against a foreign sovereign, even though he or she would otherwise be entitled to jury trial under federal maritime law. 28 U.S.C.A. § 1330. Jurisdiction over claims against foreign sovereigns is concurrent between federal and state courts, 28 U.S.C.A. § 1330, but a foreign sovereign may remove to federal court any civil action brought against it in a state court. 28 U.S.C.A. § 1441(d). There are special provisions for venue of such actions, 28 U.S.C.A. § 1391(f), and for the exercise of "long arm" jurisdiction over foreign sovereigns. 28 U.S.C.A. § 1608.

A state's immunity from suit in federal court, provided by the Eleventh Amendment, extends to maritime claims. *In re New York*, 256 U.S. 490 (1921). A state may expressly waive the immunity by statute. It also may waive the immunity if it voluntarily invokes or clearly declares that it intends to submit itself to the jurisdiction of the federal court. However, a state does not impliedly waive its immunity from suit in federal court by participating in a maritime matter, even where there is an unambiguous statement of Congressional intent to subject the state to suit. *College Sav. Bank v. Florida Prepaid Postsecondary Edu. Expense Bd.*, 527 U.S. 666 (1999). Congress also may not subject a nonconsenting state to some private suits for damages in the state's own courts. *Alden v. Maine*, 527 U.S. 706 (1999). *Compare, State of Tennessee v. Lane*, 541 U.S. 509 (2004). At least one court has held that the Eleventh Amendment does not shield a state from federal jurisdiction where the state seeks recovery of damages caused by a shipping accident when the shipowner has sought limitation of liability in federal court. *Magnolia Marine Transp. Co. v. Oklahoma*, 366 F.3d 1153 (10th Cir. 2004).

Some political subdivisions and departments perform such functions, and their finances are so intertwined with the general state treasury that they fall under the umbrella of the state's sovereign immunity under the Eleventh Amendment. The immunity of lesser governmental bodies probably will be determined by application of the general tort law governing immunity. In *Northern Ins. Co. of New York v. Chatham County*, 547 U.S. 189 (2006), the Supreme Court held that a county that does not qualify for sovereign immunity under the ''arm of the state'' test does not qualify for sovereign immunity from suit in admiralty.

CHAPTER XVII

JOINT AND SEVERAL LIABILITY, INDEMNITY AND CONTRIBUTION

Maritime tort law imposes joint and several liability upon joint tortfeasors. *Norfolk & Western Rwy. Co. v. Ayers*, 538 U.S. 135 (2003); *Edmonds v. Compagnie Generale Transatlantique*, 443 U.S. 256 (1979); *Coats v. Penrod Drilling Corp.*, 61 F.3d 1113 (5th Cir. 1995).

However, there has been a radical shift in American law regarding joint and several liability in tort cases. Once the clear majority rule was that joint tortfeasors (tortfeasors who caused indivisible injuries) were jointly and severally liable. However, many jurisdictions, either through legislative enactment or judicial decision, have moved toward several or modified several liability for joint tortfeasors. While state law has moved away from joint and several liability, maritime law has held the traditional course, preserving joint and several liability. Consequently, maritime law may be quite appealing to the plaintiff seeking full recovery. Maritime law is even more appealing when one considers the holding of *Grubart*, *see* Chapter III, *supra*, that admiralty jurisdiction over a maritime joint tortfeasor will also provide maritime jurisdiction over a land based joint tortfeasor. This raises the intriguing possibility that the land based-joint tortfeasor may be exposed to joint and several liability under maritime law even though otherwise applicable state law may no longer recognize joint and several liability.

Where one person may be jointly and severally liable with another, issues of indemnification and contribution may arise. Liability for indemnity or contribution may arise because of a contract between the parties or it may arise in tort.

When the underlying obligation is maritime, admiralty law determines the extent to which a debtor who pays the creditor can shift all or part of the loss to a third person. Generally, an indemnification clause in a contract to unload a vessel is governed by admiralty law, since the underlying contract is maritime, but an indemnification provision in a shipbuilding contract is regulated by state law because an agreement to construct a vessel is nonmaritime. Similarly, tort indemnification and contribution generally are governed by admiralty law if the underlying tort is maritime.

When the indemnity claim arises out of contract, the primary role of the law is to provide interpretation and enforcement of the agreement. Some maritime contractual indemnity provisions are invalid. The United States Supreme Court has ruled that an agreement by which a tow agrees to indemnify a tug from damages caused by the latter's negligence is invalid. *Bisso v. Inland Waterways Corp.*, 349 U.S. 85 (1955). The Longshore and Harbor Workers' Compensation Act, 33 U.S.C.A. § 905(b), invalidates any agreement by which an LHWCA employer agrees to indemnify the vessel owner for payment of damages to the employer's LHWCA employee, except for certain mutual indemnity agreements governing activities on the Outer Continental Shelf. 33 U.S.C.A. § 905(c).

Maritime law will enforce a contractual provision by which the indemnitor agrees to indemnify against the indemnitee's negligence, if the intent to do so is unequivocal. *See, e.g., Roberts v. Williams–McWilliams Co.*, 648 F.2d 255 (5th Cir. 1981). Thus state laws which invalidate such indemnity provisions in contracts involving mineral exploration have increased the importance of distinguishing between maritime and non-maritime contracts for offshore mineral development. *See, e.g., Smith v. Penrod Drilling Corp.*, 960 F.2d 456 (5th Cir. 1992). *See also,* Chapter III, *supra.*

Maritime law also has recognized an implied contractual indemnity, as an outgrowth of the *Sieracki* seaman doctrine. *See* page 297, *supra.* Prior to the 1972 amendments to the LHWCA, a longshoreman employed by a stevedore could recover damages from the vessel owner caused by an unseaworthy condition of the vessel, even though the condition was caused by the stevedore's negligence. In *Ryan Stevedoring Co., Inc. v. Pan–Atlantic Steamship Corp.*, 350 U.S. 124 (1956), the Supreme Court provided the vessel owner with a remedy against the stevedore in such a case. The Court ruled that a stevedore impliedly warranted that it would perform its services in a workmanlike manner; if breach of that warranty caused the vessel owner damage, such as the damages it was required to pay to the longshoreman for the injuries caused by the unseaworthy condition, the vessel owner could recover indemnification from the stevedore. However, the circumstances which gave rise to this *Ryan* doctrine changed in 1972, when Congress substituted a negligence action, 905(b), for the maritime employee's unseaworthiness remedy against the vessel, and also provided that the maritime employer was not liable to the vessel owner for the employee's damages, either "directly or indirectly," and that "any agreements or warranties to the contrary shall be void." 33 U.S.C.A. § 905(b).

The warranty of workmanlike performance in maritime law grew out of the *Sieracki* and *Ryan* doctrines; after their demise, its status remains uncertain. *See Fontenot v. Mesa Petroleum Co.*, 791 F.2d 1207 (5th Cir. 1986), *Bosnor, S.A. de C.V. v. Tug L.A. Barrios*, 796 F.2d 776 (5th Cir. 1986). *See also*, Chapter XI. Some courts have held that the warranty extends to all contracts for the performance of maritime services, while others have limited its application to stevedoring contracts. The importance of the survival of the warranty of workmanlike performance depends primarily upon whether it imposes upon the maritime contractor a duty more onerous than reasonable care.

Tort indemnification in maritime law may arise when the indemnitor's negligence "triggers" the indemnitee's liability (such as vicarious liability, or a shipowner's absolute liability for an unseaworthy condition or for maintenance and cure). *See, e.g., Federal Marine Terminals, Inc. v. Burnside Shipping Co., Ltd.*, 394 U.S. 404 (1969). Before the advent of comparative contribution, maritime law also provided tort indemnification when the negligence of one joint tortfeasor was "slight" and that of another was "gross." After adoption of contribution between joint tortfeasors on the basis of percentages of fault, indemnification under the "gross-slight" rule appears to serve no useful purpose and may no longer exist in maritime law. *See, e.g., Loose v. Offshore Navigation, Inc.*, 670 F.2d 493 (5th Cir. 1982).

Where two or more defendants are at fault, contribution ordinarily applies. Where the liability of one is based upon a "no-fault" theory (such as, arguably, unseaworthiness), the faulty tortfeasor may not be entitled to contribution (although the non-faulty defendant may be entitled to indemnity, as discussed above). *See, e.g., Cooper Stevedoring Co., Inc. v. Fritz Kopke, Inc.*, 417 U.S. 106 (1974).

Initially, admiralty law enforced contribution among joint tortfeasors only in collision cases; if two or more vessels were at fault, the damages were divided equally between or among them. *The Catharine: Lewis v. Dickinson*, 58 U.S. 170 (1855). In other cases, maritime law generally followed the common law rule barring contribution among joint tortfeasors, although the rule was not always followed by lower courts. The case often cited for the proposition that admiralty law did not permit contribution in non-collision cases was *Halcyon Lines v. Haenn Ship Ceiling & Refitting Corp.*, 342 U.S. 282 (1952), in which a vessel owner was denied contribution from a ship repairer for damages paid to the repairer's employee. In *Cooper Stevedoring Co., Inc. v. Fritz Kopke, Inc.*, page 365, *supra*, the Supreme Court, reviewing the jurisprudence, declared that there was a "well-established maritime rule allowing contribution between joint tortfeasors." *Halcyon*, the Court noted, did not support the opposing view, but merely represented an exception to the rule: contribution may not be enforced against a negligent party who is immune from tort liability to the victim, such as in *Halcyon*, where the maritime employee's exclusive remedy against his employer was the compensation benefits provided by the Longshore and Harbor Workers' Compensation Act. The rule derived from *Halcyon* and *Cooper* is that where a party against whom contribution is sought in an admiralty claim cannot be held liable to the plaintiff, the basis for mutual responsibility, and thus for contribution, disappears. *See In Re: McAllister Towing and Transp. Co., Inc.*, 432 F.3d 216 (3rd Cir. 2005) (no contribution as a matter of law where the United States is immunized from direct liability under the Federal Employee's Compensation Act).

The Court's opinion in the *Cooper Stevedoring Co.* case left open the question of whether contribution should be made on a per capita basis, as in the rule of divided damages, or on a percentage basis, which would be more harmonious with the maritime rule of "pure" comparative negligence. Subsequently, the Court swept away the rule of "divided damages," holding that contribution in collision cases must be made on the basis of the percentage of fault of the offending vessels. *United States v. Reliable Transfer Co., Inc.*, 421 U.S. 397 (1975). Since that decision, the courts uniformly hold that contribution in non-collision cases also is on the basis of percentages of fault.

A victim's settlement of a maritime claim with less than all of the tortfeasors presents problems at sea and on land. The settlement may not discharge the non-settling tortfeasors, since the release of a co-debtor does not discharge other co-debtors unless the parties intend such as a result. *Cates v. United States*, 451 F.2d 411 (5th Cir. 1971). The settlement does defeat the non-settling tortfeasor's right to contribution from the settling tortfeasor, but the victim's recovery against the non-settling tortfeasor is reduced by the percentage of fault assessed to the settling tortfeasor. *McDermott, Inc. v. AmClyde and River Don Castings Ltd.*, 511 U.S. 202 (1994). The assignment of a tort claim from the injured party to one tortfeasor which would permit a settling defendant to proceed against a co-tortfeasor is invalid; such a result would be inconsistent with the rule of *McDermott*, that the proportionate liability scheme bars contribution action by nonsettling tortfeasors against settling tortfeasors. *Ondimar Transportes*

Maritimos LTDA v. Beatty Street Properties, Inc., 555 F.3d 184 (5th Cir. 2009). An assignment by the victim to a co-tortfeasor of an unliquidated tort personal injury claim against a joint tortfeasor is likewise invalid. *Lexington Ins. Co. v. S.H.R.M. Catering Services*, 567 F.3d 182 (5th Cir. 2009).

There is scant authority for the proposition that where the liability of the defendants is based not on negligence but on some theory of strict liability, the defendants are not joint tortfeasors; thus where the plaintiff settles with one of the defendants, its recovery against the other is not reduced by the percentage of fault allocated to the settling tortfeasor but by the dollar amount of the settlement. *Chisholm v. UHP Projects*, 205 F.3d 731 (4th Cir. 2000). The decision seems contrary to the spirit of *McDermott*.

May a party entitled to indemnity or contribution recover his costs, including attorney's fees incurred in defense of the victim's claim, from the party paying the indemnity or contribution? In cases involving implied contractual indemnity or tort indemnity, the courts have answered the question in the affirmative; the opposite result has been reached in contribution cases.

CHAPTER XVIII

LIMITATION OF LIABILITY

A. GENERALLY

When a voyage or event subjects the owner of a vessel to liability, maritime law sometimes permits him to limit his liability arising out of the voyage or event to the value of his vessel (and "pending freight") at the conclusion of the voyage or event. This remedy, called limitation of liability, is found in the maritime law of many nations and was adopted by Congress as part of American admiralty law in the mid-nineteenth century.

In addition to limiting liability, limitation also permits the owner or operator to provoke interpleader or concursus through which all claimants are required to litigate their claims against him in a single proceeding in federal court, without trial by jury. The vessel owner or operator may institute limitation proceedings without admitting liability to the claimants, i.e., the owner may institute the proceeding to seek exoneration or, alternatively, limitation. Ordinarily, he will provoke limitation but deny liability; if he is exonerated, he owes nothing, but if he is found at fault, he nevertheless may be able to limit his liability to the value of his vessel.

Limitation of liability was originally adopted by Congress in 1851 before the corporate device developed into an effective method of doing business, before comprehensive insurance protection was generally available, and before modern forms of bankruptcy evolved. Limitation serves an analogous function to the corporate vehicle: encouraging investment of funds in a venture by permitting the investor to limit his personal financial responsibility to the amount that he has invested. With universal acceptance of the corporate device, the general availability of liability insurance, the adoption of other liability-limiting statutes such as the Carriage of Goods by the Sea Act, *see* Chapter IV, and the prevalence and relative ease of bankruptcy, the modern need for limitation as a means of encouraging investment in maritime commerce is questionable. Even if there once was a need, the American limitation proceeding is nevertheless subject to criticism because it extends to situations which have little or no connection with maritime shipping and commerce and the investment inducement purpose of limitation, such as non-collision accidents aboard small pleasure craft.

Moreover, even if limitation has some value in the promotion of maritime shipping and commerce, limitation has developed in ways that make it an inequitable remedy. The operator of a vessel entitled to limitation need surrender only the vessel or its value after the occurrence; if, as is frequently the case, the vessel is sunk or heavily damaged, the limitation fund available to the claimants may be insignificant. In most states, a liability insurer is required to pay only the damages which the insured becomes legally obligated to pay to third persons; since limitation reduces the legal obligation of the insured, the beneficiary of the remedy usually is an insurer that has been compensated for underwriting the particular risk which has occurred, and thus the limitation may be viewed as a boon to the liability insurer. Additionally, the vessel's owner or operator generally fares better than the claimants his vessel has injured. The owner's or operator's hull insurance does not form part of the limitation fund. *Place v. Norwich and N.Y. Transportation Co. (The City of Norwich)*, 118 U.S. 468 (1886). The vessel owner may retain the proceeds of such insurance, although those damaged by his vessel recover little or nothing. It is not surprising, then, that limitation is unpopular. Gilmore & Black note that in modern (and post-modern) times "the limitation principle has been attacked by many and defended by almost none," and that calls for its repeal have "become a commonplace." Gilmore & Black, *supra*, page 822.

While it remains, however, limitation plays an important role in allocation of damages resulting from maritime catastrophes and perhaps an even more important role in the tactics and strategies of maritime personal injury litigation. Limitation permits the owner to surrender the vessel and pending freight (or a sum equal to their value) and walk away from the debts of the voyage in which the accident occurred, or, if there is no voyage, from the debts arising out of the accident. The owner must surrender the vessel, or its value at the end of the voyage or after the accident, free of all liens arising prior to the voyage or accident. The 1976 Convention on Limitation of Liability for Maritime Claims bases the limitation fund upon the vessel's tonnage and not its post-casualty value. However, that Convention, effective in 1986, has not been adopted by the United States.

In nearly all courts, the underlying contract or wrongful conduct that provokes the limitation policy will fall under admiralty jurisdiction. *See, e.g., Grubart, supra*; *Sisson, supra*. However, there is some authority for the proposition that the limitation statute provides an independent basis of federal jurisdiction. *See, e.g., In re Bernstein*, 81 F.Supp.2d 176 (D. Mass. 1999); *see also*, Chapter XIX. The United States Supreme Court has left the question unanswered. *Grubart, supra*.

The owner and demise charterer, whether individual, partnership or corporation, may claim the benefits of the limitation statute. A part owner may limit his liability to an amount equal to the value of his share of the vessel. Limitation is available to the owners of "all seagoing vessels and vessels used on lakes or rivers or in inland navigation, including canal boats, barges, and lighters." 46 U.S.C.A. § 30502. Thus the owner of a pleasure boat or of an 18–foot rowboat is entitled to limitation if the accident falls within admiralty jurisdiction. Since most pleasure boat accidents will have maritime "flavor," *see* Chapter III, pleasure boat owners (including jet ski owners) usually are entitled to limitation of liability if the accident occurs on navigable waters. *See, e.g., Matter of Guglielmo*, 897 F.2d 58 (2d Cir. 1990). The result has not escaped criticism and some judicial dissent. *See Matter of Lowing*, 635 F.Supp. 520 (W.D.Mich. 1986), and the cases cited therein.

If two or more ships owned by the same person are involved in the incident for which limitation is sought, the owner in some instances may be required to surrender both vessels, and not merely the offending one. The "flotilla doctrine" requires the surrender of all vessels involved in performance of a contract when those vessels are subject to common ownership and are engaged in a single enterprise under a single command. *See, e.g., Valley Line Co. v. Ryan*, 771 F.2d 366 (8th Cir. 1985). The "pure tort" exception to the "flotilla rule" provides that if the injury is to a third person to whom the shipowner does not owe a duty based upon consent, he may limit his liability to the ship against which a maritime lien would arise from the wrong, as opposed to the value of the entire "flotilla." *See, e.g., In re Libel of Kristie Leigh*, 168 F.3d 206 (5th Cir. 1999).

Under the original American limitation statute, the limitation fund encompassed only the value of the vessel at the conclusion of the voyage. After a marine disaster in 1934 which claimed 135 lives, the vessel owner petitioned to limit his liability to the salvage value of his vessel, about $20,000. The resulting public outcry prompted Congress to enact legislation increasing the shipowner's responsibilities for vessel accidents causing death or personal injury. The most notable legislation was the so-called "Loss of Life Amendments," 46 U.S.C.A. §§ 30506, 30707(2). These sections define a "seagoing vessel" and provide that if the owner of such a vessel is entitled to limitation and there are claims for personal injury or death, the limitation fund must provide a total minimum payment of $420 per ton (raised from $60 per ton by a 1984 amendment) to such claimants. For example, if limitation is sought and the vessel, after the occurrence, has a salvage value of only $20,000, but the vessel weighed 10,000 tons and there are personal injury and death claims, the limitation fund would be calculated in the following manner: (1) the personal injury and death claimants would receive their proportionate share of the distribution from the general limitation fund of $20,000; (2) if the amount received from that fund was insufficient to satisfy their claims, the personal injury and death claimants would be protected by an additional fund consisting of the difference between $4,200,000 ($420 per ton times 10,000 tons) and the total amount that they together received from the general limitation fund of $20,000.

The owner is liable for the $420 per ton fund on each "distinct occasion" in which loss of life or bodily injury occurs. 46 U.S.C.A. § 30506(d). Although § 30505(a) permits the owner of any "vessel" to limit liability, the Loss of Life Amendments apply only to owners of "seagoing vessels," the definition of which excludes pleasure yachts, tugs

and towboats, fishing boats and other vessels usually not engaged in carrying passengers for hire. The
statutory and jurisprudential definitions would exclude most pleasure boats, creating the anomaly
that a water venture which bears a minimum relationship to maritime shipping and commerce may
be treated by admiralty law more favorably than
oceangoing commercial vessels.

As for what exactly is a "seagoing vessel," one
court has defined a "seagoing vessel" as used in the
Loss of Life Amendments as one that, considering
its design, function, purpose and capabilities, may
normally be expected to engage in substantial operations beyond the boundary line (set by the Coast
Guard) dividing inland waters from the high seas.
Matter of Talbott Big Foot, Inc., 854 F.2d 758 (5th
Cir. 1988). In *In re Complaint and Petition of King
Fisher Marine Service, L.P.*, 2008 WL 4900382 (S.D.
Tex. 2008), the court held that a vessel was not
seagoing where the vessel's design, function, and
purpose was to conduct dredging operations in the
inland waterways, and the vessel did not, was not
intended to, and was not capable of navigating or
operating beyond the boundary line of twelve nautical miles from the Gulf Coast.

Additionally, Congress has made state medical
malpractice limitations on recovery applicable in
certain maritime medical malpractice cases. 46
U.S.C.A. § 30510.

Ordinarily, the claimants in a maritime catastro-
phe will proceed against the shipowner and will not

join his insurer, since the shipowner's liability policy will contain a "no action" clause barring suit
against the insurer until judgment has been rendered against the insured. However, some states
have adopted "direct action" statutes which nullify
"no action" clauses and permit a claimant to institute suit against the insurer without first obtaining
judgment against the insured. The issue of whether
a "direct action" may be maintained against the
vessel owner's liability insurer when the vessel
owner has provoked limitation came before the Supreme Court in *Maryland Casualty Co. v. Cushing*,
347 U.S. 409 (1954). Four members of the Court
concluded that the "direct action" statute conflicted
with limitation and could not be applied. Their
reasoning was that if the insurer's liability was
exhausted through payment of judgments in "direct
actions" prior to a determination of the limitation
proceeding, the owner would be required to pay the
limitation fund that his insurer otherwise would
have paid. This would mean that maintenance of a
"direct action" would deny the owner the benefit of
his insurance, violating the long-standing maritime
policy that the owner in a limitation proceeding is
entitled to the benefit of his insurance. *See The City
of Norwich, supra.* Four dissenters saw no conflict
and would have permitted the claimant to maintain
a "direct action." The ninth member of the Court,
Justice Clark, proposed the solution that the "direct
action" be stayed until determination of the limitation proceeding; if the policy limits were not exhausted by the limitation fund or the matter was

not mooted by exoneration of the vessel owner, the claimants then could continue the "direct action" for whatever insurer liability remained under the policy. Most of the subsequent cases have arisen in the U.S. Fifth Circuit, where intensive maritime activity and the Louisiana "direct action" statute coalesce. That court has instructed its lower courts to permit the "direct action," but to devise effective procedures, such as stay or consolidation, to assure that the owner is not deprived of the benefit of his insurance.

When the "direct action" is permitted, another issue arises: is the defense of limitation personal to the insured shipowner, or may it be urged by the insurer in a "direct action"? The Fifth Circuit initially held that the defense is personal to the insured. However, it later upheld, under the applicable state law, a policy provision which limited the underwriter's liability to the dollar amount for which the shipowner-assured was liable after it successfully maintained the right to limit liability. *Crown Zellerbach Corp. v. Ingram Indus., Inc.*, 783 F.2d 1296 (5th Cir. 1986).

B. DEBTS INCURRED WITHOUT PRIVITY OR KNOWLEDGE

The vessel owner may only limit his liability for those debts which were incurred without his privity or knowledge. 46 U.S.C.A. § 30505(b). As Gilmore & Black observe, the words "privity or knowledge" are "empty containers into which the courts are free to pour whatever content they will." Gilmore & Black, *supra*, page 877. Because of the harshness of the limitation remedy and the vagueness of the terms "privity or knowledge," it is not surprising that most limitation litigation has centered around whether there is "privity or knowledge." While the concept remains elusive, some general rules have evolved.

The initial inquiry is whether the claim for which limitation is sought sounds in tort or in contract. If the claim is in tort, "privity or knowledge" means the owner's personal participation in the negligence or fault that caused the damage. The negligence that constitutes privity, however, is not necessarily the same as some other forms of maritime negligence, such as in Jones Act claims. *See, e.g., Brister v. A.W.I., Inc.*, 946 F.2d 350 (5th Cir. 1991). If the owner is an individual, he usually fares well under the "privity or knowledge" test. He is not required to supervise his vessel, either at sea or in port. If he selects competent personnel and gives them adequate instructions, he will not be charged with "privity or knowledge" of their subsequent negligent acts. *Complaint of Signal Int'l, LLC*, 579 F.3d 478 (5th Cir. 2009). There are a number of exceptions to the rule, however. The first is that the individual owner of a "seagoing vessel" who seeks to limit liability for personal injury or death is charged with the "privity or knowledge" of the master of the vessel or of the owner's superintendent or managing agent at or prior to the commencement of each voyage. 46 U.S.C.A. § 30506(e).

The second is that if the individual owner delegates all management and control of his vessel to another, the delegate may become the owner's "alter ego," and the owner may be chargeable with the delegate's "privity or knowledge." Finally, the owner may be chargeable with "privity or knowledge" if he is in active control of the vessel at the time the claim arises. *See, e.g., Complaint of Ingoglia*, 723 F.Supp. 512 (C.D. Cal. 1989). If the owner is aboard the vessel but not in active control when the claim arises, he probably will be entitled to limitation only if he could not reasonably be expected to have discovered or prevented the negligent acts of his employees under the circumstances of the case. In one recent case involving negligent entrustment of a jet ski, the court held that mere subjective belief in the competence of the operator to whom the jet ski was entrusted was insufficient to establish lack of privity or knowledge. The owner had to establish some objective basis for his belief in the operator's competence. Of course, in that case the operator was towing the owner on an inner tube which struck plaintiff. *Complaint of Messina, supra.*

If the shipowner is a corporation, application of the "privity or knowledge" exception is exceedingly difficult. As the Supreme Court has observed, "[a] corporation necessarily acts through human beings. The privity of some of those persons must be the privity of the corporation else it could always limit its liability." *Coryell v. Phipps*, 317 U.S. 406 (1943). There is, of course, the other side of the coin: if the "privity" of every corporate employee is "privity" of the corporation, then a negligent corporate shipowner could never limit its liability. The Act offers no aid in the solution of this problem; its drafters in the mid-nineteenth century understandably were thinking of shipowners as individuals, and not as corporations. Other than to rule that a corporation is entitled to limit its liability, the Supreme Court has provided little guidance. *See generally, In re Vulcan Materials*, 369 F.Supp.2d 737 (E.D. Va. 2005) (summing up the current jurisprudence).

Without help from higher authority, the lower courts have struggled with the problem. Generally speaking, courts will deny limitation of liability if the corporate fault that contributed to the damage was that of "high level managerial personnel," i.e., an officer or employee vested with discretion or authority with respect to the corporate activity that produced the damage. The employee's responsibilities, rather than his or her title, are critical. *In re Hellenic Inc.*, 252 F.3d 391 (5th Cir. 2001). This may, in some circumstances, include the master. *See, e.g., Potomac Transp., Inc. v. Ogden Marine, Inc.*, 909 F.2d 42 (2d Cir. 1990). Unlike the individual owner, the corporate owner may not escape liability for negligent conduct occurring in port by delegating a task to another; the corporate "high level managerial personnel" probably will be charged with whatever they could have discovered in the exercise of reasonable care in supervising the vessel's activities. A corporate owner that sends out an unseaworthy vessel may be denied limitation because "high level managerial personnel" failed to discover the condition prior to sailing or were negligent in their supervision of those persons charged with making the vessel seaworthy. Failure to enforce a rule or custom by a sufficiently high ranking officer in the relevant entity may constitute "privity or knowledge." *In re City of New York*, 522 F.3d 279 (2d Cir. 2008). If the claims involved in the limitation are personal injury or death claims, the corporate owner, like the individual owner, is chargeable with the "privity or knowledge" of the master, superintendent or managing agent at or prior to the commencement of each voyage, pursuant to the Loss of Life Amendments. 46 U.S.C.A. § 30506(e).

In *Richardson v. Harmon*, 222 U.S. 96 (1911), the Supreme Court ruled that an owner who is entitled to limitation nevertheless remains liable for "his own fault, neglect, *and contracts*." (emphasis added). This language led to the creation of the amorphous "personal contract" doctrine, i.e., the shipowner may not limit his liability for those contracts which are deemed "personal." A "personal contract," however, is not necessarily one which is executed personally by the owner. Charter parties are personal contracts but bills of lading are not, even though personally executed by the owner. Contracts for supplies or repairs which are entered into at the vessel's home port, and probably those entered into elsewhere, are personal contracts. There is authority for the proposition that the owner will be denied limitation under the "personal contract" doctrine only if the contract and the breach of the contract are both personal. *The Soerstad*, 257 F.

130 (S.D.N.Y. 1919). For example, although a contract to tow is "personal," the breach of the tower's duty to tow in a non-negligent manner may not be a "personal" one. The Limitation Act, 46 U.S.C.A. § 30505(c), excludes wages from limitation, and it is arguable that a seaman's maintenance and cure claims arise out of the owner's "personal contract" with the seaman and are not subject to limitation.

There are cases holding that claims for wages and for damages to cargo through deviation of the voyage are not subject to limitation. Claims under the Wreck Act and the Rivers and Harbors Act (*See* Chapter XII) also are not limitable.

One particular provision of the limitation statute was an enigma. In 1884 Congress added former 46 U.S.C.A. § 189, which provided cryptically that "[t]he individual liability of a shipowner shall be limited to the proportion of any ... debts that his individual share of the vessel bears to the whole." Read literally, this section could have eliminated the "privity or knowledge" exception. It did not receive such an interpretation, however, and generally was ignored by the courts. In the recent recodification of maritime statutes, the section was amended and incorporated into 46 U.S.C.A. § 50505(a) to read: "If the vessel has more than one owner, the proportionate share of the liability of any one owner shall not exceed the owner's proportionate interest in the vessel and pending."

To clarify the liability of the owner who seeks limitation but is sued in a capacity, other than as owner, new 46 U.S.C.A. § 30512 provides:

This chapter does not affect the liability of an individual as master, officer, or seaman, even though the individual is also an owner of the vessel.

On a slightly different note, claims brought under the Oil Pollution Act of 1990, 33 U.S.C.A. §§ 2701–61, are not subject to limitation. Likewise, limitation does not apply to the United States' right to recover under The Wreck Act. *Southern Scrap Material Co., LLC v. ABC Ins. Co., supra.*

C. PROCEDURE IN LIMITATION OF LIABILITY

46 U.S.C.A. § 30511(a) provides that

The owner of a vessel may bring a civil action in a district court of the United States for limitation of liability under this chapter. The action must be brought within 6 months after a claimant gives the owner written notice of a claim.

This provision is jurisdictional; thus the right to limit liability through a concursus or interpleader proceeding in federal admiralty court is lost if the owner does not seek the relief within six months after receipt of the first claim in writing against him arising out of the occurrence. Supplemental Rule F(1), Admiralty and Maritime Claims, 28

U.S.C.A.; *Esta Later Charters, Inc. v. Ignacio*, 875 F.2d 234 (9th Cir.1989). The period may be extended if the claims arise out of "distinct occasions." *Exxon Shipping Co. v. Cailleteau*, 869 F.2d 843 (5th Cir. 1989). The period may not necessarily commence when the shipowner receives notice of a claim against him; arguably, it does not begin until he has notice that the claims urged against him exceed the value of his vessel. A letter setting forth key sufficient facts can constitute notice for purposes of commencing the six-month period. *Paradise Divers, Inc. v. Upmal*, 402 F.3d 1087 (11th Cir. 2005).

It seems clear that the vessel owner does *not* lose the right to seek limitation as an affirmative defense if he fails to provoke the concursus proceeding within the six-month period. There are cases upholding the use of limitation as a defense in an action in federal court after the six-month period has expired, *but* there is some dicta, including some from the Supreme Court, to the contrary. *M/S Bremen v. Zapata Off–Shore Co.*, *supra*.

If the vessel owner who has failed to seek limitation in admiralty within the six-month period is sued in state court, he encounters the additional argument that a state court may lack jurisdiction to apply limitation, even as a defense. *See, e.g.*, *Vatican Shrimp Co., Inc. v. Solis*, 820 F.2d 674 (5th Cir. 1987). However, the better view seems to be that limitation should be available as a defense in either state or federal court. *Karim v. Finch Shipping Co., Ltd.*, 265 F.3d 258 (5th Cir. 2001). There is, of course, another danger to the shipowner who permits the six-month period to elapse without commencing a limitation concursus proceeding; even if he is permitted to urge limitation as a defense in separate suits, he may be required to make separate deposits of the total amount of the limitation fund in each of the suits. *Signal Oil & Gas Co. v. Barge W–701*, 654 F.2d 1164 (5th Cir. 1981).

The limitation concursus proceeding is governed by 46 U.S.C.A. § 30511, Supplemental Rule F, Admiralty and Maritime Claims, and by local court rules. The shipowner provoking limitation must surrender title to the vessel, or file a bond in the amount of the value of the vessel. The posting of the bond probably is not jurisdictional and thus the failure to file it within the six-month period is not fatal. *See, e.g., Guey v. Gulf Ins. Co.*, 46 F.3d 478 (5th Cir. 1995). When a petition for limitation is filed, the court enjoins the commencement or continuation elsewhere of claims arising out of the voyage or event for which limitation is sought and fixes a time for the filing of claims in the limitation proceeding. Notice is given to the known claimants and is published. Claimants must file their answers and claims within the designated delay. When that delay has expired, each claimant who has filed a claim is notified of the other claims that have been filed, and the matter proceeds to trial in the normal course of litigation. The delay for filing claims is not jurisdictional; the court may excuse a late filing.

The party provoking the limitation and the claimants may file counterclaims and cross claims against each other, so that all of the claims arising out of the maritime disaster may be litigated in one proceeding. *British Transp. Comm'n v. United States (The Haiti Victory)*, 354 U.S. 129 (1957).

In most cases, the vessel owner will deny liability and will urge his right to limitation in the alternative. When this occurs, the claimants initially bear the burden of establishing the vessel owner's liability. If they fail to do so, the owner is exonerated, and the limitation proceeding is mooted. If the claimants are successful in establishing liability, the burden shifts to the owner to prove that the liability was incurred without his "privity or knowledge" and that he is otherwise entitled to limit his liability to the value of his vessel. *See, e.g.*, *Suzuki of Orange Park, Inc. v. Shubert*, 86 F.3d 1060 (11th Cir. 1996).

Since jurisdiction over a limitation proceeding is within the exclusive jurisdiction of the admiralty "side" of federal court, limitation issues are not triable to a jury. Thus limitation conflicts with the maritime policy of granting a claimant the option of trial by jury, a policy espoused by Congress (the "saving to suitors" clause) and by the judiciary. *Romero v. International Terminal Operating Co.*, *supra* and *Fitzgerald v. United States Lines Co.*, 374 U.S. 16 (1963). *See also* Chapter XIX. What has emerged in the jurisprudence is an accommodation in which a claimant is permitted to obtain jury trial (as a law claim in federal court, or in state court) on the issues of liability and damages if such a trial would not undermine the protection to which the shipowner is entitled under limitation. Thus a claimant may obtain a modification of the injunction against "other proceedings" provided by Supplemental Rule F(3) so that he may prosecute his claim in state court or at law in federal court if (1) his claim is the only claim against the vessel owner, *Ex parte Green*, 286 U.S. 437 (1932), *Langnes v. Green*, 282 U.S. 531 (1931), or (2) the total amount of all claims does not exceed the limitation fund. *Lake Tankers Corp. v. Henn*, 354 U.S. 147 (1957). In such cases, one of the reasons for the concursus or interpleader in limitation is absent: either there is no exposure of the shipowner to liability beyond the value of his vessel, or no possibility of duplicative or conflicting fact finding on the issues of liability and damages. In either case, however, the litigants must return to federal court for determination of the limitation issues, if those issues are not mooted by the disposition made in the other court.

Since injunctive relief ordinarily is discretionary, it is arguable that a judge may lift the injunction and permit litigation in state court whenever equitable considerations justify such action. Some jurisprudence suggests that the judge may modify the injunction and permit litigation in state court only if the "single claim" or "adequate fund" criteria described above are present. However, courts generally are liberal in finding a "single claim," *see, e.g.*, *Complaint of Midland Enterprises, Inc.*, 886 F.2d

812 (6th Cir. 1989), and in lifting the injunction
when the claimant makes stipulations that eliminate any prejudice to the limitation defense by
allowing the matter to proceed first in another
court. The stipulations are becoming uniform and
complex. *See, e.g., Texaco, Inc. v. Williams*, 47 F.3d
765 (5th Cir.1995); *Complaint of Dammers & Van-
derheide*, 836 F.2d 750 (2d Cir. 1988). Defendants
had sometimes argued that in order to be allowed to
proceed in state court, a claimant had to stipulate
that the federal court had exclusive jurisdiction over
both exoneration and limitation. The United States
Supreme Court implicitly rejected that argument in
Lewis v. Lewis & Clark Marine, Inc., 531 U.S. 438
(2001). The Fifth Circuit expressly did so in *In re
Tetra Applied Technologies, L.P.*, 362 F.3d 338 (5th
Cir. 2004). In *Inland Dredging v. Sanchez*, 468 F.3d
864 (5th Cir. 2006), the court noted that there is no
principled reason to read the Limitation of Liability
Act to preclude the traditional right of an aggrieved
party to seek redress in the forum of his choice. A
single claimant's choice of forum is a sufficient
interest to warrant the dissolution of an injunction
if the claimant files stipulations that adequately
protect the shipowner's rights under the Act. Moreover, in *Norfolk Dredging Co. v. Wiley*, 439 F.3d 205
(4th Cir. 2006) the district court did not set the
limitation fund amount pending the outcome of a
state court personal injury action, but claimant
stipulated to the amount of the litigation fund,
whatever that should turn out to be. The vessel
owner argued that unless claimant stipulated to a

particular amount, the claimant should not be allowed to proceed in state court. The court disagreed and allowed claimant to prosecute the action in state court.

Supplemental Admiralty Rule F(8) provides that "the fund ... shall be divided pro rata, subject to all relevant provisions of law, among the several claimants in proportion to the amounts of their respective claims, duly proved, saving, however, to all parties any priority to which they may be legally entitled." The uncertainty of lien rankings thus carries over into the distribution of the limitation fund. Some courts have used equitable principles in distributing an inadequate limitation fund.

D.   CHOICE OF LAW IN LIMITATION PROCEEDINGS

While limitation is a generally accepted principle of maritime law, there are no uniform international rules. Many nations adhere to the 1957 Brussels Convention rules, while the United States and Great Britain each has its own limitation scheme, with differing methods of calculating the limitation fund. For example, American law is more favorable to the death or personal injury claimant than British law.

Read literally, 46 U.S.C.A. § 30502 would make American limitation law applicable to foreign vessels. Thus a foreign shipowner may seek limitation in an American admiralty court; when this occurs, the question of choice of limitation law arises. As a general proposition, the American courts treat limitation as procedural, rather than substantive, and apply the law of the forum, i.e., the American law. There is at least one qualification, however. Congress has prescribed the application of foreign limitation law in some wrongful death actions. 46 U.S.C.A. § 30306 provides:

> When a cause of action exists under the law of a foreign country for death by wrongful act, neglect, or default on the high seas, a civil action in admiralty may be brought in a court of the United States based on the foreign cause of action, without abatement of the amount for which recovery is authorized.

Thus under certain circumstances, if the death is caused by injury occurring outside American territorial waters, the American limitation act may not be applied to reduce recovery.

The "substance-procedure" rule arose out of the decision of the United States Supreme Court in *Oceanic Steam Navigation Co. v. Mellor (The Titanic)*, 233 U.S. 718 (1914). At that time the "substance-procedure" distinction was of great significance in the choice of laws. Its application nearly a century later to make a choice of law that determines the amount of damage a tortfeasor must pay seems incongruous. The matter would best be resolved under modern choice of law principles, and, in fact, nearly all the decisions since *The Titanic* are consistent with the application of those principles. Under such principles, the court should evaluate the interests of the forum state and other sovereigns in applying their limitation law to the claims involved. If limitation is sought in an American court, and the vessel is American owned or operated or the accident occurred in American waters, American limitation law ordinarily should be applied. If the accident occurs on the high seas, a federal court should apply American law as the law of the forum, unless there is some other sovereign with an overriding interest in the outcome of the litigation, such as where the vessel and claimants are of the same nationality. If the accident occurs within the territorial waters of another sovereign, that sovereign's law ordinarily should apply, particularly if that sovereign treats limitation as part of its substantive law. *See, e.g.*, *Karim v. Finch Shipping Co., Ltd., I & II*, 374 F.3d 302 (5th Cir. 2004 and 2001); *In re Korea Shipping Corp., Ltd.*, 919 F.2d 601 (9th Cir. 1990).

CHAPTER XIX

JURISDICTION AND PROCEDURE IN MARITIME CLAIMS

A. HISTORY

Prior to the American Revolution, English law developed three court systems—law, equity and admiralty—which exercised jurisdiction over different types of controversies. The admiralty court was the outgrowth of the informal "port courts," which initially resolved maritime disputes. The concept of separate courts of law, equity and admiralty was imported into the colonies and subsequently survived the Revolution and the adoption of the Constitution. In the early days of the federal judiciary, however, a single judge performed all three functions in a given geographical area; as a result, each federal court had three dockets or "sides"—law, equity and admiralty. If a matter was brought before the court and jurisdiction was based upon the federal admiralty power, the case would be placed on the admiralty docket and would be processed through application of special admiralty rules by a judge "sitting in admiralty" and lawyers sometimes called "proctors in admiralty."

The first major change came in 1938, when the Federal Rules of Civil Procedure were adopted and made applicable in all cases of law and equity. This produced a unification of the law and equity "sides" of federal court, but admiralty remained separate. The special admiralty rules continued to govern cases on the admiralty "side." In 1966, the Federal Rules were made applicable to cases in which the federal court is exercising jurisdiction through the admiralty power. This seemingly sounded the death knell for the admiralty "side" of the federal court, but, to borrow a phrase, the news of its death was greatly exaggerated. The 1966 effort at unification made nearly all of the Federal Rules of Civil Procedure applicable in admiralty matters, but the rule-makers retained a number of special rules that apply only when the federal court is exercising jurisdiction through the admiralty power. For example, amended Rule 38(e) provides that "[t]hese rules shall not be construed to create a right to trial by jury of the issues in an admiralty or maritime claim," and amended Rule 14(c) continues, in maritime claims, a unique admiralty third party practice. The merged rules do not affect venue; thus the special admiralty venue rules continue in maritime matters. Finally, special supplemental rules for certain maritime matters were adopted as an appendix to the general rules. Thus despite the 1966 "unification," significant procedural differences still exist if the jurisdiction of the federal court is premised upon the admiralty power. Accordingly, it still is appropriate to speak, in a limited sense, about the admiralty "side" of federal court, and the term continues as a shorthand way of referring to a case pending in federal court in which jurisdiction is based upon the federal admiralty power, i.e., when it is brought as an admiralty claim. In the remainder of this chapter, we explore the situations in which a matter may or must be brought as an admiralty claim in federal court and discuss some of the procedural issues that arise out of the selection of the forum.

B. SUBJECT MATTER JURISDICTION

If a claim falls within the federal admiralty power, Congress can prescribe which courts may adjudicate it. *See* Chapter I, *supra*. Congress made the primary allocation of subject matter jurisdiction over matters "in admiralty" in section 9 of the Judiciary Act of 1789, now 28 U.S.C.A. § 1333, which provides:

The district courts shall have original jurisdiction, exclusive of the courts of the States, of:

(1) Any civil case of admiralty or maritime jurisdiction, saving to suitors in all cases all other remedies to which they are otherwise entitled....

Thus if a matter falls within the federal admiralty power, a federal district court has subject matter jurisdiction by virtue of section 1333. If the court's only basis of jurisdiction is section 1333, the case properly may be said to be on what remains of the admiralty "side" of federal court after the attempted unification in 1966. The primary feature of this admiralty "side" is that there is no constitutional or statutory right to trial by jury.

The "saving to suitors" clause in 28 U.S.C.A. § 1333 initially provided that what was "saved" was "the right of a common law remedy, where the common law is competent to give it." Section 9, Judiciary Act of 1789, 1 Stats. 76, 77. For over a century, argument raged over whether what was "saved" was the common law cause of action or the right to proceed in common law courts to enforce the maritime cause of action. It now is settled that what is "saved" is the right to enforce the maritime cause of action in a law court, which may be either the state court or a federal court that has jurisdiction at law by virtue of diversity of citizenship or the existence of an independent federal question. *See* Chapter I. Thus if a matter is "in admiralty," maritime substantive law applies, regardless of the court in which it is heard.

It also is settled that the common law "is competent to give" all maritime remedies except *in rem* proceedings. The term "*in rem* proceeding" is used here in the strict and not the broader sense. The distinction, as pointed out in *Pennoyer v. Neff*, 95 U.S. 714 (1877), is that:

> In a strict sense, a proceeding *in rem* is one taken directly against property, and has for its object the disposition of property, without reference to the title of individual claimants; but, in a larger and more general sense, the terms are applied to actions between parties, where the direct object is

to reach and dispose of property owned by them, or some interest therein. Such are cases commenced by attachment against the property of debtors, or instituted to partition real estate, foreclose a mortgage, or enforce a lien.... They are substantially proceedings *in rem* in the broader sense.

Maritime law authorizes the use of the *in rem* proceeding—in the strict sense—to enforce a maritime lien or a preferred mortgage against a vessel; the vessel is made the defendant, and a judicial sale in the proceeding conveys title "good against the world." Section 1333, then, conveys exclusive jurisdiction to the federal court, sitting in admiralty, over all proceedings *in rem* to enforce a maritime lien or preferred ship mortgage. All other maritime matters are those in which "the common law is competent to give" a remedy and therefore may be brought in state court, unless Congress by some other statute has vested exclusive jurisdiction in federal courts or a federal administrative agency.

There is one notable exception to the rule that all maritime *in rem* proceedings must be brought as admiralty claims in federal court. In *C.J. Hendry Co. v. Moore*, 318 U.S. 133 (1943), the Supreme Court upheld a state forfeiture proceeding (the functional equivalent of an *in rem* proceeding in the strict sense) in state court against a net which had been used for fishing in navigable waters in violation of state law. The Court reached this conclusion after determining that common law courts historically exercised jurisdiction *in rem* in the enforcement of forfeiture statutes, concurrently with the courts of admiralty; thus, this was an *in rem* remedy that "the common law is competent to give."

The admiralty "side" of federal court has exclusive jurisdiction over limitation of liability concursus proceedings, 46 U.S.C.A. § 185, *see* Chapter XVIII, and suits against the sovereign, either under the Suits in Admiralty Act, 46 U.S.C.A. § 741 et seq., *see* Chapter XVI, or under the Public Vessels Act, 46 U.S.C.A. § 781 et seq., *see* Chapter XVI. There is strong dicta in *Offshore Logistics, Inc. v. Tallentire*, page 329, *supra*, that jurisdiction over DOHSA claims is concurrent between the federal court sitting in admiralty and state court. Jurisdiction over Jones Act claims, 46 U.S.C.A. § 688, is concurrent between federal and state courts.

If a federal law is enacted which regulates substantive admiralty rights but does not make an express grant of subject matter jurisdiction, the case may be brought in federal court, either as an admiralty claim under 28 U.S.C.A. § 1333 ("civil case of admiralty or maritime jurisdiction") or at law, under 28 U.S.C.A. § 1331 (it "arises under" a federal statute), or in state court (under the "savings to suitors" clause of section 1333).

A general maritime law claim (within the admiralty power but not arising out of a federal statute) may be brought as an admiralty claim under 28 U.S.C.A. § 1333, and, unless the litigant seeks enforcement of a claim *in rem*, it also may be brought in state court under the "savings to suitors" clause. It may not be brought as a law claim in federal court unless there is diversity jurisdiction (complete diversity of citizenship and an amount in controversy exceeding $75,000). 28 U.S.C.A. § 1332. The Supreme Court has rejected the contention that a maritime common law claim may be brought in federal court as a law claim because it "arises under" the Constitution (Art. III, Sec. 2). Although the federal power to prescribe general maritime law stems from the Constitution, a general maritime law remedy does not "arise under" the Constitution within the meaning of the statute conveying "federal question" jurisdiction, 28 U.S.C.A. § 1331. *Romero v. International Terminal Co.*, page 5, *supra*. Examples of these kinds of claims which may not be brought as law claims in federal court unless there is diversity jurisdiction are general maritime tort and contract claims and the seaman's remedies of maintenance and cure and unseaworthiness.

The most important distinction between the law and admiralty "sides" of federal court is that trial by jury is guaranteed for law claims through the Seventh Amendment, but if the case is maintained as an admiralty claim, the litigant has neither constitutional nor statutory right to a jury trial. The one exception is the "Great Lakes rule," a special statute providing

> In any case of admiralty and maritime jurisdiction relating to any matter of contract or tort arising upon or concerning any vessel of twenty tons or upward, enrolled and licensed for the

coasting trade, and employed in the business of commerce and navigation between places in different states upon the lakes and navigable waters connecting said lakes, the trial of all issues of fact shall be by jury if either demands it. 28 U.S.C.A. § 1873.

With this exception, a litigant may not demand trial by jury in federal court if jurisdiction is premised solely upon the admiralty power.

Litigation of a matter as an admiralty claim in federal court frequently provides a judge who is skilled in and sympathetic to maritime concerns, but, except when Title 28 U.S.C.A. section 1873 applies, it does not provide trial by jury. When a maritime matter is brought in state court, there may be trial by jury (depending upon state law), but the state judge is not likely to be as attuned to federal admiralty concerns or as conversant with the intricacies of maritime law, as his federal counterpart. Understandably, a maritime litigant may want to present his maritime common law claim to a jury in federal court. There is one important way in which that goal may be attained. While a litigant in federal court whose claim is premised solely upon admiralty common law may not demand trial by jury, there is no constitutional or statutory bar to a jury trial of such a claim. If the maritime claim is the only claim before the court, trial by jury is inappropriate; the federal policy generally favoring jury trials is counterbalanced by the goal of judicial efficiency, since granting trial by jury in such a case would burden the federal judiciary with an otherwise unnecessary jury trial. But what if a matter which is cognizable at law is properly joined with a matter brought as an admiralty claim and the litigant seeks trial by jury on the law claim? The trial may be bifurcated, with the judge sitting as trier of fact in the maritime claim. However, if the claims are properly joined, they ordinarily will arise out of the same factual situation, and permitting a jury trial on both claims will not burden the federal judiciary with an additional jury trial on those facts. Thus the federal policy favoring jury trials can be served without a corresponding disservice to the goal of judicial economy. Accordingly, the Supreme Court has ruled that if a "federal question" claim is properly joined with a maritime claim brought on the admiralty "side," and both "grow out of a single transaction or accident," the litigant may obtain trial by jury of both matters. *Fitzgerald v. United States Lines Co.*, page 386, *supra*. One typical case is joinder of a Jones Act negligence action, for which trial by jury is statutorily provided, with claims for unseaworthiness and maintenance and cure. If there is diversity jurisdiction over the unseaworthiness and maintenance and cure claims, and they are brought at law, the parties are entitled to trial by jury. If there is no diversity jurisdiction over them, the two claims can be brought in federal court only as admiralty claims. However, under Fed. Civ. Proc. Rules 18 or 20, the unseaworthiness and maintenance and cure claims may be joined with the Jones Act claim, which can be brought at law under 28 U.S.C.A. § 1331, and thus under

Fitzgerald a litigant may have jury trial on all three claims. If the Jones Act claim that provides the trial by jury is dismissed prior to trial, the litigant probably will lose his right to jury trial on the appended maritime claims. If the Jones Act claim is dismissed during trial, the judge has discretion to submit the remaining claims to the jury.

The result may be different if the jurisdiction at law is based upon diversity of citizenship. If all of the defendants, including those against whom admiralty claims are asserted, are of diverse citizenship from the plaintiff, there is complete diversity and all of the matters may be tried to a jury if a party so elects. But if one of the admiralty claim defendants is not of diverse citizenship from the plaintiff, then arguably the complete diversity required by *Strawbridge v. Curtiss*, 7 U.S. 267 (1806), is lacking, and the court is without subject matter jurisdiction at law over the non-maritime claims. Thus *Fitzgerald* should not apply because there is no "law" claim entitled to jury trial to which the "admiralty" claim can be pended. The counterargument, of course, is that what has occurred is merely a joinder of a maritime claim with a non-maritime claim, and that since complete diversity exists over the nonmaritime claim, both claims may be tried to a jury under the *Fitzgerald* doctrine. *Compare Powell v. Offshore Navigation, Inc.*, 644 F.2d 1063 (5th Cir. 1981), with *Vodusek v. Bayliner Marine Corp.*, 71 F.3d 148 (4th Cir. 1995).

Some actions may be brought in federal court either as admiralty claims or as law claims. One example is a Jones Act claim; another is an unseaworthiness or maintenance and cure claim in which there is diversity of citizenship and the requisite jurisdictional amount. In such cases, Fed. Civ. Proc. Rule 9(h) provides that the claim will be processed as a law claim unless the pleading setting forth the claim contains "a statement identifying the claim as an admiralty or maritime claim for the purposes of Rules 14(c), 38(e), 82, and the Supplemental Rules for Certain Admiralty and Maritime Claims."

C. JURISDICTION OVER THE PERSON

In a maritime *in rem* action, jurisdiction over the person of the "defendant," the vessel, is premised upon the presence of the vessel within the district in which the court sits. Jurisdiction usually is perfected by seizure of the vessel. Seizure, however, may not be essential to jurisdiction; the courts have upheld *in rem* jurisdiction if the vessel owner takes some action which fairly may be construed as a waiver of the lack of jurisdiction over the vessel, such as a "letter of undertaking" by which the owner agrees that the claimant's rights are the same as if the vessel had been seized and subsequently released by the filing of a claim and a release bond. *See, e.g., Panaconti Shipping Co., S.A. v. M/V Ypapanti*, 865 F.2d 705 (5th Cir. 1989). After jurisdiction *in rem* has attached, it generally is not lost if the res is removed from the control of the seizing court. *See, e.g., Republic National Bank v. United States*, 506 U.S. 80 (1992).

When a maritime matter is brought in state court or on the "law side" of federal court, the general rules governing jurisdiction over the person in those courts apply. The rules applicable to proceedings brought at law in federal court also govern jurisdiction over an *in personam* action brought as an admiralty claim, since there are no special statutes or rules governing jurisdiction over the person in maritime matters. A defendant may be compelled to litigate in a federal court if (1) he is "amenable," i.e., the exercise of jurisdiction is consistent with the Constitution and laws of the United States, and (2) he may be served with process by the court asserting jurisdiction. In many instances the nonresident shipowner or other admiralty defendant will have sufficient contacts to satisfy the requirement of amenability, and the issue of jurisdiction will turn upon whether service may be effected upon him within the district. The more important rules governing service upon nonresident shipowners are (1) Rule 4(e), providing for personal or domiciliary service upon a defendant within the district or through use of the state's "long arm" statute; (2) Rule 4(f), providing methods for service upon individuals in foreign countries; (3) Rule 4(h), providing for service in the district upon a corporation or partnership by delivering a copy of the complaint to "an officer, a managing or general agent, or to any other agent authorized by appointment or by law to receive service of process"; and (4) Rule 4(k)(2), providing for service of process and personal jurisdiction in any district court for cases arising under federal law where the defendant has minimum contacts with the United States as a whole sufficient to satisfy due process concerns, but defendant is not subject to jurisdiction in any particular state.

A forum selection clause may confer personal jurisdiction over a party in some circumstances. A federal court sitting in admiralty also may assert a kind of *quasi in rem* jurisdiction over a nonresident through attachment, a traditional maritime remedy that has been continued in Supplemental Rules B and E, Admiralty and Maritime Claims. Under those rules attachment is proper if the defendant is not "found within the district." Supp. Rule B(1), Admiralty and Maritime Claims. "Found," in this context, means that the defendant is both subject to the jurisdiction of the court *and* can be served within the district. *See, e.g.*, *STX Panocean (UK) Co., Ltd. v. Glory Wealth Shipping Pte. Ltd.*, 560 F.3d 127 (2d Cir. 2009), holding that registering to do business in a state and appointing an agent for service of process within a district of the state constitutes being "found" within that district for purposes of Rule B. *See, also, LaBanca v. Ostermunchner*, 664 F.2d 65 (5th Cir. 1981). If the defendant has not engaged in sufficient activity in the district to make him amenable to suit there under due process and the applicable state or federal statutes exerting jurisdiction over the person, he can not be "found" in the district in the jurisdictional sense, and attachment is proper. Even if the defendant is amenable to suit *in personam* and thus is "found" within the district in the geographical sense, non-resident attachment may be effected if he may not be "found" for service of process, i.e., if service may not be effected upon him within the district in the manner provided by Rule 4. Since "nonresidency" for attachment in admiralty is nonresidency within the district and not within the state, a claimant may attach property within a district in which the defendant cannot be served, although the defendant is amenable to service in, and can be served elsewhere in, the state. This permits the claimant to use nonresident attachment as a means of obtaining security for the judgment that subsequently is rendered. That result has been subject to some criticism but apparently was a deliberate choice of the rulemakers. *See, e.g., Aqua Stoli Shipping Ltd. v. Gardner Smith Pty. Ltd.*, 460 F.3d 434 (2d Cir. 2006), holding that a court may set aside an otherwise valid attachment if the defendant is subject to personal jurisdiction in a convenient adjacent district or if the defendant is located in the same district as the plaintiff and is subject to personal jurisdiction in that district. *See* notes of advisory committee, Supp. Rule B, Admiralty and Maritime Claims. Supplemental Rule B also permits a plaintiff to utilize in admiralty court the attachment procedures provided by the state in which the court sits. Use of *quasi in rem* jurisdiction may permit a marine supplier to enforce his claim against a "sister ship" of the vessel he supplied.

When a defendant whose property has been seized in an *in rem* or *quasi in rem* action gives security for the plaintiff's claim and asserts a counterclaim "arising out of the same transaction or occurrence," the court has the power to order the plaintiff to "give security in the usual amount and form to respond in damages to the claims set forth in such counterclaim." Supplemental Rule E(7), Admiralty and Maritime Claims. When the court exercises its discretion to require such security, the proceedings on the original claim are stayed until the security is given. *See, e.g., Chan v. Society Expeditions, Inc.,* 39 F.3d 1398 (9th Cir. 1994). Under 28 U.S.C.A. § 2464(B) and Supplemental Rule E(5)(b), the court may require "further security" at any time; however, that may be limited to replacement security and not an increase in the amount of security originally fixed by the court. *Moore v. M/V Angela,* 353 F.3d 376 (5th Cir. 2003).

Since the admiralty *in rem* and *quasi in rem* actions are devices by which jurisdiction is asserted through prejudgment seizure of property, the constitutionality of each has been challenged, under the due process "amenability" requirements of *Shaffer v. Heitner,* 433 U.S. 186 (1977), and the due process "fair notice" rules laid down in *Fuentes v. Shevin,* 407 U.S. 67 (1972), and its progeny. Under *Shaffer,* prejudgment seizure may not be used to effect jurisdiction unless there is a sufficient relationship among the forum state, the property and its presence in the state, the defendant, and the claim to make it reasonable for the forum state to exercise jurisdiction through seizure of the property. The *in rem* action frequently meets the *Shaffer* test, since the claim enforced in an *in rem* proceeding, the maritime lien, usually will have a close connection with the property and the "defendant," i.e., the property itself. Nonresident attachment appears more constitutionally vulnerable, since there is no requirement of a relationship between the property attached and the claim sought to be enforced.

The *Fuentes* doctrine generally condemns prejudgment seizure unless there is a special need for prompt action, and the person initiating the seizure is a government official responsible for determining under standards of a narrowly drawn statute that the particular seizure is justified. Supplemental Rules B, C and E, Admiralty and Maritime Claims, initially did not require pre-seizure judicial supervision, making the maritime *in rem* and *quasi in rem* procedures suspect under *Fuentes*. Most admiralty courts determined that the admiralty prejudgment seizures passed constitutional muster because the international and mobile character of vessels satisfied the *Fuentes* requirement of a need for prompt seizure, and because a speedy post-seizure hearing was available, either through a Rule 12 motion or through local court rules. Concern for constitutionality, however, led to 1985 amendments to Supplemental Rules B and C. The amended rules require judicial scrutiny before the issuance of attachment, garnishment or a warrant of arrest of a vessel, unless "exigent circumstances make [pre-seizure] review by the court impracticable." Process may issue by the clerk if the plaintiff or his attorney certifies that "exigent circumstances" exist; in such a case, the vessel owner is entitled to a post-seizure hearing, Rule E(4)(f), at which the plaintiff has the burden of establishing that exigent circumstances did exist.

Service of process in an *in rem* proceeding must be made "forthwith," Rule E(4)(a); however, untimely but accomplished service may not defeat the court's jurisdiction. *United States v. 2,164 Watches, More or Less, Bearing a Registered Trademark of Guess?, Inc.*, 366 F.3d 767 (9th Cir. 2004).

D. VENUE

There is no general venue requirement for an action brought as an admiralty claim in federal court; if the court has jurisdiction over the person, venue is proper. However, some maritime actions brought in federal court under the admiralty jurisdiction are subject to special venue rules; examples include proceedings for limitation of liability, Supplemental Rule F(9), Admiralty and Maritime Claims, and suits against the United States, 46 U.S.C.A. §§ 742 (now 30903), 782 (now 31101).

The provision in the Jones Act, 46 U.S.C.A. § 688(a), that "[j]urisdiction ... shall be under the court of the district in which the defendant employer resides or in which his principal office is located" has been interpreted as prescribing venue, and not jurisdiction. *Panama Railroad Co. v. Johnson*, 264 U.S. 375 (1924). Despite this venue provision, if the Jones Act case is brought as an admiralty claim, the plaintiff may avail himself of the admiralty rule that venue is proper wherever jurisdiction over the person can be obtained.

When the Jones Act was adopted, its venue provision was broader than the general provision for venue in suits brought at law in federal court against corporations. However, the general venue provision, now 28 U.S.C.A. § 1391(c), was amended in 1948 to permit a corporation to be sued "in any judicial district in which it is incorporated or licensed to do business or is doing business." The Supreme Court has ruled that a claimant pursuing a Jones Act claim at law may avail himself of the now broader provisions of 28 U.S.C.A. § 1391(c), and is not restricted to the venue provided in the Jones Act. *Pure Oil Co. v. Suarez*, 384 U.S. 202 (1966). A subsequent amendment to 28 U.S.C.A. § 1391 has further liberalized the venue rules for civil actions in which jurisdiction is not founded solely upon diversity, and those rules also should apply to Jones Act claims.

Statutes permitting transfer to a proper (28 U.S.C.A. § 1406) or more convenient (28 U.S.C.A. § 1404(a)) forum apply in actions brought as admiralty claims in federal court. *Continental Grain Co. v. The FBL–585*, 364 U.S. 19 (1960). Transfer to a more convenient forum merely moves the claim to another federal court. It must be distinguished from *forum non conveniens*, in which an action is dismissed and the parties are required to pursue the matter in the courts of another sovereign. *See also,*

Sinochem Int'l Co., Ltd. v. Malaysia Int'l Shipping Corp., 549 U.S. 422 (2007) (a court may determine dismissal on the grounds of *forum non conveniens* without first determining whether the court has personal jurisdiction over the parties). The federal *forum non conveniens* rule, *see* Chapter XIII, *supra,* is not binding on a state court in a maritime matter. *American Dredging Co. v. Miller,* 510 U.S. 443 (1994).

E. PROCEDURE IN MARITIME CLAIMS

When a maritime claim is brought in state court or at law in federal court, the applicable procedure is that procedure used in processing other claims in the same courts, with one important exception: if there is an admiralty procedural rule which is an integral part of the substantive maritime right, that rule must be applied when the claim is processed in other courts. This principle is illustrated by *Garrett v. Moore–McCormack Co.,* 317 U.S. 239 (1942), in which a seaman who had executed a release of his maritime claims subsequently brought an action on the claims in Pennsylvania state court. The maritime rule is that a party relying upon a seaman's release has the burden of proving the validity of the release, but Pennsylvania law placed the burden of proving the invalidity of the release upon the claimant who executed it. The Supreme Court held that the Pennsylvania courts erred in applying the state rule, noting:

The right of the petitioner to be free from the burden of proof [of the invalidity of the release] imposed by the Pennsylvania local rule inhered in his cause of action. Deeply rooted in admiralty as that right is, *it was a part of the very substance of his claim and cannot be considered a mere incident of a form of procedure....* Pennsylvania having opened its courts to petitioner to enforce federally created rights, the petitioner was entitled to the full scope of those rights. (Emphasis added).

This is the converse of the rule, pronounced in *Byrd v. Blue Ridge Rural Electric Cooperative, Inc.*, 356 U.S. 525 (1958), that a federal court sitting in diversity must apply state procedural law which is an integral part of the state cause of action. There are few illustrations of the application of the *Garrett* rule in maritime law. The most common one is that if a Jones Act claim is brought in state court, the plaintiff's "featherweight" burden of proving causation applies, rather than a more stringent state court rule. One important issue is whether the non-availability of trial by jury in certain circumstances is an integral part of the maritime remedy. If a Jones Act claim is brought in state court, the seaman has a right to trial by jury without regard to state law. However, if there is an absence of diversity or federal question jurisdiction, a suit on any other maritime claim brought in federal court must be brought as an admiralty claim, and there is no trial by jury. Some litigants have argued that if the same claim is brought in state court, the parties should not be entitled to trial by jury, even though jury trial otherwise would be available under state law, because trial to a judge alone is an integral part of the federal maritime right. This argument has been rejected by a state supreme court. *Lavergne v. Western Co. of North America, Inc.*, 371 So.2d 807 (La. 1979).

When a maritime claim is brought in federal court and jurisdiction is premised upon the admiralty power, the Federal Rules of Civil Procedure apply, with several important exceptions. One of these exceptions, the lack of jury trial, previously has been discussed. Another exception is that the Supplemental Rules for Certain Admiralty and Maritime Claims apply in *in rem* and *quasi in rem* actions; in possessory, petitory and partition actions; and in actions for exoneration from or limitation of liability. A third exception is that when the federal court's jurisdiction is based upon the admiralty power, a special third party practice is available under the provisions of Fed. R. Civ. P. 14(c). The original federal third party rule, now Rule 14(a), permits a defendant to call in a third party who may be liable to the defendant in indemnity or contribution. Under Rule 14(a) a defendant may "pass on" to the third party all or part of defendant's liability to plaintiff, but plaintiff may not recover judgment directly against the third party unless he amends his complaint to assert a claim against the third party. Former Admiralty Rule 56 permitted the defendant to use third party practice to "pass on" his liability, but also permitted the defendant to assert the plaintiff's claim directly against the third party defendant, thus making the third party an "additional defendant" subject to judgment in favor of the plaintiff without any further pleadings on the part of the plaintiff. Fed. R. Civ. P. 14(c), adopted as part of the unification in 1966, makes this "additional defendant" procedure available if the federal court is sitting in admiralty.

If jurisdiction over a claim brought in federal court may be sustained both under the admiralty power and under some other basis of jurisdiction, the matter is at law unless the plaintiff makes the declaration contemplated by Fed. Civ. Proc. Rule 9(h), identifying the claim as an admiralty or maritime claim. A court may permit a plaintiff to amend his complaint to add or delete the Rule 9(h) declaration and transfer the case into or out of the admiralty docket, at least where jurisdiction at law is premised solely upon the Jones Act and the defendant is not entitled to jury trial in his own right. *See, e.g.*, *Rachal v. Ingram Corp.*, 795 F.2d 1210 (5th Cir. 1986).

It is not clear whether a plaintiff may provoke an *in rem* proceeding and obtain a jury trial on a joined personal injury claim to which trial by jury ordinarily would be available. *See, e.g.*, *Haskins v. Point Towing Co.*, 395 F.2d 737 (3d Cir. 1968).

F. REMOVAL

The general provision for removal of civil actions from state to federal court, 28 U.S.C.A. § 1441, applies to maritime actions commenced in state court, but not all such actions may be removed. Section 1441(a) provides:

Except as otherwise expressly provided by Act of Congress, any civil action brought in a State court of which the district courts of the United States have original jurisdiction, may be removed....

Congress has expressly provided, in Title 28 U.S.C.A. section 1445, that a FELA claim commenced in state court is not removable; the adoption of the FELA by the Jones Act has been interpreted to include this prohibition against removal. Accordingly, a Jones Act claim commenced in state court is not removable, even if there is federal jurisdiction independent of the Jones Act, such as diversity jurisdiction.

The traditional rule was that if the state court did not have subject matter jurisdiction, the matter could not be removed. Thus if a maritime *in rem* action was brought in state court, the appropriate remedy was dismissal. A 1986 statute, now 28 U.S.C.A. § 1441(e), now permits removal of *in rem* cases brought in state court.

Other maritime cases commenced in state court ordinarily may be removed to the law "side" of federal court, if the requisites for diversity jurisdiction are present or if there is "federal question" jurisdiction. However, a maritime common law claim does not fall within the court's "federal question" jurisdiction under 28 U.S.C.A. § 1331, although it "arises under" the Constitution. *Romero v. International Terminal Operating Co.*, page 386, *supra*. When such a claim is brought in state court under the "saving to suitors" clause, may it be removed to the admiralty "side" of federal court, thus perhaps depriving the litigant of trial by jury? *Romero* bars removal as a "federal question," under section 1441(b). However, section 1441(a) provides that "any civil action brought in a State court of which the district courts of the United States have original jurisdiction, may be removed." An *in personam* maritime claim brought in state court is a civil action over which the federal court, sitting in admiralty, has original jurisdiction, and thus it seemingly is removable under the general language of section 1441(a), as long as the condition of section 1441(b)—that all of the defendants are nonresidents—is met. *See, e.g., Morris v. T E Marine Corp.*, 344 F.3d 439 (5th Cir. 2003). There are strong arguments to the contrary, however. One is that the "saving to suitors" clause is an express provision by Congress against such removal; this argument finds support in the dictum in *Romero* that permitting such removal would destroy the historic option that the "saving to suitors" clause gives to maritime claimants to pursue their claims in either state or federal court.

One maritime removal problem arises out of the jurisprudence holding that a 905(b) claim does not produce federal question jurisdiction. *See* Chapter XIII, *supra*. Thus in those cases in which the injured worker's duties place him on the borderline between seaman status and LHWCA coverage, the defendant's right to remove depends upon the worker's status. Because a Jones Act claim is not removable, a state court plaintiff seeking to avoid federal court may allege a frivolous seaman's claim and an alternative 905(b) claim. Courts generally avoid a determination of the worker's status upon trial of the motion to remand by imposing upon the defendant a heavy burden of proving that the Jones Act claim is frivolous.

If a maritime claim brought in state court is removable under 28 U.S.C.A. § 1441(a), it may lose removability when it is joined in that court with a claim which is not removable. Section 1441(c) permits removal of a removable claim that is joined with a nonremovable claim only if the claims are "separate and independent," a criterion not usually met when an unseaworthiness claim is joined with a Jones Act claim.

G. JOINDER AND SUPPLEMENTAL JURISDICTION

The federal rules of initial joinder (joinder of claims under Fed. Civ. Proc. Rule 18, 28 U.S.C.A., and joinder of parties under Fed. Civ. Proc. Rule 20) and subsequent joinder (counterclaims and cross claims under Fed. Civ. Proc. Rule 13, third party actions under Fed. Civ. Proc. Rule 14, and intervention under Fed. R. Civ. P. 24,) apply in an action in a federal court in which jurisdiction is premised upon the admiralty power. Where the Federal Rules of Civil Procedure permitted joinder of a claim over which a federal court had subject matter jurisdiction with a claim over which it did not have such jurisdiction, the federal courts developed the theory of "ancillary jurisdiction" or "pendent jurisdiction," under which a federal court sometimes would exercise jurisdiction over the nonfederal claim. In such cases, the court's jurisdiction over the state law claim was said to be an "ancillary" to the federal claim. Congress' creation of supplemental jurisdiction, 28 U.S.C.A. § 1367, continues the concepts of ancillary and pendent jurisdiction in maritime law. *See, e.g., Jerome B. Grubart, Inc. v. Great Lakes Dredge & Dock Company*, page 41, *supra*. Under *Grubart*, a tort claim that ordinarily would not be maritime may be so connected with a maritime claim that it will also be deemed a maritime tort. Thus damage-causing conduct that otherwise would be evaluated under state tort principles may arise out of or coalesce with maritime tort conduct and thus could be pursued in federal court either as a maritime tort under 28 U.S.C.A. § 1333, or as a state tort claim over which the federal court hearing the maritime claim could exercise supplemental jurisdiction.

Supplemental jurisdiction poses an additional problem in a maritime setting. When jurisdiction in a federal court is premised solely upon the admiralty power, the parties are not entitled to trial by jury. If a party to a maritime claim brought as an admiralty claim is permitted to "pend" a nonfederal (state law) cause of action, the whole case presumably will be tried in federal court without a jury. However, since the "pended" or nonfederal claim arises out of state law, the litigants usually would have been entitled to try the claim to a jury in state court. Thus application of supplemental jurisdiction in a federal court sitting in admiralty could deprive a litigant of the trial by jury to which he otherwise was entitled.

The expansive interpretation of the supplemental jurisdiction statute provided by the Supreme Court may impact upon the jurisprudential difficulties between maritime and supplemental jurisdiction. *Ortega v. Star–Kist Foods, Inc.*, 545 U.S. 546 (2005).

Res judicata probably will not apply in a maritime claim unless both parties are identical to or in privity with the parties to the prior suit. *Gulf Island–IV, Inc. v. Blue Streak–Gulf Is. Ops.*, 24 F.3d 743 (5th Cir.1994). Courts also may apply "judicial estoppel," i.e., a party is estopped from changing positions in a case to gain an unfair advantage over an opponent where the later position is clearly inconsistent with the earlier position and the first tribunal accepted and relied upon the prior position. *New Hampshire v. Maine*, 532 U.S. 742 (2001).

H. APPEALS

A final judgment in a suit brought as an admiralty claim in federal court is reviewable in the same fashion as judgments in other cases. 28 U.S.C.A. § 1291. The standard for review on appeal is that provided for all bench trials by Fed. R. Civ. P. 52(a): "Findings of fact shall not be set aside unless clearly erroneous, and due regard shall be given to the opportunity of the trial court to judge ... the credibility of the witnesses."

An interlocutory judgment of a federal court sitting in admiralty may be reviewed under Rule 54(b), which permits the trial court to convert into a final judgment an order disposing of all of the claims of one party in a multiparty suit, or an order disposing of one of several claims between the same parties. Another method of review of an interlocutory judgment is through certification by the district court that the decision involves a "controlling" question of law or fact under the provisions of 28 U.S.C.A. § 1292(b). In addition, 28 U.S.C.A. § 1292(a)(3), a special provision for admiralty cases, provides appeal of "[i]nterlocutory decrees of ... district courts ... determining the rights and liabilities of the parties to admiralty cases in which appeals from final decrees are allowed." The purpose of the provision is to continue the traditional admiralty practice of separate trial and appeal on the issue of liability, with subsequent trial of the damage issue before a commissioner. However, some courts have given the provision broader application. *See, e.g.*, *Estate of Hager v. Laurelton Welding Service, Inc.*, 124 Fed. Appx. 104 (3d Cir. 2005) (jurisdiction to hear interlocutory appeals in admiralty cases narrowly construed and only applies in a case in which liability has been determined).

Some states apply their own appellate standards in reviewing appeals in maritime matters. This practice arguably is acceptable in "saving to suitors" cases, but not in review of Jones Act jury trials, since the right to a jury verdict is an integral part of the seaman's substantive rights under the act, and the weight of the jury's verdict should not be diminished by a state appellate review standard.

I. REMEDIES

The struggle between the English law and equity courts and that struggle's impact upon admiralty has been recounted earlier in this chapter and in Chapter I. One of the outgrowths of the struggle was the rule that maritime courts could not grant equitable relief. This limitation developed in American maritime law into a rule that a federal court sitting in admiralty lacked "jurisdiction" over equitable matters, with the result that such a court could not grant injunctions or specific performance, enforce a trust, reform a contract because of fraud or error, or entertain an action for an accounting or an action based on an equitable title or an equitable right.

The rule was not without detractors or exceptions. One exception was that an admiralty court could entertain an equitable defense to a maritime claim. By 1966 it was clear that there were other exceptions, although the boundaries of admiralty's

permissive intrusion into traditional equity matters
were far from clear. Two Supreme Court cases
merit special attention. In *Swift & Co. Packers v.
Compania Colombiana Del Caribe, S.A.*, 339 U.S.
684 (1950), the plaintiff seized a vessel allegedly
owned by one defendant; a second defendant sought
to vacate the attachment on the grounds that it had
acquired the vessel from the first defendant prior to
the seizure. When the plaintiff then sought to set
aside the transfer as fraudulent, the district court
concluded that it was without jurisdiction to inquire
into sale of the vessel, since reformation of contracts for fraud was an equitable remedy. Reversing, the Supreme Court observed:

> Unquestionably a court of admiralty will not en-
> force an independent equitable claim merely be-
> cause it pertains to maritime property.... But
> that is not the case before us. Libellants went
> into admiralty on a claim arising upon a contract
> of affreightment supplemented by charges of neg-
> ligence in the nondelivery of a sea cargo—matters
> obviously within the admiralty jurisdiction. As an
> incident to that claim, in order to secure respon-
> dents' appearance and to insure the fruits of a
> decree in libellants' favor, they made an attach-
> ment.... *The issue of fraud arises in connection
> with the attachment as a means of effectuating a
> claim incontestably in admiralty.* To deny an ad-
> miralty court jurisdiction over this *subsidiary or
> derivative issue in a litigation clearly maritime*
> would require an absolute rule that admiralty is
> rigorously excluded from all contact with nonmar-

itime transactions and from all equitable relief, even though such nonmaritime transactions come into play, and such equitable relief is sought, in the course of admiralty's exercise of its jurisdiction over a matter exclusively maritime. (Emphasis added).

More significant to the issue of the demise of the rule is the Court's decision in *Archawski v. Hanioti*, 350 U.S. 532 (1956), in which it upheld admiralty jurisdiction over a suit for restitution. Recognizing that the issue was "to prevent unjust enrichment from a maritime contract," the Court observed that "so long as the claim asserted arises out of a maritime contract, the admiralty court has jurisdiction over it."

Archawski may have heralded the end of the concept that admiralty courts do not have the power to grant equitable remedies. It also is arguable that the concept did not survive the unification of law and admiralty rules in 1966. That unification extended federal rules pertaining to injunction and other equitable remedies to courts sitting in admiralty. The view that unification cured any lack of equity powers by admiralty courts was artfully expressed by Judge Brown of the Fifth Circuit in these words:

The Chancellor is no longer fixed to the woolsack. He may stride the quarterdeck of maritime jurisprudence and, in the role of admiralty judge, dispense, as would his landlocked brother, that which equity and good conscience impels.

Compania Anonima Venezolana De Nav. v. A.J. Perez Export Co., 303 F.2d 692 (5th Cir. 1962).

However, the limitation on the power of a court sitting "in admiralty" to grant equitable remedies traditionally has been phrased in terms of "jurisdiction," and Rule 82 provides that the federal rules "shall not be construed to extend ... the jurisdiction of the United States district courts." Thus it is not clear that unification has removed all limitations on equitable remedies in maritime law.

Through the admiralty power, a federal court may adjudicate claims to the ownership or possession of vessels, cargo and other maritime property. Supplemental Rules for Certain Admiralty and Maritime Claims, Fed. R. Civ. P. D. A petitory action is one in which title to the property is adjudicated independently of possession. The traditional rule is that the plaintiff in the petitory action must assert legal title to the vessel or other property, and not merely an equitable interest. The possessory action is one in which the right to possess the vessel or other property is at issue.

Prior to 1954, there was doubt whether a federal court sitting in admiralty had jurisdiction to partition a vessel. In addition, the admiralty substantive rule was that a court that had jurisdiction could not partition a vessel unless the parties in disagreement were the owners of equal shares. If the owners of unequal shares disagreed about the use of the vessel, the decision of the majority owners prevailed, but the minority owners could require a bond to secure the return of the vessel from any voyage undertaken without their consent. In *Madruga v. Superior Court*, 346 U.S. 556 (1954), the Supreme Court ruled that under the "saving to suitors" clause of 28 U.S.C.A. § 1333, federal and state courts have concurrent jurisdiction to order the partition of ships in a proceeding *in personam,* and that there is no federal admiralty rule barring judicial partition of a vessel unless the ownership interests are deadlocked. Accordingly, Supplemental Rule D, Admiralty and Maritime Claims, provides for partition actions as well as petitory and possessory actions.

The Federal Arbitration Act makes any written provision in a maritime transaction valid and enforceable except for "such grounds as exist at law or in equity for the revocation of any contract." 9 U.S.C.A. § 2. A seaman's employment contract is exempted from the application of the FAA (9 U.S.C. Sec. 1). *Brown v. Nabors Offshore Corp.*, 339 F.3d 391 (5th Cir. 2003). However, an injured seaman may be bound by an informed agreement he enters into with his employer to arbitrate any future claims related to the injury. *Terrebonne v. K–Sea Transportation Corp.*, 477 F.3d 271 (5th Cir. 2007).

The American courts generally uphold agreements to submit to foreign arbitration. *Vimar Seguros y Reaseguros, S.A. v. M/V Sky Reefer*, 515 U.S. 528 (1995). Foreign awards are enforced through the 1958 Convention on the Recognition and Enforcement to Foreign Arbitral Awards, which the United States has ratified.

INDEX

References are to Pages

425

HELD COVERED CLAUSE, 129

HIMALAYA CLAUSE, 84

HONOR POLICY, 128

INDEMNITY, 361

INLAND RULES, 186

INSURANCE ACT OF 1906, 127

INTERNATIONAL CONVENTION ON SALVAGE, 143

INTERNATIONAL RULES, 186

JASON CLAUSE, 162

JOINT AND SEVERAL LIABILITY, 361

JONES ACT
See Seamen

†